THE EARLY ANGLO-SAXON KINGS

THE EARLY ANGLO-SAXON KINGS

TONY SULLIVAN

PEN & SWORD HISTORY

AN IMPRINT OF PEN & SWORD BOOKS LTD.
YORKSHIRE – PHILADELPHIA

First published in Great Britain in 2023 by
PEN AND SWORD HISTORY
An imprint of
Pen & Sword Books Ltd
Yorkshire – Philadelphia

Copyright © Tony Sullivan, 2023

ISBN 978 1 39908 417 8

The right of Tony Sullivan to be identified as Author of this work has been asserted by him in accordance with the Copyright, Designs and Patents Act 1988.

A CIP catalogue record for this book is available from the British Library.

All rights reserved. No part of this book may be reproduced or transmitted in any form or by any means, electronic or mechanical including photocopying, recording or by any information storage and retrieval system, without permission from the Publisher in writing.

Typeset in Times New Roman 10/12 by SJmagic DESIGN SERVICES, India. Printed and bound in the UK by CPI Group (UK) Ltd.

Pen & Sword Books Limited incorporates the imprints of Atlas, Archaeology, Aviation, Discovery, Family History, Fiction, History, Maritime, Military, Military Classics, Politics, Select, Transport, True Crime, Air World, Frontline Publishing, Leo Cooper, Remember When, Seaforth Publishing, The Praetorian Press, Wharncliffe Local History, Wharncliffe Transport, Wharncliffe True Crime and White Owl.

For a complete list of Pen & Sword titles please contact
PEN & SWORD BOOKS LIMITED
47 Church Street, Barnsley, South Yorkshire, S70 2AS, England
E-mail: enquiries@pen-and-sword.co.uk
Website: www.pen-and-sword.co.uk

Or
PEN AND SWORD BOOKS
1950 Lawrence Rd, Havertown, PA 19083, USA
E-mail: Uspen-and-sword@casematepublishers.com
Website: www.penandswordbooks.com

Contents

Acknowledgements		viii
Introduction		ix
Chapter One	Fifth-century Britain	1
Chapter Two	The First Kingdom	32
Chapter Three	Ælle, the First Bretwalda	58
Chapter Four	Weapons and Warfare of the Fifth and Sixth Centuries	92
Chapter Five	The Empire Strikes Back	137
Chapter Six	The Rise of Wessex	161
Chapter Seven	Kings and Kingdoms	169
Sources for Maps		193
References		197
Endnotes		204
Figure 1	Map of fourth-century Roman Britain	5
Figure 2	Map of major concentration of Roman villas	6
Figure 3	Map of major Roman roads of Britain	7
Figure 4	Map of infrastructure and Romanisation of the fourth century	8
Figure 5	Map of provinces of Roman Britain c. 400	9
Figure 6	Administrative organisation of the late Western Roman Empire	9
Figure 7	Map of Anglo-Saxon cemeteries in post-Roman Britain	15
Figure 8	Map of battle locations of the HB and ASC	44
Figure 9	Map of early Anglo-Saxon cemeteries in Kent	46
Figure 10	Map of the Battle of Crecganford 457	51
Figure 11	Map of the Revolt and partition	52
Figure 12	Map showing coastline around Anderitum c. 491	60
Figure 13	Map of Roman fort of Anderitum c. 491	61
Figure 14	Map of Ælle and the South Saxons	62
Figure 15	Map showing Ælle's *imperium*	65
Figure 16	Map showing Saxon, Angle and Jute homelands	77
Figure 17	The Anglo-Saxon genealogies	90

Figure 18	Cross section of earthwork	110
Figure 19	The 'Boar's Head' formation	116
Figure 20	Vegetius general battle tactics	118
Figure 21	Map showing Mercian raid 'as far as Ashdown'	148
Figure 22	Map showing most likely locations of Arthur's battles	151
Figure 23	Map of early battle sites of the Anglo-Saxon Chronicles	164
Figure 24	Family tree of the kings of Bernicia and Deira	186

Table 1	Battles in Kent in the *Anglo-Saxon Chronicle* and *Historia Brittonum*.	43
Table 2	Timeline for Hengest	47
Table 3	Early Kentish Kings	48
Table 4	Earliest Anglo-Saxon kings	84
Table 5	Estimate of warrior numbers from the Tribal Hidage	97
Table 6	The conversion of Anglo-Saxon kingdoms	182
Table 7	Battles of the early sixth century	187

Picture 1	Outer ditch and wall at Richborough Roman Fort, East Kent (by author)	122
Picture 2	Exterior wall at Pevensey Roman Fort, East Sussex. Taken by Ælle in 491 (by author)	122
Picture 3	Interior of Pevensey Roman Fort, East Sussex (by author)	123
Picture 4	Highdown Hill, Sussex. Fifth century Anglo-Saxon cemetery (by author)	123
Picture 5	Outer ditch at Cissbury Hillfort, Sussex (by author)	124
Picture 6	Cadbury Castle Hill Fort (Wikimedia Commons)	124
Picture 7	Warriors outside reconstruction of a King's Hall c. 700 in Lejre near Roskilde (Ivanowich)	125
Picture 8	A dark age Lord in reconstruction of hall c. 700 in Lejre near Roskilde, Denmark (Ivanowich)	125
Picture 9	Shield bosses, bowls and brooches found at Highdown Hill fifth-century Anglo-Saxon cemetery (Worthing Museum)	126
Picture 10	Glassware found at Highdown Hill (Worthing Museum)	126
Picture 11	Glassware found at Highdown Hill possibly c. 400 from Egypt (Worthing Museum)	127
Picture 12	Two swords and spear found at Highdown Hill (Worthing Museum)	127
Picture 13	Quoit military style brooches found at Highdown Hill (Worthing Museum)	128

Contents

Picture 14	Replica of Vendel helmet at Worthing Museum (Worthing Museum)	128
Picture 15	Evidence of sword cut to thighbone of a fifth-century warrior. From Highdown Hill (Worthing Museum)	128
Picture 16	James Sainsbury Curator at Worthing Museum compares the thighbone of a fifth-century warrior (Worthing Museum)	129
Picture 17	Skull from early Anglo-Saxon period showing likely fatal blow from axe. From Highdown Hill (Worthing Museum)	129
Picture 18	Replica of the c. seventh century Benty Grange helmet (Wikimedia Commons)	129
Picture 19	Spangenhelm (iron), helmet from the Migration Period (Wikimedia Commons)	130
Picture 20	Late Romano-British warrior from fifth century (Sean Poage, author of 'The Retreat to Avalon')	130
Picture 21	Dark Age warrior (Wikimedia Commons)	130
Picture 22	Taeppa's Mound, Taplow, Buckinghamshire (Wikimedia Commons)	131
Picture 23	Drinking horns, late sixth century from Taplow (Wikimedia Commons)	131
Picture 24	Burial mound 2 at Sutton Hoo (Wikimedia Commons)	132
Picture 25	Model of Sutton Hoo ship-burial (Image by Wikimedia Commons)	132
Picture 26	Burial chamber of the Sutton Hoo ship-burial (Wikimedia Commons)	133
Picture 27	Replica of Sutton Hoo Helmet (Wikimedia Commons)	133
Picture 28	Shield from Sutton Hoo burial mound (Wikimedia Commons)	134
Picture 29	Shoulder clasps from Sutton Hoo (Wikimedia Commons)	134
Picture 30	Helmet from the seventh-century ship-burial at Vendel (Wikimedia Commons)	135
Picture 31	Migration period sword from Saint-Dizier (Wikimedia Commons)	135
Picture 32	Anglo-Saxon warriors from the migration period (Yahushan Ram, Seaxia Dark Ages Re-enactment Group)	135
Picture 33	Anglo-Saxon warrior (Yahushan Ram, Seaxia Dark Ages Re-enactment Group)	136
Picture 34	Anglo-Saxon warrior (Yahushan Ram, Seaxia Dark Ages Re-enactment Group)	136
Picture 35	Two early period Anglo-Saxon warriors (Yahushan Ram, Seaxia Dark Ages Re-enactment Group)	136

Acknowledgements

Many thanks to Yahushan Ram of the Seaxia Dark Ages Re-enactment Group for the photographs of Anglo-Saxon Warriors. Also to James Sainsbury, curator at Worthing Museum, for giving up his time to show me the exhibits and allowing me to take photographs. Also to Ivanowich of Kobbeaa for photographs of the reconstruction of the King's Hall from c. 700 in Lejre near Roskilde, Denmark.

Introduction

There are many books on the early medieval period and Anglo-Saxons in general. A few have made a valiant attempt at piecing together what little we know of the emergence of the first kingdoms in the fifth and sixth centuries. Inevitably this has involved looking at the different models for the arrival of Germanic settlers in the fifth century. I recall being taught at school, over forty years ago, that waves of Anglo-Saxons warriors arrived in Britain and pushed the indigenous population to the north and west. The implication being that they killed and enslaved those that remained and simply took over the land. We now know this is far from the truth. Recent advances in genetics have revealed a significant continuation of the population. Additionally archaeology has shown equally significant evidence for continuation of land use, while at the same time little support for any wide-scale destruction and displacement, despite the lurid tales of some of the literary sources such as Gildas, in the early sixth century, and Bede c. 730.

This has led to a vigorous debate about the nature of the Anglo-Saxon take-over. This book will argue that, far from a one-off event, it was in fact a process lasting many decades. At the start of this process, at the beginning of the fifth century, Roman Britain had a functioning civil and military structure which held authority over much of the island of Britain, certainly south of Hadrian's Wall. In addition many Britons had a distinctly Roman cultural identity. By the end of the sixth century this had all been swept away. The diocese and provincial structure had fragmented and a number of petty kingdoms emerged, many possibly based on the former *civitates* and tribal areas. The west and north of the former diocese evolved a distinct Romano-British cultural identity. Ironically the more Romanised regions in the south and east developed a more Germanic culture. We should not assume these two groups or regions and areas were homogenous, ethnically, politically or culturally. As we shall see, the term 'Anglo-Saxon' is a late one and applied retrospectively. Instead I will argue that a combination of influences and events, together with increased levels of settlement, helped create different cultural identities. Not just within the indigenous population but also within the various different peoples settling in Britain.

In contrast with these different emerging cultural identities an important similarity is often overlooked: the emergence of the war-band as a principal building block of an increasingly militarised society. By the beginning of the seventh century, both the Britons and Germanic peoples came to share the common institution: The *comitatus* or war-band. We will investigate how this impacted society and use some of the earliest literary sources and sagas. Poems such as the old English *Beowulf*, or Old Welsh *Y Gododdin* give us a vivid picture of great Halls, shield walls and warriors. We can contrast this with the apparently still Roman world of Saint Germanus and the Roman general Aetius in the first half of the fifth century.

The term *Bretwalda* is first used by the ninth-century ASC and is more likely to mean 'wide ruler' rather than 'Britain ruler'. Importantly, Bede doesn't use the word 'Bretwalda' at all. The actual word he uses is *imperium*, which suggests some sort of overlordship, or simply someone exerting influence or authority over a large area. The extent of this early imperium was possibly the Humber which formed a natural divide for a 'confederacy of Southern English peoples'.[1] We see a similar political context in sixth-century Frankia: 'For since Clovis's death the Bretons have always been under the dominion of the Franks and their rulers have been called counts, not kings.'[2] The question arises, did our first Bretwalda, Ælle, hold dominion over a large area? This could include not only a significant number of Germanic peoples settling in the south and east, but also the indigenous Romano-British population in the *civitates* and provinces of the former Roman diocese. Out of these political structures emerged the early Anglo-Saxon kingdoms at the end of the sixth century.

The term Heptarchy, or seven kingdoms (Kent, Sussex, Essex, Wessex, East Anglia, Mercia and Northumbria) was first used by Henry of Huntingdon in the twelfth century. In the fifth and sixth centuries this was not the political reality. Instead we see a complex and inconsistent fragmentation of old structures together with the forging of new. Some of these emerging power blocks were based on the former Roman administrative boundaries. We also see evidence of continuation and evolution of some *civitates* into petty kingdoms. The how, when and why of this process is what this book will attempt to uncover.

This book will focus on the first of the Anglo-Saxon Kings, an ethnic description I will continue with for ease rather than accuracy. For as we shall see, the first of our arriving warriors, Hengest, or Hengist, was alleged to be neither Angle or Saxon, but a Jute. I will use the former spelling as a version of this, *Hengestes*, is found in the *Finnesburg Fragment* which we will discuss later. Despite being named as leading the first band of warriors he was not described by Bede as holding *imperium* over a substantial part of the island. Few books have tackled Bede's first 'Bretwaldas' mainly due to lack of evidence. This book aims to address that gap and will also look at the emerging Brittonic kingdoms. Inevitably it will focus on conflict and wars. We will thus look at weapons, armour and warfare of the time as well as contemporary accounts of battles. What will emerge is something far more complex and nuanced than our traditional view of the Romano-British fighting back against invading Anglo-Saxons.

The book will cover the roughly two-and-a-half centuries from the end of Roman authority in Britain to the emergence of the Anglo-Saxon kingdoms in the seventh century. Some names readers will be familiar with and we will address the historicity of the more debatable figures: Hengest and Horsa, the first leaders of the Angles according to Bede; Vortigern, the alleged leader of the council that invited them; Vortimer, who the *Historia Brittonum* describes as driving the invaders out of Britain; and Ambrosius Aurelianus, described by Gildas as: 'a gentleman who,

Introduction

perhaps alone of the Romans, had survived the shock of this notable storm'. We will meet *Ælle* of the South Saxons and Ceawlin, Bede's first and second kings to hold imperium.

Any book of this period will have to mention King Arthur. I have dealt with the evidence for and against his historicity in my previous book, *King Arthur, Man or Myth*. I don't intend to spend too much time on the topic, but one of his alleged battles, Mons Badonicus, is worthy of investigation as it is confirmed in other sources. Whether this really was Arthur's victory or erroneously added to his exploits centuries later is for another book. Other battles will also be covered, some are attested, others only known from poems and legends, such as Catraeth and Arfderydd. The Anglo-Saxon Chronicle gives us a number of early battles alongside several origin stories for some of the early kingdoms.

As we get closer to the end of the sixth century we are on firmer historical footing. *Æthelberht* of Kent, number three on Bede's list, is well known partly due to the mission of Saint Augustine. But also because he gives the first written law code in English.[3] There appears to have been few speakers of Latin or practitioners of Roman Law in the south and east by the late sixth century, consequently the Anglo-Saxon law codes are unique among continental Germanic law codes in being written in the vernacular and owing nothing to Roman law.[4] East Anglia was one of the earliest regions affected by major levels of settlement. However, there is a distinct Scandinavian influence in contrast to other areas. One of its kings, Rædwald, is number four on Bede's list. The magnificent finds at Sutton Hoo are thought to be part of his burial. Numbers five to seven were all from the north, as was Bede, and they fought a succession of bloody wars in the mid-seventh century against Penda of Mercia and Cadwallon of Gwynedd. We will end with the death of Penda, the last pagan Anglo-Saxon king, at Winwaed in 655. All dates will be AD, or in modern terms CE, unless stated otherwise.

The intention of this book is to bring to life the atmosphere of the period. It is a time of great conflict and bloody battles. It is also a time of great change. Kingdoms emerged from the fragmented Roman provinces and *civitates*. One battle, or even one man, could change the destiny of a kingdom. The great halls of these kings and warriors rang with the sound of feasting and songs. Their echoes are caught in the poems of both the Welsh and Anglo-Saxons centuries later. Tales of Vortigern and Hengest, Arthur and Beowulf, but also Cadwallon and Penda. The first chapter will set the historical scene before we meet Hengest and Horsa. Mercenaries and adventurers arriving in troubled times to help fight off the Picts and Irish raiders. Below is a brief list of the main sources used.

Main sources

I have listed this roughly in order of date.
Chronica Gallica (The Gallic Chronicle): Two anonymous versions thought to have been written in southern Gaul are dated to c. 452 and 511.

De Excidio et Conquestu Britanniae (On the Ruin and Conquest of Britain): Written by a British monk, Gildas. Dating is unclear but the consensus is for the second quarter of the sixth century.

De origine actibusque Getarum (The Origin and Deeds of the Goths): Written mid-fifth century by Jordanes. This is often abbreviated to Getica.

Historia Francorum (The History of the Franks): Sixth-century work by Gregory of Tours

Historia ecclesiastica gentis Anglorum (Ecclesiastical History of the English People): Written by a northern British monk, Bede, in c. 731.

Historia Brittonum (History of the Britons): Written c. 828 in North Wales commonly attributed to Nennius.

Anglo-Saxon Chronicle: Thought to be late ninth century and probably compiled in Wessex.

Annales Cambriae (The Welsh Annals): Compiled in South West Wales in the tenth century, earliest copy twelfth century.

Historia regum Britanniae (The History of the Kings of Britain): A pseudo-historical tale written in c. 1136 by Geoffrey of Monmouth.

Abbreviations

AC *Annales Cambriae*
ASC *The Anglo-Saxon Chronicle*
DEB *De Excidio et Conquestu Britanniae*
GC *Gallic Chronicle*
HB *Historia Brittonum*
HE *Historia ecclesiastica gentis Anglorum*
HF *Historia Francorum*
HRB *Historia regum Britanniae*

Chapter One

Fifth-century Britain

Splendid this ramparts is, though fate destroyed it
The city buildings fell apart, the works of giants crumble.
Tumbled are the towers, ruined the roofs, and broken the barred gate.
Frost in the plaster, all the ceilings gape
Torn and collapsed and eaten up by age.
And grit holds in its grip, the hard embrace
of earth, the dead departed master-builders.
Until a hundred generations now
of people have passed by. Often this wall
stained red and grey with lichen has stood by
surviving storms while kingdoms rose and fell.
And now the high curved wall itself has fallen.
  The Ruin, tenth century, Anglo-Saxon poem
    from the *Exeter Book*.

Roman Britain

Before Julius Caesar invaded in 55 BC and 54 BC, Britain was a patchwork of tribal kingdoms. The invasion of AD 43 under Emperor Claudius was the start of 350 years of Roman rule over much of the island. Many of these tribal areas formed the basis of *civitates* and over thirty towns and cities grew within a provincial structure. We must not assume a direct continuity from pre-Roman kingdoms to later *civitates* and to later fifth-century kingdoms.[1] Nevertheless there are strong hints that some, such as the Cantii, did just that, and evolved into the later kingdom of Kent. The basic building block of the Empire was the *civitas*. It is necessary to remember this because it became a particularly important 'socio-political unit' in the fifth century and formed an important layer of Roman identity.[2]

No surviving document or source defines the provincial or *civitas* boundaries.[3] Our understanding of political structures is also poor.[4] What we do know is that by the early fourth century, Britain had been split into four provinces with a fifth added after 367. Two provinces were headed by Consuls: Maxima Caesariensis and Valentia. Three were headed by a *Presidii*: Britannia prima, Britannia secunda and Flavia Caesariensis. All five reported to the *Vicarius Britanniae* who ruled the diocese of Britain under the praetorian prefect of the Gauls based at Trier. The five provinces contained several *civitates*, many likely to be similar to the pre-Roman tribal areas. Each *civitas* had a large town with its own administrative structure. Civilian posts included *Decurions* on town councils, *aediles* responsible for public buildings and services and *quaestors* in charge of finance and magistrates. A town senate, *ordo*, consisted of up to 100 representatives from the local community. Late Roman military commands included *tribunes, praefectus* and *protectors*.

These roles and structures did not disappear over night after Roman rule ended. When and how they disappeared are important points in our investigation. As we shall see, faint echoes may have survived into later centuries such as when Bede describes Paulinus of York being greeted by a *praefectus* in Lincoln. c. 625. Back in the fourth century Britain had become Romanised and urbanised. This urbanisation was marked by activities other than subsistence farming; the urban centres became hubs for economic activity and trade, but also civilian and military control. This had a transformational affect on the surrounding rural countryside.[5] The growth of urban centres become inextricably linked with the monetary and tax system.[6]

In the second half of the fourth century Britannia was seen as an economically 'prosperous diocese'.[7] Some described it as 'very wealthy'.[8] While there was a significant urbanisation, up to 90 per cent of the population remained rural.[9] In the mid-fourth century there is evidence for construction and maintenance within towns.[10] Many luxurious and large villas were built in the second half of the fourth century.[11] It has been called the 'heyday or Romano-British villas' within a 'wealth producing agricultural economy'.[12] However, by the 360s many of Britain's 'middling villas' had deteriorated or been abandoned, whereas larger and grander houses were being improved and enlarged.[13] The evidence suggests the very rich were getting richer and the less wealthy were suffering difficulties. Additionally, by the end of the fourth century, towns had become poorer and politically weaker.[14] There was already signs of a weakening economy. Thus Britain was already in decline when Constantine III left Britain in 407 with much of the army.

One could place the beginning of the end of Roman Britain a generation earlier with the usurper Magnus Maximus. It was during the reign of Theodosius I (379–395) that Maximus was declared Emperor in Britain in 383 and crossed into Gaul taking much of the British garrison with him before being killed in 388. Britain had also been subject to a number of major incursions. Most notably the *barbarica conspiratio* (barbarian conspiracy) of 367, described by contemporary Roman historian Ammianus Marcellinus. The northern frontier was overrun and Fullofaudes, the *dux Britanniarum* and Necttaridus the *comes maritime tractus* (possibly synonymous with the later *comes litoris Saxonici*) were killed.[15] Further raids occurred in 382 and 398. It is important to note that after this later raid was dealt with, General Stilicho pulled troops, and much of the coinage, out of Britain. Thus by the beginning of the fifth century, the provinces of Britannia had experienced significant raids and political upheavals alongside a seemingly declining economic and urban situation.

In the winter of 406 the Rhine froze over and multiple tribes crossed into a relatively undefended northern Gaul. These included Vandals, Burgundians,

Alemanni, Alans, Saxons and Gepids. The Britons soon rebelled and appointed three leaders in quick succession. First they proclaimed a certain Mark as emperor, but soon murdered him. Next came Gratian, but within four months he too was killed. Finally, c. 417, Orosius tells us Constantine, 'a man of the lowest military rank, on account of the hope alone which came from his name and without any merit for courage, was elected'. Once appointed, Constantine crossed over to Gaul with his forces and became 'master of Gaul as far as the Alps'.[16]

At first Honorius accepted Constantine as co-emperor. In 409, with Constantine in Gaul, we hear from the Gallic Chronicle of 452: 'The Britains were devastated by an incursion of the Saxons.' The Britons rebelled again, this time against Constantine. They requested help direct from Honorius, who famously declined with *The Rescript of Honorius.* Interestingly the reply, to look to their own defences, was to the *civitates* and not to the provinces. Was the provincial structure still intact? or could Honorius not trust the provincial governors? There is some debate whether the intended recipients were in Britain, or Bruttium in Italy.[17] However, this is academic as the Romans never regained the former diocese.

Zosimus, writing c. 500, records that the 'barbarians' crossed the Rhine and 'reduced' the Britons and some of the Celtic peoples causing them to defect from Roman rule and live their lives 'disassociated from the Roman law'. The Britons took up arms and 'freed their own cities from barbarian threat'. His next statement is of interest:

> likewise all of Armorica and other Gallic provinces followed the Britons' lead: they freed themselves, ejected the Roman magistrates, and set up home rule at their own discretion.
> Zozimus book VI.5[18]

The Britons, it would seem, had broken free of Roman rule and much of Gaul had followed suit. This is not the first time such an event occurred. In the third century a short lived Gallic Empire survived between 260–274. A decade later, Carausius declared himself Emperor in Britain but was murdered by his treasurer Allectus, who assumed the title before Roman rule was restored three years later. In the fourth century, Magnentius ruled in Britannia, Gaul and Hispania between 350–353 and Magnus Maximus controlled the Western Empire from 383–388. The events of c. 410 were thus the last in a long line of examples of political turmoil and civil war.

These incidents coincided with the sack of Rome by the Visigoths in 410. A year later Constantine suffered the same fate as Allectus, Magnentius and Maximus. Sozomen, writing in 439, records that after Constantine's defeat the province returned its 'allegiance to Honorius'. Sozomen is likely referring to Gaul and makes no mention of Britain at this point. Later sources seem to agree this was a turning point for Britain. Procopius, writing in 540, records: 'However the Romans never succeeded in recovering Britain, but it remained from that time on under tyrants.'[19] At the time, of course, the Britons, and Romans, may well have thought this was a temporary political situation. One wonders at what point the penny started to drop that this was something entirely different?

To understand the events of the later fifth century we need to know what sort of civilian and military structure was in place at the beginning of the fifth century. We can only go back to the last known situation when Constantine was declared emperor. We get some clues from the *Notitia Dignitatum*, an early fifth-century manuscript of uncertain authority.

The governors of the five provinces of Britannia were as follows:

> *Consularis per Maxima Caesariensis*
> *Consularis per Valentia*
> *Praesidis per Britannia prima*
> *Praesidis per Britannia secunda*
> *Praesidis per Flavia Caesariensis*

These five governors reported to the *Vicarius Britannarum*, The Vicar of the Britons, based in London. In turn he reported to the Praetorian Prefect of the Gauls. The military commands were as follows:

- *Dux Britannarium* controlled *Limitanei* (literally frontier troops) in the North, including Hadrian's wall. Consisting of eight cavalry and twenty-nine infantry units based at York, with approximately 4,000 cavalry and 15,000 infantry.
- *Comes Litoris Saxonici per Britanniam* (count of the Saxon shore) also utilised *Limitanei* across the forts along the southern and eastern coast. Consisted of two cavalry and seven infantry units, approximately 1,000 cavalry and 3,500 infantry
- *Comes Britanniarum* who controlled the main field army consisting of four infantry units and six cavalry units, suggesting a mobile force to combat raiders, with approximately 3,000 cavalry and 2,000 infantry.

This equates to a paper strength of 20,000 infantry and 8,000 cavalry in c. 400. However, the reality may be two thirds of that. Estimates range from as low as 6,000 to as many as 20,000 before Constantine depleted the forces further in 407.[20]

Figure one shows a map of the main towns, tribal areas and *civitates* alongside the likely position of the provinces. The second map shows the main distribution of known Roman villas. This indicates the spread of Romanisation across the provinces. The third map shows the main roads in Roman Britain. M.C. Bishop's book, *The Secret History of the Roman Roads of Britain*, finds not only were many of the Anglo-Saxon battles associated with Roman roads but so too were nearly all later battles on English soil.[21] It is estimated 40 per cent of the 3,000 miles survived into the medieval period.[22] It is thus likely a significant percentage were still usable in the fifth and sixth centuries.

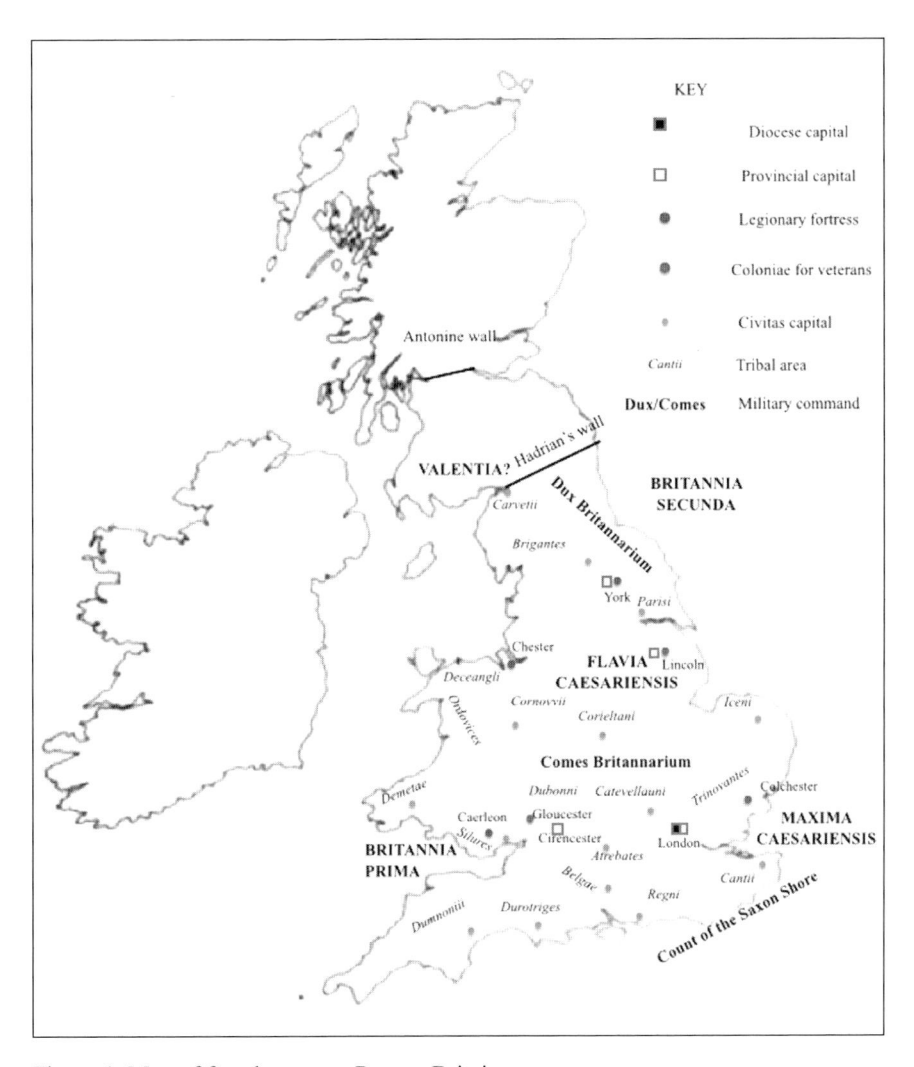

Figure 1. Map of fourth-century Roman Britain.

Our fourth map shows the concentration of urban areas, infrastructure and Romanisation at the turn of the century. This highlights an important point. Unsurprisingly this correlates with the distribution of Roman villas in map two. However as we shall see it also corresponds roughly with the earliest distribution of Germanic material culture and early evidence of settlement. This is not to say the evidence is uniformly spread across the region. Instead we shall see it was confined to specific areas: the coast, river valleys and close to urban and economic centres. The last map in this section is a simplified provincial map. This is quite speculative as we don't know the exact boundaries. However, it is worth considering how much of this structure was maintained into the fifth century.

Figure 2. Map of major concentration of Roman villas.

    This point is perhaps one of the most crucial in our investigation. The fifth century began with a functioning civil and military structure across much of the island. Within 200 years this had fragmented into a series of petty kingdoms. The question arises when and how did this fragmentation occur? Figure six gives us a very simplified version of the civil and military hierarchy. With Roman authority gone after 410, what then replaced the higher level, if anything? We will see later writers suggest there was a council of sorts that lasted until the mid-fifth century. Bede names its leader as Vortigern. We must view this with caution, but it is unlikely that 350 years of Roman rule and structures disappeared overnight. In fact the next section suggests some continuity.

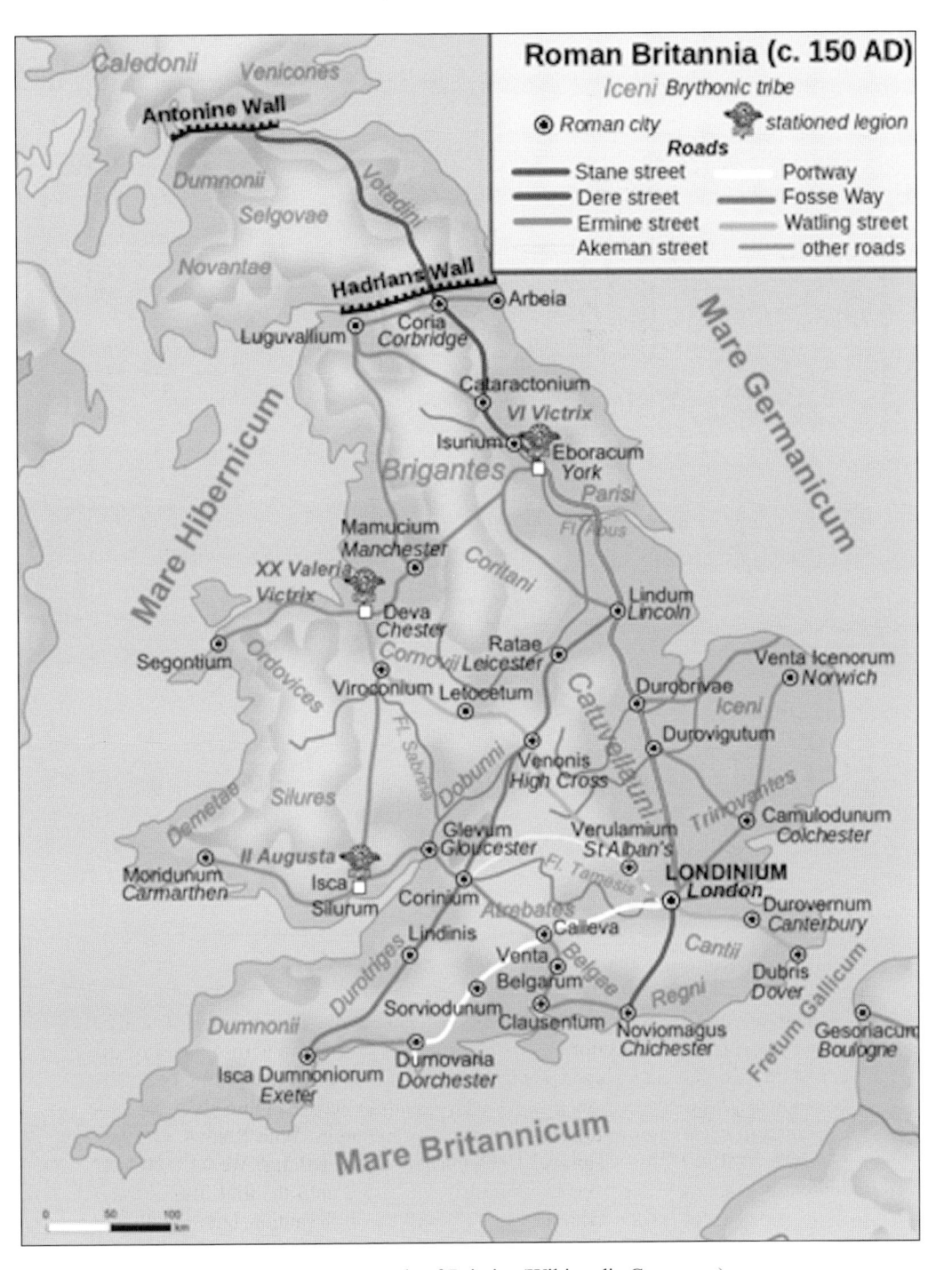

Figure 3. Map of major Roman roads of Britain. (Wikimedia Commons)

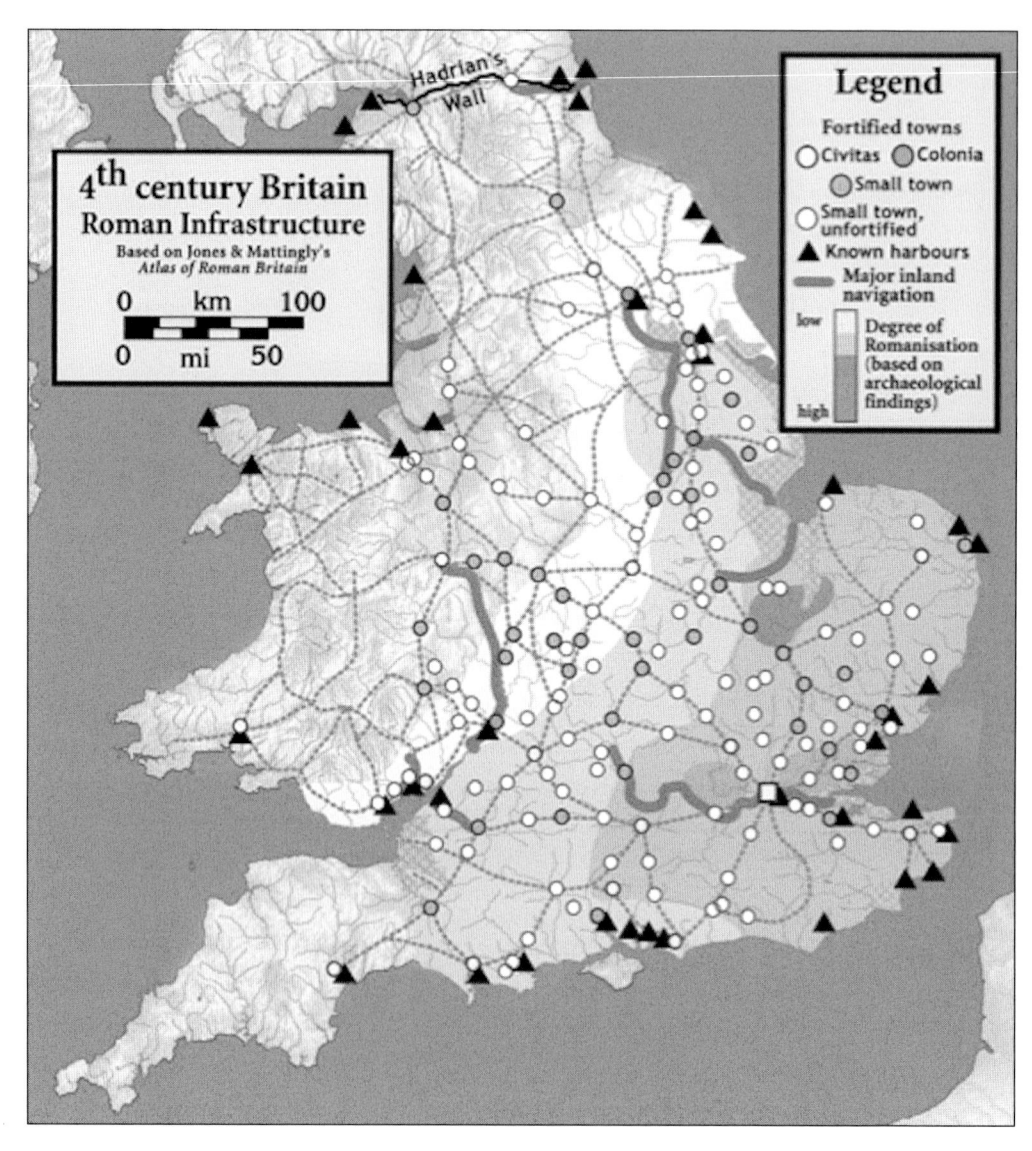

Figure 4. Map of infrastructure and Romanisation of the fourth century. (Wikimedia Commons)

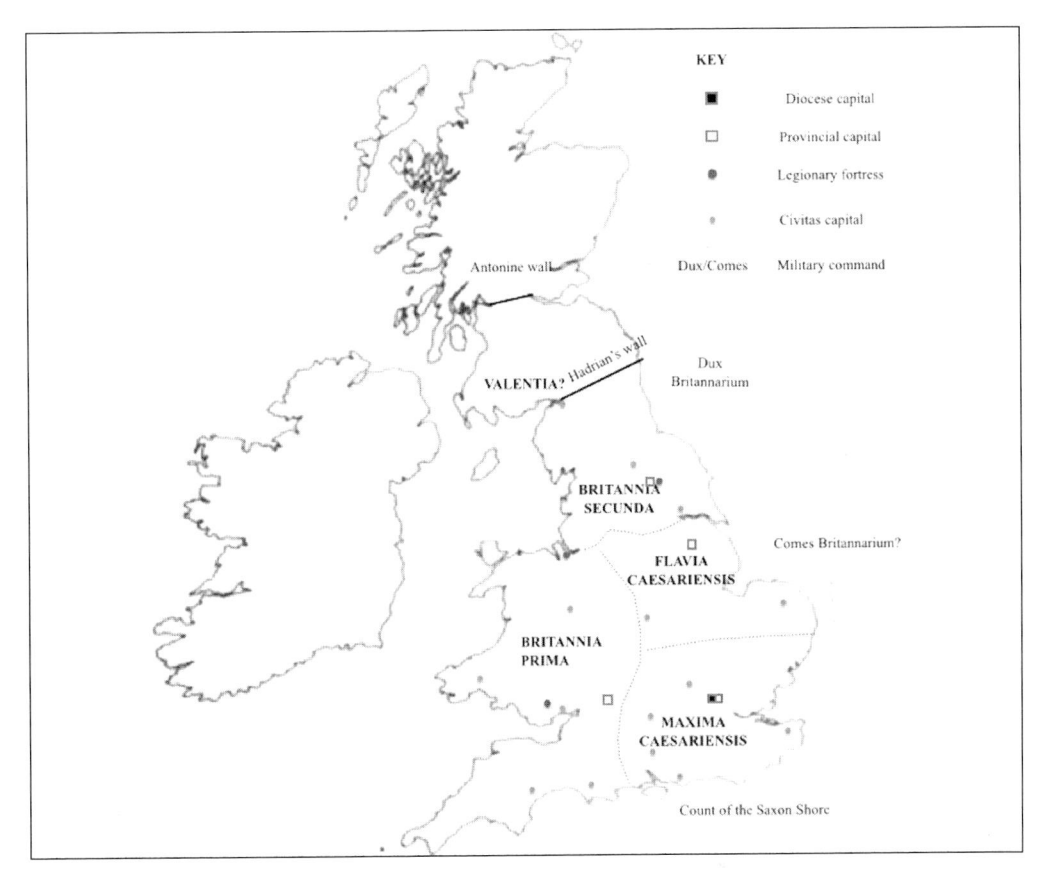

Figure 5. Map of provinces of Roman Britain c. 400.

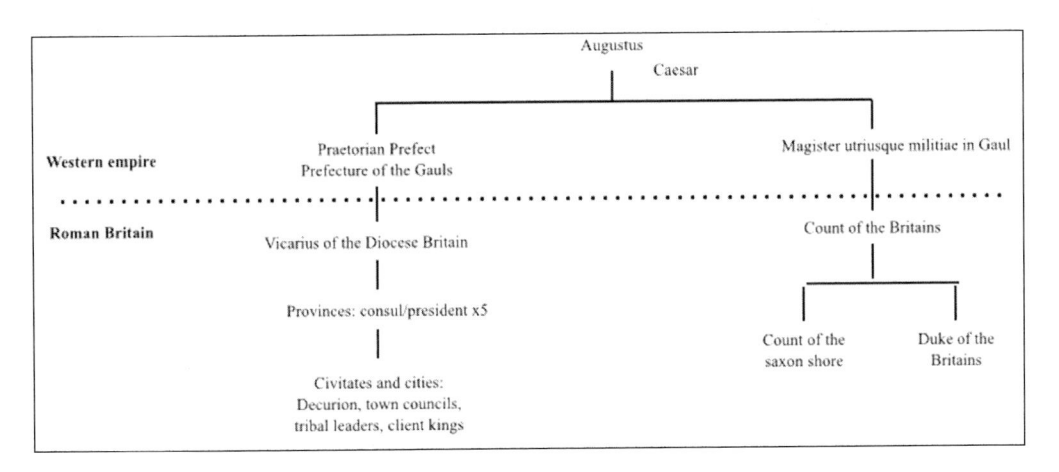

Figure 6. Administrative organisation of the late Western Roman Empire.

Post-Roman Britain

Someone living in Britain after these tumultuous events would be forgiven for thinking the apparent break from Roman rule was a temporary situation. There was certainly nothing certain about subsequent events. However, it is true to say that many of the structures which held Romano-British life together were severely weakened. Urban life had certainly deteriorated, even before the end of the fourth century. In the decades either side of 400, 'urban life, industrial scale manufacturing of basic goods, the money economy and the state collapsed'.[23] Towns and villas appear to have prospered more in Gaul compared to Britain in the fifth century.[24] Some historians state town life in Britain did not survive past c. 430,[25] others accept that life in towns continued even if 'town life' did not.[26] One view argues that villas appeared to be abandoned in the early fifth century and urban life ended around the same time.[27] Those living between 375–425 witnessed 'crippling economic and political dislocations' which had a 'profound impact' on their lives.[28] Industries such as pottery, ceramic and glass making, brick and quarried stone and metal production all suffered significant loss of production and knowledge. The end of the coin supply, and of Roman governance, severely disrupted the economic cycle, causing parts of Roman life to fail suddenly and irrevocably.[29] One view is this caused a collapse in the infrastructure of Roman Britain that was more sudden and more complete than elsewhere in the western empire.[30] The success of the imperial enterprise depended on the state's ability to collect for itself much of the surplus created by those living within the Empire.[31] With the end of the coin supply and the the collection of taxes, villa estates, towns and military settlements, and large-scale cereal production, all had ceased to function by 425.[32] Given the discrepancy between the 'plentiful and varied' fourth-century evidence and the dearth of later finds, the end of Roman Britain has been described as a 'mass extinction' in terms of archaeological material.[33] The question is, does this reflect historical reality?

James Gerrard in *The Ruin of Roman Britain* offers three possibilities: A systemic shock; 'slide and bump'; and a soft landing.[34] On one hand there was an unparalleled economic collapse seen nowhere else in the Western Empire other than northern Gaul. Coin use, pottery and other imported luxury items declined. With taxation ceasing, urban centres deteriorated and the general fragmentation was accelerated by plague, famine and war. On the other hand, the removal of the tax burden and requirement to produce a grain surplus, while a significant economic readjustment, actually may have improved the lives of the general population. The bulk of production was local and agricultural and the 'over-fixation' on visible finds skews the evidence.[35]

Pam Crabtree summarises the debate in her book *Early Medieval Britain, The Rebirth of Towns in the Post-Roman West*.[36] One view is that 'the principal towns of Roman Britain were deserted by the mid-fifth century, and remained so for at least a hundred years.' An alternative view is they 'retained a real presence and vitality in the landscape until the seventh century'. Which view is correct? Are they mutually exclusive? There is some evidence for surviving enclaves within areas otherwise surrounded by Anglo-Saxon finds such as Lincoln, Silchester and Verulamium.[37] Evidence of continuation of town life also includes the following:[38] a new water main and maintenance of the aqueduct at St Albans; the town fountain in Carlisle was still working in the seventh century; paved streets at Winchester; new floor at the temple in Bath; flood prevention work and new sluice gate at Cirencester; and Mediterranean imports at London and Wroxeter.

Archaeological evidence from Aquae Sulis, Bath, offers some clues:[39] a recognisable Roman lifestyle was grinding to a halt in the late fourth and early fifth centuries; after c. 410 it is likely that Bath formed part of a new political entity based around Cirencester; this area may have been the basis of the Hwicce, which itself evolved from the former Roman Civitas Dobunnorum; Bath retained a 'political meaning' into the late sixth century. There is evidence that the precinct and spring at the baths were still being used in the mid-fifth century. The baths themselves are likely to have been abandoned by c. 370.[40] Evidence exists of timber buildings being erected while the temple fell out of use. The Baths themselves may have become the barracks or headquarters of a local king or warlord.

The rural fabric of the diocese certainly survived into the fifth century.[41] The removal of the tax burden allowed the agricultural economy to transform. With the need for a grain surplus to supply the empire removed, conditions likely improved for some rural communities and we have substantial evidence of continued occupation and land use. Yet every significant Roman urban settlement of note saw deterioration in post-Roman Britain.[42] The last phase of occupation in many villas appear to be 'squatter occupation' of people living in ruined or semi-derelict buildings.[43] We see no evidence for occupation of these villas by Germanic settlers.[44] Additionally, despite much evidence of continuing land use in rural areas, there is little sign of Roman infrastructure being exploited by the Germanic settlers.[45]

We do have evidence at York of Alemmanic troops or civilians as early as the fourth century and in the fifth century the legionary fortress was still occupied, although evidence for survival of the town is lacking.[46] Concerning Hadrian's Wall, neither archaeology nor contemporary literary sources suggest it was abandoned at the end of the fourth century.[47] Indeed, several sites show continued occupation and use in the fifth century: South Shields, Vindolanda, Birdoswald, Carlisle and south of the wall at Binchester, Piercebridge and York.[48] In fact, Piercebridge on the River Tees shows the defences were used until the late sixth century.[49]

Hill forts start to be reoccupied in this period: South Cadbury, and Crickley Hill near Gloucester.[50] Additionally, other strongholds such as Tintagel and Cadbury Congresbury too. Dinas Powys in Wales was occupied from the fifth century, fortified in the sixth and abandoned by around 700.[51] Reoccupied hillforts are a feature of fifth-century Britain in the South West too, such as a stone enclosure at Trethurgy in Cornwall.[52]

We also see Mediterranean trade links with some of these sites, such as Tintagel in Cornwall or Dunadd hillfort in Dal Riata.[53] By the end of the fifth century we see a series of similar settlements in the north and west.[54] These are distinct from the more Romanised south-eastern areas.[55] It is odd that that the least Romanised areas in the north and west have a striking amount of Mediterranean and continental imports.[56] These same areas also show the links to the Roman past.[57] In contrast, the south-east, despite the greater Romanisation and infrastructure, shows a greater presence of Germanic cultural material, and later in the century shows far fewer links with the Roman world.

We are getting a little ahead of ourselves here. The generation after the end of Roman authority still maintained links with, and were very much part of, the Roman world. Economic and urban life appears to have deteriorated. The evidence suggests some towns continued, albeit in a reduced state. The northern military sites appear to have been maintained. The greatest evidence of continuation comes from rural areas which may even have prospered without the burden of tax. We have one contemporary source who actually visited Britannia twice and we will meet him shortly. First, however, we will look at the apparent increase in Germanic material culture and settlement that archaeology suggests occurred within a generation of the end of Roman rule.

Earliest Germanic settlement

By the fourth century there were significant numbers of Germanic troops in the Roman army. It is thus highly likely there were already a number of people of Germanic heritage in Britain. As early as the third century the field army of Allectus in the province contained many Germanic mercenaries and his predecessor, Carausius, was himself a native of the Belgic coast in Gaul.[58] Alamanni troops based there in the 370s were said to be 'distinguished for their numbers and strength'.[59] The title of The Saxon Shore command suggests the possibility of Saxon *foederati* or settlers. It is possible, though less likely, the stretch of defences was named after those raiding rather than those guarding. In Caistor-by-Norwich cremation burial vessels suggest a Germanic presence before 400.[60]

The earliest Germanic cruciform brooches start to appear in Wessex around 425. We then see a wide range of goods spreading throughout southern Britain in the second quarter of the fifth century.[61] The greatest volumes of finds occur in the midlands and eastern areas.[62] We also see a distinct difference in burial practices. Angles tended to cremation and Saxons to inhumation.[63] Where Saxon cremations do occur they are similar to finds in the Elbe-Weser triangle in Germany. Anglian types are similar to an area just north of this in the German/Danish border region of Schleswig-Holstein.[64]

At this point in our chronology we must make a distinction between the first half of the fifth century and the second half. The reason being, as we shall see, the literary sources point to the mid-fifth century for a pivotal point in the history. The GC dates this to 441, whereas Bede suggests sometime after the arrival of Hengest in 449. Much later, in the eighth century, Bede famously describes the 'three Germanic tribes': Saxons in Wessex, Sussex and Essex; Jutes in Kent and Hampshire; and Angles in East Anglia, Mercia and Northumbria. The archaeological evidence broadly supports this up to a point.[65] Bede describes their original homeland of Angeln as still being unpopulated in his day.[66] We do indeed have evidence for a depopulation of that region in the fifth century. However, we should remember that evidence of material culture does not equate to evidence for settlement or invasion. It could simply reflect the adoption of practices, customs or goods. Additionally, it is often forgotten that Bede lists several other peoples who settled in Britain: Frissians; Rugians; Danes; Huns; Old Saxons; and Bructeri.[67]

While we see a marked increase in evidence after the mid-fifth century, there is a pattern that emerges for the period between the end of Roman Britain and the *adventus saxonum* described by the sources. The earliest evidence for settlement is in the east between the Thames and the Humber.[68] Most notably East Anglia, Essex and Lincolnshire. Interestingly, the majority of Anglian finds occur in Flavia Caesariensis, which covers Lincolnshire, the East Midlands and possibly Norfolk. Saxon finds predominate in Maxima Caesariensis including Kent, Sussex and Essex.[69] The East Anglia region is likely the earliest to be settled by significant Germanic immigration from early in the fifth century.[70] Recent analysis suggests this area had a separate socio-economic identity as early as the first half of the fifth century.[71] Trade between eastern Britain and north Germany and Scandinavia was 'almost non-existent in Roman times', yet after the mid-fifth century we see the emergence of a 'new zone of exchange' across the North sea.[72] It is possible there were different patterns of settlement, or different *foederati* arrangements between the different provinces or even *civitates* in Britannia.

The cemetery at West Heslerton in North Yorkshire is instructive. The lower-status female burials indicate a Scandinavian or Baltic origin. Many of the females buried with Germanic material culture had spent their childhoods locally. Local people were more likely to be buried with grave goods. Only seven of the nineteen skeletons were not local and six of those were from other parts of Britain. At Berinsfield in Oxfordshire, three quarters were local people and only one of the remaining from outside Britain. In general, what we see is a significant amount of movement from within Britain, many coming from the west to settle at places such as Wasperton, Warwickshire, and West Heslerton, North Yorkshire. The grave goods were not always an indication of ethnicity.

Alongside this we also have very significant levels of continuation of population and land use. There is no evidence, for example, of large areas returning to woodland. The early settlement appears to be confined to coastal areas and rivers and marginal areas. Two examples in Sussex include Portchester and Bishopstone.[73] In Essex a site at Mucking shows evidence of settlement predating the end of Roman Britain. The implication is that they were being placed, or allowed to settle, in unused areas, by a British authority. In fact some areas, such as Lincoln, show a ring of settlements around an urban centre with much evidence for continuation of use by the Romano-Britons. The Anglo-Saxon ingress appears to be 'patchy and opportunistic'.[74] Settlement was inconsistent and irregular with complex and different timescales.[75]

The origin of this settlement can be identified by pottery, metalwork and burial goods and rites.[76] Gildas describes the first settlement as 'in the east' and Nennius specifies Thanet in east Kent. Recent scholars have suggested the first settlements were in East Anglia and spread westwards towards Dorchester and Oxford.[77] Others cite Yorkshire and Lincolnshire as well.[78] Similarly, early evidence exists at Thurmaston near Leicester, Ancaster in Lincolnshire and Great Casterton in the East Midlands. It may well be that the literary sources are referring to something more specific within the context of increasing settlement. The group Gildas refers to are a mercenary group hired by the *superbus tyrannus*, whom Bede names as Vortigern. The archaeological evidence can be summarised as follows:[79]

- Saxons from west of the River Elbe in Germany settle in the Thames Valley and the South from the early fifth century.
- Jutes from Jutland in the mid-fifth century settle in East Kent.
- Angles from the Schleswig-Holstein region between modern Germany and Denmark and the island of Fyn settled in central, eastern and north of England with some Saxons.
- Further late fifth-century influx from western Norway into Norfolk and Humberside.

A whole range of grave goods show a marked difference between south and eastern England and western areas: amber beads, ivory rings, rick crystals and glass vessels.[80] We also find differences in the distribution of inscribed stones and rune markings, appearing in Angle and Jutish areas but not supposed Saxon ones.[81] Other examples of distinctive Jutish material are found in Kent.[82]

The region that became known as Wessex is particularly instructive and we see a marked contrast between west and east Wessex:[83] Early settlement is found in the east, particularly around the River Meon in East Hampshire. This is the likely western border of the *civitas* of the *Regnii*. It is possible it was also a provincial border between *Maxima Caesariensis* and *Britannia Prima*. Artefacts dated prior to 475 are only found in eastern Wessex and the earliest is 425.[84] The towns of Abingdon and the area around Winchester are especially notable for early settlement as well as Reading, Mildenhall, Andover, Pewsey and Maidenhead. The finds are centred on the *civitas* of the *Atrebates* as well as eastern *Belgae* and western *Regnenses*. Anglo-Saxon cemeteries as early as the second quarter of the fifth century are found at Abingdon and from around 475 at Wallingford, Reading, West Hendred, Harwell, East Shefford and Long Wittenham with a more isolated case at Market Lavington.[85] What emerges is a patchwork of settlements in the period c. 425–450, mainly in the east but also down the Thames Valley. These appear to expand after the mid-fifth century. One interesting point is the Germanic material culture from the early to mid-fifth century was relatively homogenous.[86]

Recent DNA studies have given us some interesting data although it is sometimes difficult to be exact about the very specific period, c. 400–450, this chapter is investigating. In the Northeast, East Anglia and the Thames Valley, 'continental influences' could account for as much as 38 per cent of DNA content.[87] More localised studies have suggested a male immigrant population of 10 per cent

Fifth-century Britain

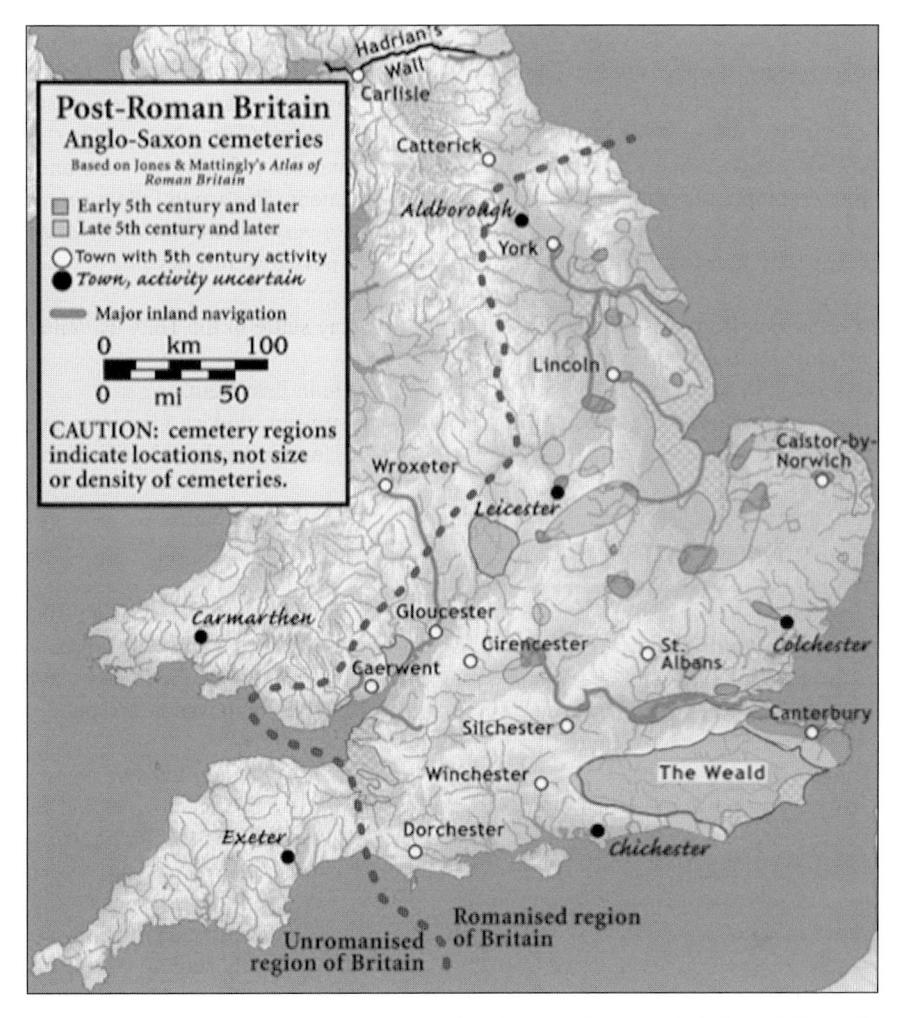

Figure 7. Map of Anglo-Saxon cemeteries in post-Roman Britain. (Wikimedia Commons)

in the Wessex area compared to 20 per cent in East Anglia.[88] Interestingly, one study found a warrior elite of only 10 per cent, spread over many decades, could account for up to 50 per cent towards the gene pool within five generations due to reproductive advantages.[89] Taking a generation as twenty-five years we can see how the arrival of such an elite in c. 425–450 could influence the political situation by c. 550–575. Interestingly, this is precisely when we get literary sources recording the expansion of the early Anglo-Saxon kingdoms.

Estimates for the total Germanic immigrant population in the mid-fifth century suggest 100,000 to 250,000 in to a population of 2 million, while skeletal data for just the south and east estimates the percentage of immigrants range from around

15–25 per cent.[90] Cunliffe summarises the evidence, stating both the genetic and archaeological finds suggest 'a significant level of immigration into south-eastern England during the fifth century in the order of between 10 and 20 per cent'.[91]

Much of this evidence includes data from after the mid-fifth century. We can, however, suggest the following: in general, the archaeological and DNA evidence does not support a military invasion and widespread population displacement.[92] It should also be noted that ethnicity is complex and as much socially rather than biologically constructed.[93] There were likely a range of different Germanic peoples in Britain before the end of Roman rule, most notably in the military. Germanic material culture and settlement appear to have increased after c. 425. However this was isolated to specific areas and some sort of Romano-British polity appears to have still been in control. Ethnic labels of people and material culture in fifth-century Britain are 'anachronistic and misleading'.[94]

The map in figure 7 shows early and late Anglo-Saxon burials of the fifth century.

It appears that Roman Britain continued after the end of Roman authority being just that, Roman in nature. Despite the disruption to the economy and deterioration of urban centres much of the rural population continued cultivating their fields. The increase in immigration is 'an insufficient explanation for the development of the new, post-Roman material cultural package because it does not take into account the collapse of Roman systems of material production'.[95] One contemporary account allows us a brief snapshot of what life was like in post Roman Britain a generation after Constantine III had taken much of the army to Gaul and ultimate defeat.

Saint Germanus

Constantius of Lyon (born c. 420) writing in c. 480 describes St Germanus in glowing terms.[96] He was 'born of parents of the highest rank, and was from the earliest childhood given a liberal education'. He studied Law in Gaul and Rome, and as a barrister 'became the ornament of the law courts'. He married a woman of high birth, wealth and character. Then the state appointed him to the official office of *dux* to rule over more than one province. Constantius tells us around this time a deputation from Britain came to Gaul to complain the heresy of Pelagius had 'taken hold of the people over a great part of the country'. A synod was convened with a 'large number of bishops'. The result was that two 'apostolic priests', Germanus and Lupus, were sent to help.

Pelagius is thought to have been a British monk who favoured the concept of free will over that of original sin. This was in contrast to Augustine of Hippo who emphasised God's grace as the only path to salvation. Pelagius visited Rome in the early fifth century. We know of his thoughts mainly from writings of his supporters, such as Caelestius, and that of his opponents, such as Jerome, who described him as a 'portly Scot, stuffed with Scottish porridge'. There has been some debate over whether he was a Briton or Irish. Bury, in 1904, proposed he was perhaps both, coming from one of the Irish settlements in western Britain.[97] An anonymous Pelagian treatise, *De divitiis* (On Riches) was written between 408–414.[98] It was highly critical of wealth and the concept of almsgiving which Augustine supported in North Africa. Emigres to North Africa after the sack of Rome in 410, including Pelagius himself, brought these ideas with them. Pelagius was eventually called before the council of Carthage in 418 to answer to a charge of heresy.

Anti-Pelagian legislation appeared after this date and subsequently a Pelagian called Agricola fled to Britain suggesting it was relatively safe for supporters compared to the Continent.[99] We then hear from Prosper in 455:[100] 'at the persuasion of the deacon Palladius, Pope Celestine sent Germanus, bishop of Auxerre, as his representative, and having rejected the heretics, directed the British to the catholic faith'. A similar deputation was sent to Ireland in 431 indicating the presence of Christianity prior to St Patrick's later mission: 'Palladius was sent by Pope Celestine to the Scots who believed in Christ, and was ordained as their first bishop.'

Constantius was writing a generation or more after Prosper and describes a violent storm nearly swamping the ship and miraculously being calmed by Germanus. On arrival they were met with 'great crowds' and their fame, preaching and miracles soon spread. We then hear the following:

'they ruled through consciences, taught through letters and worked miracles through their holiness. Preached by such men, the truth had full course, so that whole regions passed quickly over to their side.' This suggests a period of time elapsed. Perhaps more interestingly it suggests a religious schism across a still Romanised Britain. The Pelagians laid low 'for a time' but 'after prolonged consideration ... came forth flaunting their wealth, in dazzling robes, surrounded by a crowd of flatterers'. This could indicate the heresy was prevalent among the aristocracy.

We then hear a remarkable story of a great debate, at the 'meeting-place a crowd of vast proportions, wives and children among them, drawn by the occasion'. The usual landing point for travellers would have been Richborough in Kent, and the logical location for a such a debate with a large crowd would have been London. Constantius tells us of course that Germanus wins the debate and goes on to cure the blind daughter of a 'Tribune', suggesting a continuation of Roman administrative or military structures. Next he visited the shrine at St Albans about twenty-six miles to the north-east of London. So far we get a picture of a very Roman-sounding province. Some historians suggest Britannia was in fact still considered part of the empire.[101]

However, Constantius then tells us the Saxons and the Picts had 'joined forces to make war upon the Britons'. Germanus obviously is the hero once more. The army requested help from the bishop and on arrival he baptised many of the soldiers and appointed himself *Dux Proelii* (leader for battle). Germanus was able to win the battle without bloodshed by directing his forces to hide and shout 'Alleluia' repeatedly scaring the enemy many of who drowned in a river.

It is worth noting some of the details of the 'battle'.[102] First, it describes the presence of a functioning military force a generation after the end of Roman rule.

This implies recruitment, training, resourcing and maintenance within a military structure continued. Gildas in DEB described the Britons 'worthlessness', yet here the army had already marched out, located the enemy and were in camp when Germanus was sent for. The request was due to apprehension 'judging their resources to be utterly unequal to the contest' rather than being panic stricken or cowardly as Gildas suggests. The question arises: what resources did Germanus bring, if any? It could be that Constantius simply exaggerated. There is a contradiction between Saxons and Picts joining forces to make war and a force small enough to be frightened by a ruse. The barbarians learn of the Britons' location and advance to attack. The Britons demonstrate 'decisive superiority in reconnaissance' and lay an ambush. Germanus leads lightly armed men across country presumably leaving the bulk of heavy infantry behind. In 'a valley enclosed by steep mountains', Germanus laid out his ambush. On their approach the bishops chanted 'Alleluia' three times and directed their soldiers to repeat the battle cry.

Constantius emphasises the lack of bloodshed and the fact that no blow was struck. Whatever the truth, it suggests the Britons had a functioning military force c. 430 and were willing and able to to use it. But who were these Saxons? It could well be they were raiders from outside Britain. Constantius could be using the term generically as Roman writers often did. Sidonius Apollinaris in fifth-century Gaul, a contemporary of Constantius, describes Saxon pirates in the North Sea as 'the most ferocious of enemies'. It is possible Constantius simply used the term to mean raiders rather than an accurate ethnic description. In c. 553 Procopius writes that Britain was populated by three 'populous nations', each ruled by their own king: *Anglii, Frissones,* and *Britonnes*. He doesn't mention Saxons at all. The main point here is we cannot equate the relatively small amount of evidence of possible Saxon-related material culture and graves in Britain in the first half of the fifth century with other groups, whether they were Saxons or not. The 'most wealthy island' now secure, Germanus returned to Gaul.

Shortly after, the heresy returned, as did Germanus. There is some debate as to the date of this second visit, with three different years put forward: 437, 442 or 448. The earlier date is considered the most likely.[103] This is supported by events in Gaul at the time.[104] This time the heretics are banished and brought back to Gaul by Germanus himself. Constantius, writing fifty years later, tells us that after these visits the 'opulent island' was secure and peaceful.[105]

We get a number of clues about Britain from the text: Britain was stable enough to travel to and across; links with Gaul and the church had been maintained; in the first visit the Pelagians are 'confounded' but in the second they are condemned and exiled, suggesting a shifting of power towards the Roman church; raiding by Saxons and Picts occurred; and there was a functioning military force. Around this time Prosper writes praising the Pope, Celestine, for freeing Britain from the disease of the Pelagian Heresy and for sending a bishop (Palladius) to the Irish. Celestine, 'while he labours to keep the Roman island Catholic he has also made the barbarian island Christian'.[106] The impression is that in c. 430 Britain was still seen as a 'Roman island', in nature if not politically. Our next source gives a similar impression.

Saint Patrick

We have two surviving texts written by Saint Patrick, the *Confessio* and *Epistola*. From the first we learn he was born in *Bannavem*, Taburniae, an as yet unknown location, although it is likely to be in the west as he was captured by Irish raiders at the age of 16. His father, Calpurnius, was a deacon in the church and a *decurio*, a member of town council. His grandfather, Potitus, was a priest.[107] This implies a functioning town council and Christian community in the fifth century. There are some difficulties and much debate in dating his life accurately.[108] Irish annals suggest two separate floruits. The first places his death around 457 but it is likely this is confusing the mission of Palladius, sent by Pope Celestine in 431. A more accepted date is recorded in the Annals of Ulster placing his death in 493.[109] If we take the second date we can estimate his birth in c. 420 and his capture in the c. 430s. He spent six years in captivity before escaping and making his way back home, possibly through Gaul. Some later sources have him meeting St Germanus but again this is likely conflating him with Palladius.

The second text is his letter to a certain King Coroticus in response to a raid by the King's soldiers. By this time he has returned to Ireland, possibly in c. 450s following our later timeline. Patrick complains in his letter that the 'newly baptised' have been killed or captured, to be sold to their allies the 'apostate Scots and Picts'. Coroticus could be Ceretic Guletic, a fifth-century British king of Alt Clut centred on Dumbarton, but this is uncertain. Patrick makes a point of labelling him as neither a Christian or a Roman citizen. The implication is that he was in fact both and would take this as an insult. He calls the raiders 'soldiers whom I no longer call my fellow citizens', suggesting they were indeed Britons. The use of the phrase 'fellow citizens' suggests a Roman identity too.

Unfortunately, we learn very little from the manuscripts. However, it shows that communities in the west of Britain were Roman and Christian. Raiding and slaving were a real threat. In one area at least, petty kings were emerging and engaging in the same practices as their Irish and Pictish counterparts. The record then goes silent for nearly a century. The next source was not intended as history but rather a sermon, but it provides some clues as to the subsequent events that brought about the birth of the early Anglo-Saxon kingdoms.

Gildas

Our only contemporary British record of events comes about a hundred years after the two visits of St Germanus and St Patrick's capture by Irish raiders. The British monk, Gildas wrote *De Excidio et Conquestu Britanniae* (On the Ruin and Conquest of Britain) sometime between 524 and 547.[110] The text demonstrates a good level of training in Latin.[111] If the dating is correct then Gildas was born sometime in the late fifth century, which suggests Roman civilisation survived later than first thought.[112]

It cannot be viewed as an accurate historical account. It is a sermon, warning the Britons to change the error of their ways. It does, however, contain some vital clues and the nearer to his own time Gildas gets the more reliable the narrative may be.

It begins with a general description and history of Britain. The point at which it becomes relevant to our period is when the usurper Magnus Maximus 'had his evil head cut off at Aquileia'. This is the only date, 388, that we can be confident about. We then hear the Britons 'groaned aghast for many years' due to 'two exceedingly savage and over-seas nations', the Scots (Irish) and Picts. Envoys are sent to the Romans requesting aid and a legion arrives and deals with the raiders. Here Gildas possibly misdates the construction of the Antonine Wall by nearly 300 years. He tells us the Romans built a 'turf wall'. A second raid results in envoys being sent a second time and the Romans respond again. This time Gildas appears to misdate Hadrian's Wall and possibly the Saxon Shore defences. He tells us the Romans built a wall 'from sea to sea', but also towers on the south coast before bidding farewell never to return. This could reflect the *Rescript of Honorius* c. 410 when the Emperor tells the *civitates* of the Britain to look to their own defences.

It is possible Gildas is simply trying to explain the presence of structures more than a century after the Romans left. He does not mention Constantine III and it is possible the two incursions are synonymous with known raids in the last quarter of the fourth century. However, his narrative is confused and jumbled at this point. It may be that these raids are post 410 and perhaps one equates to the 'Alleluia victory' of St Germanus who he fails to mention.

The Scots and Picts return and seize 'the whole northern part of the land as far as the wall'. It is not clear which wall but he then talks of the Britons abandoning 'their cities and lofty wall'. I would suggest this makes Hadrian's Wall the most likely, which implies the previous Roman responses to various known raids from 367 to 409 may have pushed the border back temporarily to the Antonine Wall. There is much bloodshed and 'cruel massacres'. To make matters worse the country is 'stripped of every kind of food supply, with the exception of the relief that came from their skill in hunting'. This is far from the picture presented by Constantius of Lyon when writing about the first visit of St Germanus in 429. I would suggest it is either earlier, or the decade after his visits. Perhaps it is linked to the ASC entry for 418: 'This year the Romans collected all the hoards of gold that were in Britain; and some they hid in the earth, so that no man afterwards might find them, and some they carried away with them into Gaul'.

Alternatively it could be after St Germanus in the 440s because Gildas tells us the following:

> The miserable remnant therefore send a letter to Agitius, a man holding high office at Rome; they speak as follows:----To Agitius, in his third consulship, come the groans of the Britons; a little further in their request: the barbarians drive us to the sea, the sea drives us upon the barbarians; by one or other of these two modes of death we are either killed or drowned; and for these they have no aid.

He adds to this lament the 'severe and well-known famine'. Additionally, some people are yielding themselves as 'conquered to the bloodthirsty robbers', while others are continuing the war 'unceasingly'.

Agitius has been identified as Aetius and indeed this is the only figure in the fifth century who could possibly described as 'thrice council'. This would allow us to date this part of the chronology at least to 445–454 when Aetius held the consulship for the third time. However, it is possible that Gildas is simply adding the title rather than quoting direct from the letter. Thus it could have been as early as c. 425 or from 433 when Aetius became the dominant military figure in the Western Empire. Alternatively, it could be a different person entirely, such as Avitus, emperor in 455–6, or Aegidius, *magister militum per Gallias* in 458 and ruler of the breakaway Kingdom of Soissons in northern Gaul c. 461–5. Meaning Gildas perhaps assumed it was Aetius and added 'thrice consul'. The consensus is that it is indeed Aetius, and it would seem both Bede and the ASC followed this assumption as they place the arrival of the Anglo-Saxon mercenaries in the 440s and subsequent revolt and war in the 450s.

Gildas tells us the appeal is turned down but then the Britons, 'for the first time, they inflicted upon the enemy, which for many years was pillaging in the land, a severe slaughter'. The Irish return home and Gildas claims the Picts 'for the first time, in the furthermost part of the island … commenced their successive settlements'. With the 'devastation quieting down', the Britons experience a time of abundance: 'the island was becoming rich with so many resources of affluence that no age remembered the possession of such afterwards: along with these resources of every kind, luxury also grew'. Could this be the 'opulent island' Germanus visited in 429? Or is it the years after Aetius became consul for the third time in 445. Gildas then tells us the Britons turn to vice, namely the 'hatred of truth' and 'love of falsehood together with its fabricators'. Also, a 'desire of darkness in preference to the sun, the welcoming of Satan as an angel of light'. If he is referring to the Pelagian Heresy here, then this suggests his chronology is a little confused.

His next point is of interest to the evolution of kingship: 'Kings were anointed, not in the name of God, but such as surpassed others in cruelty, and shortly afterwards were put to death by the men who anointed them, without any enquiry as to truth, because others more cruel had been elected'. The implication here is that the Britons started to 'elect' kings before the mid-fifth century and they certainly sound more like petty warlords than saintly kings. We then come to the part of the tale that directly concerns the next chapter.

Rumour of further raids is followed by a plague killing so many that the 'living could not bury the dead'. We do have a record of pestilence in 442 that 'spread over almost the entire world'.[113] If this is the plague Gildas refers to, then it is three years before Aetius received the consulship for the third time. Next we read of a council led by a 'proud tyrant' inviting Saxon mercenaries to deal with 'repeated invasions and plundering'. Gildas does not name him but as we shall see Bede does. Gildas is scathing about the folly of inviting 'those wild Saxons, of accursed name, hated by God and men … admitted into the island, like wolves into folds, in order to repel the northern nations'. If the plague reached Britain in the mid-440s then this would place the subsequent arrival of mercenaries towards the end of that decade.

Three *cyulae* (keels), ships of war, arrive under full sail. A Saxon keel carried about thirty men which means a relatively small band of warriors. We must bear this in mind later when considering Hengest and Horsa's arrival. They 'first fixed their dreadful talons in the eastern part of the island', and a larger contingent joins itself 'to their bastard comrades'. The language Gildas uses implies strongly that this was an arrangement typical of Roman *foederati* being employed. They receive provisions, *annonas*, within a treaty, *foedere*.

After a 'length of time' they request more supplies and threaten to break the treaty. The ASC records no such disloyalty, so perhaps we are hearing one side of an argument. The Saxons revolt and 'fire from sea to sea … burned nearly the whole island … licking the western ocean with its fierce red tongue', and all the major towns were 'laid low'. Many are killed, enslaved or forced to emigrate. This, then, is our major turning point in the mid-fifth century. We will discuss dating a little later, but Gildas is writing possibly a hundred years after these events so it is well beyond living memory.

After 'a time', Ambrosius Aurelianus, whose parents had 'worn the purple', leads a fight back. An initial triumph leads to victories going 'back and forth' up to the siege of Badon Hill nearly 'the last defeat of the villains and certainly not the least'. Gildas states 'that was the year of my birth … the forty-fourth year since then has passed'. Much ink has been spilled on interpreting this passage. The most common interpretation is that Gildas was born in the same year as Badon and forty-four years has passed. However, it is possible to interpret the start of the forty-four years as the first victory of Ambrosius. Bede interprets it completely differently, but had access to a much earlier copy of Gildas. He places Badon forty-four years after the arrival of the Saxons, hence c. 493.

Coincidently, there is a good reason for dating Gildas forty-four years after this date. We have evidence for an extreme climatic event c. 535.[114] Tree rings and ice core studies show a marked reduction in growth and evidence for a drop in temperatures. In Italy c. 536, Cassiodorus described a dust veil or fog darkening the sky for about a year. Procopius in 536 records a 'most dread portent', the sun giving forth light 'without brightness'. John Lydus in c. 540s in Constantinople states clouds 'dimmed the light of the sun' over Europe and the produce was destroyed'. The Annals of Ulster in 536 records a 'failure of bread' and the Annals of Inisfallen date this 536–539. Widespread crop failures are reported from China to Europe. Gildas states: 'a dense cloud and black night of their sin so loom over the whole island', and uses many images of light and dark throughout the text. David Woods argues it is possible that Gildas is alluding to this and thus likely writing in 537.[115] Interestingly, a forty-four year period before 537 would place Gildas's birth, and possibly Badon, in 493. However, this connection in Gildas's text is a little tenuous and it is possible to take the opposite view that Gildas would have made far more of this event. If so, then we can narrow the date of DEB down to pre-536. If his later reference to Maglocunus is indeed Maelgwn of Gwynedd, and if his reign can be attested to 534–547, then we have a tentative date for the DEB of c. 534–6. This would place Badon, or the first victory of Ambrosius, in AD 490–2. This would be very close to Bede's estimate of 493.

We get a further clue from a reference to the adult grandchildren of Ambrosius described as 'inferior' to their forebear. If Ambrosius won his initial victory c. 480s and had a child at that time, then a grandchild might be born c. 510. This would place grandchildren in the 530s, exactly when we suspect Gildas was writing. Bede, in his *Chronica Majora*, c. 725, dates Ambrosius to 'in the time of Zeno', Eastern Emperor 474–491. None of these dates are secure and it has to be noted that some writers, such as Higham, place Gildas, Ambrosius and Badon two generations earlier. We will return to this debate later.

Gildas goes on to denounce five kings for various evils:

1. Constantine the 'tyrannical whelp of the unclean lioness of Damnonia', likely Dumnonia in the south west. His main sin was that he, 'in the garb of a holy abbot, cruelly tore the tender sides of two royal children … together with their two guardians'. This apparently occurred 'among the holy altars … with accursed sword and spear'.
2. Aurelius Caninus guilty of the 'filth of murders, fornications, adulteries', and a 'thirst for civil wars and repeated spoils'. Possibly one of the grandchildren of Ambrosius Aurelianus.
3. Vortipor, 'tyrant of the Demetae' and 'worthless son of a good king'. His sins include wickedness and 'various murders and adulteries'. He is described 'thy head is now becoming grey', suggesting he may well have been of fighting age forty-four years previously. Interesting when considering Badon.
4. Cuneglas, 'in the Roman tongue, thou tawny butcher'. He is described as wallowing in 'the old filth of thy wickedness, from the years of thy youth, thou bear, rider of many, and driver of a chariot belonging to a bear's den, despiser of God'. One of his chief sins is putting aside his wife and taking her sister who was 'under a vow to God of the perpetual chastity of widowhood'.
5. Maclocunus, possibly Maelgwn of Gwynedd c. 534–547. He is described as the 'dragon of the island … first in wickedness, exceeding many in power'. Gildas describes him as 'superior to almost all the kings of Britain, both in kingdom and in the form of thy stature'. One crime was killing his uncle, apparently in battle, but his main crime appears to have been renouncing his promise to become a monk.

There are a number of interesting points about these kings. First, Gildas addresses his sermon over the heads of these 'tyrants' and talks to his audience as though it was one polity. All five kings are likely to have been in the former province of

Britannia Prima. The earlier narrative of a council posting mercenaries suggests a diocese structure was still in place even after kings emerged. Gildas uses phrases such as 'countrymen' and the sense one gets is a surviving Roman world in the process of fragmenting. He accuses the kings of waging wars, 'civil and unjust'. Of chasing thieves 'all over the country', but rewarding thieves who 'sit with them at table'. Their 'military companions' are 'bloody, proud and murderous men'. Aurelius Caninus is accused of an 'unjust thirst for civil war and constant plunder'. This is in line with the emergence of petty kings and warlords. Yet these appear to be kings within some sort of surviving provincial structure. Importantly, paganism is not one of their faults. His audience is Christian and he appears to appeal to the Romano-British as a whole. Whether they considered themselves Roman is another matter.

He refers to the graves of holy martyrs, notably Saint Alban of Verulam, Aaron and Iulius, citizens of 'Caerleon', 'taken from us the citizens on account of our numerous crimes, through the disastrous division caused by the barbarians'. We know St Germanus visited the shrine of St Albans at Verulamium, but the location of the graves of Aaron and Julius are unknown regardless of where they came from. Some translate the 'disastrous division' as 'the unhappy partition with the barbarians', implying it affects the whole of Britain.[116] The implication is that the Britons can no longer access parts of the former diocese and St Albans appears to be one of locations along with the east of the island to which the Saxons returned after the revolt.

Gildas tells us that since Badon 'although wars with foreigners have ceased, domestic wars continue'. The cities are now 'deserted and dismantled' and lie neglected. He blames this on the domestic wars but it is possible he doesn't realise that urbanisation had deteriorated drastically a hundred years before. Yet we know some town life continued and Gildas tells us Britain has twenty-eight cities and 'some strongholds'.

He praises the generation after Badon, but the one subsequent to that are 'ignorant of that storm' and have experienced only of 'the present quiet'. This last point may be important. There has been an ending of 'foreign wars' and a period of relative peace, despite his denunciation of our five warlord kings. Ambrosius has fought a war that resulted in a victory at Badon and some sort of border or partition. Is this a fixed border or a series of enclaves? There is no indication that much of Britain has been lost, just specific areas. Gildas tells us Britain has rulers and 'watchmen' (*habet britanni rectores, habet speculatores*); Kings but they are 'tyrants'; judges, but they are 'ungodly men' (*reges habet britannia, sed tyrannos; iudices habet, sed impios*); priests, but they are 'unwise'; ministers, but many of them are 'impudent'; clerks but they are 'deceitful raveners'; pastors, but they are 'wolves prepared for the slaughter of souls'.

Gildas maybe confused about events a hundred years before but we can create a rough timeline. After the end of Roman rule the Britons suffered raiding from the Picts and Irish. The Britons managed to win a victory and there was a time of relative stability. Sometime in the mid-fifth century a council of sorts was able to post mercenaries to the 'east of the island' to combat northern raids. Sometime later there was a revolt that devastated large parts of the island. A fightback was lead by Ambrosius Aurelianus that went back and forth, culminating in the battle of Badon and some sort of division between Britons and regions controlled by the Saxon mercenaries. Forty-four years later Gildas describes, in well written Latin, a province of citizens, magistrates and priests. But he also describes civil wars and petty kings raiding and killing. What is happening in the areas controlled by those he calls Saxons he is silent about. This we shall look at in chapter two. First we will turn to Bede and the ASC.

Bede and the Anglo-Saxon Chronicle

Bede wrote *Historia ecclesiastica gentis Anglorum* (The Ecclesiastical History of the English People) in 731. He follows much from Gildas, but had access to continental and Anglo-Saxon sources as well, some stretching back to the time of Pope Gregory's mission to Kent. As a historian he is fairly well respected and where he is unsure of a fact he says so.[117] For example, he says the first leaders of the Angles 'are said to have been' the two brothers, Hengest and Horsa.[118]

He identifies the appeal to Aetius and dates it to the year after Attila's brother Blaedla died, c. 444. It is from Bede we learn the name of the 'proud tyrant'. His early version of the name, *Uuertigerno*, is suggested to be evidence of a fifth-century source.[119] The arrival of the Saxons in three ships is dated to the time of Marcian and Valentinian, 449–456. They are settled in the east but revolt and 'lay waste to every part of the island'. The Britons fight back, defeating them under Ambrosius Aurelianus. Victory then goes back and forth up to the siege of Mount Badon which he dates to forty-four years after their arrival, thus 493–500. He describes the visit of St Germanus as being 'a few years before' the arrival of the Saxons, and follows Constantius of Lyon's account in *The Life of St Germanus*.

The ASC, written in the late ninth century, appears to follow Bede. It dates the appeal to the Romans a little earlier, 443. The refusal is blamed on Attila, who was actually more of a threat a few years later. The appeal is to 'the princes of the Angle race'. It is interesting that once again the Angles are singled out. They arrive in the reign of Martianus and Valentinian, 449–456: 'In their days Hengest and Horsa, invited by Votigern, king of the Britons sought out Britain.' They land at Ebba's Creek (Thanet, Kent) and are given land in the south-east in return for fighting the Picts. It then repeats Bede's description of three tribes. Their numbers increase but there is no mention of a revolt.

We could decide at this point that, on the balance of probabilities, these sources are all roughly pointing to the late 440s for the arrival of mercenaries who subsequently revolt in the 450s. However, there is one source that throws a spanner in the works and this source is more contemporary and perhaps more reliable.

Gallic Chronicle

Sometime in the mid-fifth century an anonymous author, likely in southern Gaul, added to a chronicle of events, ending in 452. A Subsequent copyist continued this up to 511. These two records survive in ninth-century copies.[120] They are fairly reliable and accurate, though more so after 446. It records Carthage as being captured by the Vandals in 444 rather than 439. We can reduce this error to two years if the entry refers to the official cession of the city.[121] Thus the entry for Britain may well be a couple of years out.

Gallic Chronicle (452), entry for 441 'The Britains [i.e. the five provinces], which to this time had suffered from various disasters and misfortunes, are reduced to the power of the Saxons.'

Gallic Chronicle (511), entry for 440: 'The Britains, lost to the Romans, yield to the power of the Saxons.'

The earlier chronicle refers to 'disasters and misfortunes', which may be a reference to the events in Gildas. Yet there is no sense of the stable and 'opulent' island St Germanus saw in 429 and again in c. 437. We know there was an increase in Germanic material culture and settlement in specific areas from c. 425. Sources sometimes do differ in interpreting the same events. For example, with Prosper of Aquitaine writing c. 433, the barbarians are peripheral to events and he focuses on Roman matters. The chronicler of 452 views their arrival as the most important event. Importantly, he seems to know little of events far away such as the Franks or northern Gaul. Yet the content is generally accepted as reliable and contemporary.[122]

We are thus left to wonder why is there an apparent discrepancy between Gildas and Bede on one hand and the GC on the other? Gildas places the arrival of mercenaries after Aetius became 'thrice consul' and Bede dates this to 449. The subsequent rebellion comes after this and the ASC records battles in the 450s. Yet the GC records a Saxon takeover in 440, implying an earlier arrival date.

It is possible that Gildas is wrong and Bede simply copied the mistake. If one source is to be trusted, the GC is the most reliable and contemporary. The narrative in Gildas for the fifth century is certainly confused. However, it is also true that the whole of Britain did not 'fall to the power of the Saxons' for many centuries. We know the south-west continued to trade with the Continent, so perhaps there is a better explanation than a chronicler in southern Gaul being confused or in error. I would suggest it is possible these sources are actually referring to different events. The GC could be referring to a political event such as the appointment of a Germanic *magister militum* or *dux*. Or even a political marriage, such as the Visigoth King Athlauf and Galla Placidia in 414. We do get a hint from both Gildas and Bede of an initial arrival followed by a larger group sometime later. As we shall see in chapter two, one source, though unreliable, does indeed give us such a narrative with different arrivals and different treaties at different times. The *Historia Brittonum*, written in the early ninth century, has Hengest awarded Kent in return for his daughter's hand in marriage to Vortigern. We also have several groups arriving and different agreements taking place before a later breaking of a truce.

In summary the Gallic Chronicle provides an important marker. Britain appears to have remained culturally and socially Roman for much of the first half of the fifth century, despite being outside Roman authority. Yet something significant occurred c. 440. Whether this was the same event described by Gildas and later Bede and the ASC is unknown. If it wasn't, it was certainly the catalyst. By this point a whole generation had grown up outside Roman jurisdiction. One is left to speculate what effect this may have had on cultural identity. One major aspect of that is religion and it is to that we will now turn.

Religion

In 313 Constantine I issued the Edict of Milan, which gave Christianity, among other religions, legal status. It wasn't until 380, with the Edict of Thessalonica, that Christianity became the official state religion of the Roman Empire. This latter edict labelled other creeds, such as Arianism, heretical and authorised their persecution. We have seen this in action with the move against Pelagianism in the early fifth century which included the mission of St Germanus to Britain. Christianity had grown in Britain throughout the fourth century. Three British bishops attended the Council of Arminium in northern Italy in 359. Records state they were so poor they had to beg for financial help.

By the late fourth century the number of bishoprics in Britain were as high as twenty.[123] Thus by 407 when Constantine III took much of the remaining military force to Gaul, not only was the population 'mostly Christian', but the majority of major urban centres had large churches.[124] Despite this, some have suggested Christianity 'failed to emerge' in the first half of fifth-century Britain, with evidence pointing to dozens of pagan shrines.[125] One example can be seen at Sydney Park in Gloucestershire, dedicated to the Celtic deity Nodens. However, there is no evidence of pagan sites in Britain after 450.[126] The consensus is that, while paganism was widespread in the fourth century, by the beginning of the fifth century Christianity was the dominant religion. It would appear Germanic settlers were introducing Germanic paganism into Britain just as the native religions were disappearing. Additionally, at the same time Christianity had already established itself as the main religion, especially in the more Romanised and urbanised areas of the south and east. Despite the advance of Christianity there were still some in Rome who looked to the old gods.[127]

Volusianus was the son of a priestly family and he blamed the sack of Rome in 410 to the neglect of Rome's traditional gods. It was partly to answer these pagan criticisms that Augustine wrote the *City of God*. It is no coincidence that the Pelagian controversy also erupted around the same time. The denial of original sin undermined the need for baptism and the emphasis on free will undermined the importance of prayer and God's grace. Additionally, ardent Pelagians felt the rich could not be saved and should give away everything. Augustine, on the other hand, insisted alms-giving atoned for sins. For him the life of a Christian was one of continual penance.

For Augustine, pride not wealth was the true enemy.[128] He did not demand the renunciation of wealth, but rather that the wealthy should be generous.[129] The appearance of the rich of Italy and disciples of Pelagius after 410 was a significant turning point. Catholic Bishops had issued anti-Donatist Laws after 411 to drive out what they saw as heretics. A generation later the Arian Vandals used these same laws to exile Catholic bishops to Italy. What is significant is the cities of Africa did not protect their Bishops and 'chose city over alter'.[130] Did towns and people in Britain chose *civitas* over Roman church in the face of Anglo-Saxon rising power?

Around the same time as the Vandal conquest of North Africa, the visits of St Germanus in 429 and c. 437 imply a largely Christian former province. His *vitae* describes a schism with Christianity but no hint of paganism. The bishop is greeted by large crowds, presumably mostly Christian. The Pelagians were 'richly dressed' and we could speculate these were from the aristocracy and elites. Was there a schism between rich and poor, urban and rural? Germanus delivered mass to the army prior to the 'Alleluia victory', suggesting a percentage of the soldiers at least were Christian. His first visit results in his opponents being beaten in a debate. At the end of his second visit the heretics are condemned and exiled, suggesting not only a shift in power but the ability to judge and pass sentence was on the side of the church. We also recall his visit to the shrine of St Alban at Verulamium. A hundred years later Gildas complains he is unable to visit the same shrine. Is this because it has been destroyed, or is there some physical or political border or partition that prevents him?

We see links with the continental church did continue after the end of Roman authority. Pope Celestine sent Bishop Palladius to Ireland in c. 431. Prosper praises him for that and for ending the Pelagian Heresy: '[The pope] labours to keep the Roman island Catholic he has also made the barbarian island Christian.'[131] The implication here is that there is a Christian community in Ireland that needs a bishop. Further evidence of surviving Christian communities come from the letters of St Patrick.

His father and grandfather held positions in the church somewhere in the west of the island.[132] A functioning church and town council are present. In Ireland also there is a growing community, first through the work of Palladius after 431, and then from St Patrick perhaps a generation later. His letter to Coroticus indicates a Christian and Roman identity was seen as something to value. To suggest someone was neither was an insult. Perhaps this was similar to calling someone a barbarian or *bacaudae* rebel (a term we will address later) in early fifth-century Gaul. Of course we cannot assume everyone saw things this way. Some may have rejected these identities and wore their insults as a badge of pride.

Contact with the church in Rome appears to have broken down after the mid-fifth century. The Easter dates calculated c. 454 in Rome were utilised in Britain. However, that appears to be the last change that made it through to the church in Britain. After this date the British church evolved in a distinct way compared to the continent. Yet trade links with the Mediterranean continued, especially in the west.

And it was in the west and Ireland that the church survived. When he arrived in 597, St Augustine found a thriving British church in the west at least.

If we conclude that Christianity was dominant in the mid-fifth century, what can we say about the mid-sixth century, after a hundred years of a significant increase in Germanic material culture and settlement? Writing at the time, Gildas praises Ambrosius Aurelianus and it is unlikely he would do so if he was not a good Christian. He may well have been a contemporary of St Patrick if Bede is correct about dating him to 'the time of Zeno', 474–91, and Patrick's later obit is correct, c. 493. Gildas places Ambrosius and/or Badon forty-four years prior to writing. We read his grandchildren are 'greatly inferior' and he castigates five tyrant kings for various crimes. Paganism, however, is not among these sins. Given the nature of his polemic, it is unlikely Gildas would not have mentioned it if there was any hint of apostasy. It is not at all clear what the political situation is. Are there any provincial structures left? Even a council of sorts for the former diocese? Or have the five provinces already fragmented with former *civitates* evolving into petty kingdoms?

Whatever the case, his audience is unquestionably Christian and very distinct from the 'barbarians', who are described in withering terms. Gildas has no time for nuance or the complexity of cultural identity. This clear dichotomy portrayed by Gildas may not accurately reflect the political or social reality. His purpose is religious message, not historical accuracy. What is clear from the evidence is that a strong British church and Christian identity survived the end of Roman authority and beyond. This is certainly true for the fifth and sixth centuries, at least in the west and north.

What then of the south and east after the mid-fifth century? These are the areas that experienced a significant increase in cultural change and settlement. According to the literary sources these are also the areas where the initial mercenaries were posted, where the revolt spread from ('from sea to sea') and where to where they returned. The initial battles of the ASC in the fifth end sixth centuries are confined to the south coast from Kent to the New Forest, and the Thames Valley region. Germanic settlers, migrants and invaders were likely pagans. Even if they were Christians it's possible they were Arians like many Goths and Vandals, rather than followers of orthodox Nicene Creed such as the Franks, and it would appear, Romano-Britons.

In 595 St Augustine began his journey to Kent, sent by Pope Gregory on a mission to convert the Anglo-Saxons. King Æthelberht of Kent had married a Christian Frankish princess but had remained pagan. Pope Gregory writes about the 'bishops of the British', suggesting a surviving church structure and Christian community. Anglo-Saxon rulers seem to have tolerated different religious practices and similar evidence is seen in fifth-century Gaul. Here Christianity thrived despite the presence of the barbarians.[133]

By the beginning of the seventh century several Anglo-Saxon kingdoms had emerged. They started to convert, one after another, after Kent at the end of the sixth century. However, there remained a chasm between the established British church and the growing Roman church in the east and south. This was partly alleviated by the Synod of Whitby in 664. Bede, writing in 731, looks back at the crimes Gildas levels at the Britons of his day and adds this: 'they never preached the faith to the Saxons or Angles who inhabited Britain with them'.[134] This implies a distinct ethnic division by the eighth century.

In summary, we can be reasonably confident Britain remained largely Christian with a functioning church structure into the fifth century. The indigenous pagan religions appear to have been diminished to the extent that no archaeological evidence remains. The introduction of a Germanic material and social culture, along with significant levels of migration, seems to have affected cultural identity. By the end of the fifth century, Germanic paganism was prevalent throughout the east and south. yet a Christian community seems to have survived here too. Differences in religion did not necessarily equate to conflict, as we see Arians and Catholics coexisting in the fifth century in Gaul relatively peacefully.[135] It would be reasonable to suggest that the more Romanised and urbanised areas in the south and east were also the most diverse ethnically, culturally and in terms religion. In Gaul, the great Ecclesiastical offices became synonymous with high-ranking status and a hereditary right.[136] There seems to be hints of a similar situation in western Britain at sites such as Wroxeter. If bishoprics in eastern Britain did survive this might suggest an aristocratic elite allying themselves with incoming Germanic elites. The Frankish king Clovis worked with the civil administrative structure while still a pagan.

What we can conclude from this is that any British war leader was likely Christian, as was the vast majority of his soldiers and people. This would not, of course, prevent him from using mercenaries. However, a king of an emerging Anglo-Saxon kingdom may not have such a homogenous population from which to draw his forces. We simply do not know the ethnic, cultural or religious make up of armies led by warriors such as Hengest or Ælle. Bede puts these words into the mouth of Æthelberht, replying to St Augustine in 597:[137] 'These are fair words and promises which you have brought and announce to us. But as they are new and unknown, we cannot yet consent to leave those things, which we have long held with all the English race'.

The words, if taken at face value, would suggest Christianity had all but died out, in Kent at least, despite the apparent continuation of the indigenous Romano-British population. Alternatively, it may reflect a hierarchical social structure with a Germanic elite separate from an indigenous peasantry. The most likely explanation though is poetic licence on the part of Bede. Æthelberht had been married to a Christian princess and can't possibly have claimed Christianity was 'new and unknown'.

Conclusion

The experience of 300 years of Roman authority had a major impact on the society and landscape of tribal Britain. The economy, urbanisation and road network had transformed society. The population had developed a largely Roman and Christian identity. We cannot say whether a tribal identity survived but that of the *civitas* certainly did. The end of Roman authority resulted in a huge shock to the economy and urban life, which both deteriorated significantly. At the same time, Germanic material culture and settlement increased after c. 425. Yet St Germanus witnesses a very Roman-looking former province. Some sort of diocese structure also seems to have survived to allow the posting of mercenaries and we have evidence of much continuation of population and land use.

Robin Fleming, in *The Material Fall of the Roman Empire 300–525 CE*, provides some context.[138]

The population of Roman Britain in the fourth century is estimated between 2 to 3 million. Of this, about 75,000 were soldiers and dependants, mostly in the north. In addition, around 150,000 lived in urban or semi-urban communities. A further 15,000 lived in the villas and town houses of high-ranking administrators and landlords. Most of the elites would have descended from local Britons. This adds up to about a quarter of a million people living above subsistence levels and off the surplus created by others. The remaining 85 per cent of the population were rural workers. Importantly, their needs did not depend on the market economy. The Roman tax system disadvantaged the bulk of the population taking up to two thirds of what they produced in taxes, rents and tributes. The bulk of the land tax, for example, was paid for by these same people, whereas retired state officials, veterans and senators were exempt from many taxes.[139] Two parallel monetary systems operated: precious metal coins were relatively stable, used to pay officials and soldiers and required for the payment of taxes; in contrast small bronze coins, *nummi*, made up a low-value currency.[140] Fleming makes the interesting point that 'people are dependent on things', and vice-versa, and material culture has a 'profound role' in the how society evolves and changes.[141]

In the mid-fifth century there was a dramatic turning point for British history. The GC dates this to 440 while Bede suggests a little later. Gildas supplies a confusing, unreliable narrative full of fire and brimstone. Was this the point the diocese structure collapsed? Did the provinces remain intact? If so, for how long? By the end of the following century it had fragmented completely and petty kingdoms were emerging, many based on the former Roman *civitates*. This was the time of the tyrant kings of Gildas. The heroes of *Y Gododdin* and the warlords and petty kings of Britannia. Different cultural identities were emerging. Romano-British in the north and west and a Germanic-Romano-British in the south and east.

Back in the first half of the fifth century all this was in the future. Some Romano-Britons may still have hoped for the return of Roman rule. Some may have been cheered by the exploits of Aetius in Gaul. While others may have valued their independence. Whatever the case, when threatened by further barbarian raids they turned to the time and tested method of hiring mercenaries. It is to these mercenaries we will now turn. If we take the literary sources at face value, and trust Bede writing three centuries later, these mercenaries were led by two warriors. Their names were Hengest and Horsa and their arrival changed Britain forever.

Chapter Two

The First Kingdom

'Often the solitary man enjoys
The grace and mercy of the Lord, though he
Careworn has long been forced to stir by hand
The ice-cold sea on many waterways,
Travel the exile's path; fate is relentless.'
So spot a wanderer who called to mind
Hardships and cruel wars and deaths of Lords....

So I, careworn, deprived of fatherland
Far from my noble kin, have often had
To tie fetters my own troubled spirit
Since long ago I wrapped my Lord's remains
In darkness of the earth, and sadly thence
Journeyed by winter over icy waves,
And suffering sought the hall of a new patron

The Wanderer, Anglo-Saxon poem, The Exeter book,
late tenth century.

The Finnsburg Fragment

The heroic poem *Beowulf* is one of the oldest and most important examples of Old English.[1] J.R.R. Tolkien, author of *Lord of the Rings*, made a detailed study of the *Finnesburg Fragment* which forms part of the *Beowulf* epic. This part of the narrative is set in the fifth century and features various Danish, Geatish, Jutish and other characters. Importantly, it features the warrior Hengest. Tolkien estimated the timeframe for the characters involved and equates this warrior with the same figure in the HB. It's an interesting tale of a Jutish leader, Hengest, fighting in a Danish–Geat war in Friesland.

Finn, a king in Friesland, hosts the war-band of his brother-in-law, Hnæf Scylding, in a hall with his warriors, described as 'sixty war bears'. Finn's wife is Hildeburh, sister of Hnæf, called *Healfdene*, or half-Dane. Among Hnæf's band is the Jutish warrior Hengest. During the night they are treacherously attacked by their hosts, although the cause is uncertain. The *Fragment* begins in a great hall at Finnesburg with 'gables are burning' and Hnæf awakening his men: 'mortal enemies approach in ready armour'. They quickly don their mail and take up weapons. Sigeferth, a prince of Secgan, and Eaha protect one door of the hall. At the other Ordlaf, Guthlaf and Hengest. Outside, one of the attackers, Guthere, tries to dissuade a certain Garulf, likely a young noble, not to risk so 'precious a life', but this Garulf, son of Guthulf, is the first to die in the attack, surrounded by 'a host of good men, the bodies of the brave'. Tolkien suggests he may have been a prince based on a mention in the poem *Widsith*.[2]

For five days the warriors held the doors and 'so well they fought that none of the retainers fell'.

The fight 'swept away all the knights of Finn save few alone'. We get a dramatic picture of waves of attacks over several days with the defenders fighting for their lives. The attackers are unable to break through the doors and several die in the attempt. The leader of the the defenders, Hnæf, eventually falls, as does Hildeburh's son in the attack. Hildeburh is said to be 'without fault', and her husband's subsequent actions suggest he may not have been party to the attack. The text implies Hengest then took command inside the hall. Finn's warriors are unable to defeat Hengest or 'wrest the survivors of the disaster from the king's thane'. A treaty was agreed and Finn offered Hengest a 'hall and throne' to share with 'the sons of the Jutes'. Oaths were exchanged and a 'pact of peace' confirmed.

After the battle and peace treaty, a funeral pyre was prepared and Hildeburh placed her son and brother, Hnæf, upon it with the other warriors. Hnæf's warriors return home but Hengest stays, 'unhappily', throughout the winter. With the arrival of spring he was keen to leave but his thoughts turned to vengeance. Hunlaf's son placed the sword *Hildeleoma* on his lap. This was the 'best of swords – its edges were renowned among the Jutes'. This spurred Hengest to act and so he did: 'the hall was reddened with the life-blood of enemies and Finn too was slain'. The warriors of the Scyldings then took to their ships with the queen, Hildeburh, and 'all the riches of the king' back to her people.

Tolkien equates this Hengest with the same warrior recorded in the HB and Bede. He dates his birth to c. 425 and the battle at Finnsburg to 452. Tolkien suggests the tale of *Beowulf* is associated with historical figures living in the early sixth century. Hengest's arrival in Britain is placed in c. 453 and we can see a narrative taking shape. A war-band of Danes and Jutes led by Hnæf arrive at a Friesian settlement to visit his sister Hildeburh. Her husband, Finn, allows them use of a great hall. In the night a Friesian thane attacks the hall but is repulsed. For five days they hold out. In the end an uneasy peace is agreed but Hildeburh's son and brother, Hnæf, lie dead along with many others. Some of the war-band return home but Hengest remained for the winter. In the spring his obligation to avenge his lord outweighed his oaths to Finn. There is a hint of something more. Guthlaf and Oslaf are said to have returned home and reported the deadly attack, blaming Finn. Perhaps they returned in the spring and it was at this point Hengest found he 'could not refuse the warlord service'.

Finnsburg is destroyed, the Danes return home and no doubt the Friesians were out for blood. Perhaps Hengest took the surviving Jutes, and any other warriors out for adventure, and sailed north west. The coast of Britain was only a day's sail away. The imagery is one of great halls and war-bands, oaths and blood feuds. If Tolkien is correct, then this is a very different world from that of the Roman General Aetius. Just a year before Tolkien's date for Finnsburg Aetius defeated Attila the Hun at the Battle of the Catalaunian Plains. Despite the significant barbarian incursions and settlements, the general had been relatively successful in playing the different groups off against each other, even using Hunnic mercenaries to do so. Roman authority still held sway in Gaul in the first half of the fifth century.

This is the same Aetius who Gildas apparently refers to when the Britons appeal for help. In the mid-fifth century Britain was outside Roman authority but as we saw earlier still very much a 'Roman island'. How different would British history have been if it was Aetius who arrived to help the Britons and Hengest did not? Gildas stated the Saxon mercenaries initially 'fixed their dreadful claws on the east side of the island'. Bede tells us they were granted 'a place of settlement in the eastern part of the island'. After defeating the Picts 'the newcomers received from the Britons a grant of land in their midst', which implies a more widespread distribution, possibly across surviving military forts. The HB gives us more detail and it is to that we will now turn.

The Historia Brittonum

The HB was written c. 828 and is often attributed to a monk, Nennius, although this only appears in a later version.[3] Other manuscripts name Mark the Anchorite as author or interestingly, Rhun son of Urien, which suggests an earlier date is possible. It describes the ages of the world and the origins of Britain, including a tale of Trojan immigrants, before covering Roman Britain. Some view the text as 'synchronised history' written for political purposes in a ninth-century context.[4] Others, that the author is 'actively manipulating his text to create a synthetic pseudo-history'.[5] However, Charles-Edwards states: 'if such history is unhistorical, so also are all the major histories of the early middle ages'.[6] Chadwick views British leader Vortigern as the most important figure in the text and concludes there is 'no reasonable doubt' he is historical.[7] Another important figure is Ambrosius/Emrys (Emrys is simply the Welsh version of the name), undoubtedly the same figure Gildas highlights, and later used by Geoffrey of Monmouth to construct his figure of *Merlinus*.

The text tells us that after the death of the Emperor Magnus Maximus and the end of the Roman Empire in Britain the Britons 'went in fear for forty years'. Vortigern reigned in Britain and in his fourth year three ships led by Hengest and Horsa arrived and were settled in Thanet, east Kent. It is unfortunate that the text gives us a number of contradictory dates:[8]

- Chapter 16: 'From the year when the Saxons first came, to the fourth year of King Mervyn, 429 years are reckoned', i.e. 399.

- Chapter 31: 'the British went in fear for 40 years'. It is unknown if this is from the death of Maximus (388), killing of the 'generals' (407), or end of Roman Britain (410). Thus pointing to 428, 447 or 450.
- Chapter 31: 'When Gratian ruled for the second time with Equitius, the Saxons were received by Vortigern, 347 years after the Passion of Christ', i.e. 375.
- Chapter 66: 'Vortigern, however, held empire in Britain in the consulship of Theodosius and Valentinian and in the fourth year of his reign the English came to Britain, in the consulship of Felix and Taurus, in the 400th year from the the Passion of our Lord Jesus Christ', i.e. 428.
- Chapter 66: From the year when the English came to Britain and were welcomed by Vortigern to Decius and Valerian are sixty-nine years. Unidentified figures and unknown date.
- Chapter 66: From the reign of Vortigern to the quarrel between Vitalinus and Ambrosius are twelve years, that is Guoloppum, the battle of Guoloppum (possibly Wallop in Hampshire), an unknown date.

Unlike in Gildas and Bede it is stated they were exiled rather than hired: 'In the meantime, three vessels, exiled from Germany, arrived in Britain. They were commanded by Horsa and Hengist, brothers.' Bede uses the variant spelling, Hengist, but could this be after the destruction of Finnsburg? Vortigern receives them and an agreement is struck to supply 'clothing and provision' to fight against 'the enemies of his country', presumably the Scots and Picts mentioned earlier. The HB then relates how St Germanus deposed a tyrannical and wicked king, named Benlli, and replaced him with a certain Catel Drunlue. This is possibly a foundation-legend supporting a specific dynasty of Powys in the ninth century. It certainly doesn't feature in the Life of Saint Germanus by Constantius of Lyon. It has been suggested Germanus has been confused with St Garmon, who is known to have been in Wales in the 460s and died on the Isle of Man in 474.[9] The text then returns to Hengest.

 The mercenaries 'greatly increased in number' and the Britons have trouble fulfilling their bargain. The emphasis is slightly different from Gildas, who places the blame squarely on the barbarians who make false claims and then break the treaty. Here it is the Britons who end the treaty: 'Your number is increased; your assistance is now unnecessary; you may, therefore, return home, for we can no longer support you.' But Hengest does a deal with Vortigern and a second group of mercenaries arrive with sixteen ships. They bring with them the beautiful daughter of Hengest and he prepares a feast and has his daughter serve the guests. Vortigern is besotted and promises Hengest whatever he asks in return for her hand. Her father 'requests the province, called in English, Centland, in British, Ceint'. We are told this was done without the knowledge Guoyrancgonus, who reigned in Kent. While Guoyrancgonus is described as a king, we must consider whether this is a ninth-century interpretation of a civilian or military post. Perhaps he was the governor of a *civitas* or a military commander on the Saxon Shore. Hengest says to Vortigern, 'I will be to you both a father and an adviser.' By military advisor he may well mean a *magister militum*, a role several Germanic generals held in the Western Empire in the fifth century. Perhaps Hengest was appointed *comes* or *dux*. Recalling the GC it is worth considering if a chronicler in southern Gaul would consider this event as 'falling to the power of the Saxons'? We then get a third major arrival of mercenaries, this time in forty ships, which would give us a late legionary sized force of around 1,000 troops. Hengest's son Octha, and nephew Ebissa, are settled 'near the wall' to fight the Irish.

The text returns to Saint Germanus. A council condemns Vortigern for having a child with his own daughter and he flees to modern Gwynedd, North Wales, where he attempts to build a fortress. Continual collapses cause his wizards to advise sacrificing a 'child without a father'. They find a young boy, Ambrosius, in Glywysing, South Wales, and take him north. But Ambrosius tells Vortigern his wizards are fools and says the real reason for the failure is that there are two 'worms', or dragons, lying underneath, one red, one white causing the collapse. These are discovered and Ambrosius makes various prophecies. Vortigern then cedes the fortress and the 'western part of the island' to 'Emrys the overlord', before heading north to the region called Gwynessi. Ambrosius describes himself as the son of a Roman consul, a clear reference to the Ambrosius Aurelianus in Gildas.

Meanwhile, Vortigern's son Vortimer had taken the throne and had a very different policy towards Hengest and his mercenaries. At this point the Britons are the aggressors and Vortimer drives them out of Kent and back to Thanet three times: 'Vortimer fought vigorously against Hengest and Horsa … expelled them and besieged them as far as the island called Thanet.' Three times he 'shut them up and besieged them, attacking, threatening and terrifying them'. Hengest's response was to send envoys to Germany to 'summon a vast number of fighting men'. The battles go back and forth and the Saxons 'sometimes victoriously advanced their frontiers, sometimes being defeated and expelled'. The HB then lists Vortimer's four battles, three of which are named. Whether these are separate from the previously mentioned war is not made clear: Deguentid (Darent in Kent?); Episford (Aylesford, Kent) where Cateyrn, Vortimer's brother, dies along with Hengest's brother Horsa; and a third, a victory, in 'open country by the inscribed stone on the shore of the Gallic Sea' (the south east coast?). The fourth battle is not named. This sounds very much like Gildas's account of Ambrosius: 'From then on victory went now to our countrymen, then to their enemies.' Interesting too that they were 'sometimes expelled'. Another interesting similarity is with the description after Arthur's battles in the HB: After their defeats the 'English sought help from Germany and continually and considerable increased their number.'

Soon after this war Vortimer dies. The twelfth century HRB embellishes the tale by claiming Hengest's daughter poisoned her new son-in-law. The Saxons return and Hengest asks for peace which Vortigern, back in power, persuades the council to accept. At the subsequent peace conference the Saxons treacherously kill 300 British nobles, capture Vortigern and force him to cede Essex, Sussex, Middlesex and 'other districts'. This sounds remarkably like the south east province of Maxima Caesariensis. This would include not only the largest city in Britannia, Londinium, but also the shrine of Saint Albans at Verulamium. We are at once reminded of the 'unhappy partition' with the barbarians, referred to by Gildas, which had been in place since the time of Ambrosius forty-four years before.

The HB then has Vortigern fleeing to Dyfed, pursued by Germanus, where he is destroyed by fire 'with all his wives', although 'others have different versions' of his death. After this Germanus returns to his own country suggesting that either all these events occurred before c. 440 as the GC suggests, or that the narrative is hopelessly confused. Hence why some have suggested Saint Garmon as a possible explanation, although we have no evidence to support this.

Next the HB turns to the life of St Patrick, who it seems to conflate with Palladius, sent to Ireland c. 431. It gives him an implausibly long life of 120 years and states he preached in Ireland for eighty-five years. Crucially for our timeline, it then places the death of Saint Patrick around the same point as the death of Hengest. We have read that the more likely obit of the saint was 493 and it is interesting the ASC places Hengest's death in 488 although neither date can be confirmed. Then 'at this time' the English increased their numbers. After Hengest's death his son Octha came down from the north to Kent, and from him 'sprung the kings of the Kentishmen'. We then get the famous important passage: 'Then Arthur fought against them', and his twelve battles are listed. However, the English then sought help from Germany and brought over their kings to rule over them until the time when Ida reigned (approximately 547), the first king of Bernicia.

The HB goes on to say much more, but for our purposes at this point we note a number of points. First, there is a very clear sense that Vortigern holds authority over the whole of the former diocese and is able to allocate land and appoint military and civil posts from Kent to Hadrian's Wall. Second, while there are some differences, it doesn't contradict what other sources such as Gildas or Bede says. What it does is provide a plausible explanation for the discrepancies in dating between the GC and Bede. Here we have several different arrivals and events:

- The initial arrival of Hengest and Horsa in three ships.
- A second group arrives in sixteen ships.
- Hengest's daughter arrives and Vortigern cedes Kent to Hengest.
- A third group in forty ships arrive and are settled near the wall.
- A war with Vortimer ending in the mercenaries being besieged three times in Thanet and eventually driven out.
- Hengest returns after Vortimer's death and Vortigern agrees a new treaty.
- Finally, we get the massacre at the peace conference and ceding of much of the south east.

We must consider whether the GC could refer to one of the earlier events such as the ceding of Kent. If we follow this thinking then perhaps Hengest did arrive earlier as the HB suggests such as 428 but did not rise to power until 440. This would allow St Germanus to visit twice in 429 and 437 and still regard the the diocese as essentially Roman. The subsequent war with Vortimer would then be in the 440s and the appeal to Aetius in response to that rather than Picts and Scots. The return of Hengest is followed by 'ratifying the treaty'. This might be an official *foederati* status which Bede was able to date to 449. The revolt of Gildas and Bede may be synonymous with the massacre at the peace conference in the HB.

This is of course speculation, but there is some consistency in the sources. Some time passes after Roman authority ends. We then get an arrival of mercenaries and a subsequent revolt around the mid-fifth century. This is followed by a war going back and forth. Gildas and Bede name Ambrosius Aurelianus. The HB places him as a child protege in the time of Vortigern and names Arthur as the warrior fighting the barbarians a generation or more after Hengest. All three sources mention the battle of Mons Badonicus. Importantly at the end of this period there is a 'partition' of some sort. The important thing at this point in the narrative is that a relatively small group of Germanic warriors were hired just before the mid-fifth century and their subsequent revolt was to prove a turning point in history. Let us now see how Bede names and describes their leaders.

Bede

Bede, writing in c. 731, nearly 300 years after the events, follows Gildas for most of this part of his history. He has no doubt the appeal is to Aetius in response to Irish and Pictish raids in the north. Again we have a famine and a fight back and victory over the invaders. A time of abundance, affluence and luxury is followed by vice and 'every kind of foul crime'. A plague ravages Britain so there was 'not enough people to bury the dead'. Vortigern requests help from Saxon mercenaries to fight the Irish and Picts. He then goes on to describe the 'three Germanic tribes', Saxons in Wessex, Sussex and Essex, Jutes in Kent and Hampshire and Angles in East Anglia, Mercia and Northumbria.[10] Their original homeland of Angeln is said to be still unpopulated in his day.[11] Concerning the warriors, Bede seems slightly unsure or suspicious of his sources, as he states their names 'are said to have been two brothers, Hengest and Horsa'. Another interesting point is that Hengest and Horsa are the first leaders of the Angles, not the Saxons. He mentions Horsa being slain in battle, which is referenced in both the HB and ASC.

Bede then tells us that the Barbarians entered into a 'league' with the Picts and turned 'their weapons against their allies'. They first asked for more provisions then threatened to break the treaty. The subsequent revolt 'ravaged all the neighbouring cities and country, spread the conflagration from the eastern to the western sea, without any opposition, and overran the whole face of the doomed island'. Public and private buildings were 'overturned', priests were slain 'before the altars' and 'the prelates with the people were destroyed with fire and sword'. The enemy then 'returned home to their own settlements', presumably in the east of the island.

But the Britons fought back under the leadership of Ambrosius Aurelianus, 'a man of worth, who alone, by chance, of the Roman nation had survived the storm, in which his parents, who were of the royal race, had perished'. The war went back and forth, 'till the year of the siege of Badon-hill, when they made no small slaughter of those enemies, about forty-four years after their arrival in England'. Given he dates the arrival to 449, he is suggesting Badon occurred in c. 493. This could be a misinterpretation of Gildas who states Badon, or the first victory of Ambrosius, was forty-four years before his writing. However, Bede was usually careful in his claims and had access to other sources. In his *Chronica Majora*, written in c. 725, he dates Ambrosius Aurelianus to 'the time of Zeno', 474–91. It is thus possible that Bede had the date from another source and assumed that's what Gildas meant because it was coincidently forty-four years after their arrival. Unfortunately, regarding these events, Bede writes no more.

He clearly has access to the *Life of Saint Germanus* by Constantius of Lyon as he repeats much of that including the 'Alleluia victory'. When he returns to the later fifth century narrative he simply copies Gildas again. Britain is free from foreign but not civil wars. The cities remained abandoned and in ruins. His main criticism of the Britons is that they 'never preached the faith to the Saxons, or English, who dwelt among them'. This throwaway line could be crucial. The Saxons and English are described as 'dwelling among' the Britons. We cannot assume the 'unhappy partition' of Gildas means a fixed border with Anglo-Saxons one side and Romano-British on the other.

Annales Cambriae

The AC is a tenth-century chronicle, although our earliest copies are from the twelfth century. A number of different versions exist and while the A text makes no reference to Hengest, the B text does, c. 444:[12] *aduentus anglorum · horsi et hengisti tempore wortigerni regis*. Both the A and B text does include references to Badon, Arthur and Camlann. As even the original manuscripts likely post-date Bede, ASC and the HB, they could be later additions. But it is interesting that the AC dates Badon to 516, a generation later than implied by Bede. Some have suggested a misdated Easter cycle would push the date back nineteen years. Others point out that early Welsh legends rarely associate Arthur with Badon at all, or even fighting Saxons. In those tales he is a far more mythical character, visiting the underworld, stealing magic cauldrons and fighting giant boars. Thus perhaps Badon has been erroneously added to Arthur's battle list.

On the other hand, Camlann is attested in various other Welsh sources and is always associated with Arthur. Perhaps the date for Camlann, 537, is accurate and a copyist brought Badon forward in time in order to to place Arthur there. In my previous books, *King Arthur, Man or Myth* and *The Battles of King Arthur*, I argued for an alternative explanation for the dating in the AC. The earliest manuscript is found attached to the HB. If we look at that text it places Arthur and Badon after the death of Saint Patrick. However, it appears to conflate him with Palladius, and has Pope Celestine sending him to Ireland. A copyist during the Dark Ages would know that Celestine died in 432 and the Irish mission of Palladius was c. 431. The HB then states Patrick preached for eighty-five years. Directly after this passage we get the famous battle list of Arthur. It is possible the copyist simply added eighty-five years to the assumed date of Patrick's mission, 431. This equates to 516, exactly the date given in the AC.

Whatever the true date, over 600 years later Geoffrey of Monmouth appears to follow roughly the AC dating along with the narrative in the HB. The only date he gives is that for Camlann, which he places in 542. However, one can calculate a date for Badon from the text, around 520, although it has to be noted we cannot trust a source with so many historical errors written 600 years later.

What this means for Hengest is that his floruit is always placed before the battle of Badon. Whether he arrived in c. 428 or 449, the ASC date for his death, 488, if inaccurate, is likely to be at the later end of the range of dates. He may well have outlived Vortigern and been middle-aged or older when Ambrosius Aurelianus rallied the Romano-Britons. However, there is no tradition connecting him to Badon which appears to be dated to c. 490–520.

Geoffrey of Monmouth

The *Historia Regum Britanniae*, The History of the Kings of Britain, or HRB, was written in c. 1136. In this fantastical mythical tale, full of historical errors and contradictory dates, Geoffrey adds some more details to the story in the HB. We will leave aside the parts concerning King Arthur and focus purely on Vortigern and Hengest. He gives a garbled and ahistorical version of Magnus Maximus and the end of Roman Britain. Maximus invades Gaul and makes a certain Conanus Meridiadocus the first king of Armorica. There are a fair number of positive references to Bretons and it has been suspected Geoffrey may have had connections with the region. Many of his Norman audience would have, as about a third of William the Conqueror's force was composed of Bretons seventy years before at Hastings.

Geoffrey follows much of Bede and Gildas, citing barbarian raids and a subsequent appeal to the Romans. This having been rejected, the Archbishop of London, Guithelinus, travels to Armorica and enlists the help of the brother of King Aldroneus, great-grandson of Conanus. Constantine is crowned and reigns in Britain for ten years, followed by his son Constans. The infant brothers of Constans are called Aurelius Ambrosius and Uther Pendragon. It is tempting to equate this Constantine with Constantine III. However, other than a son called Constans, there are no other similarities and analysis of the text suggests a mid-fifth century date for this figure.

Vortigern is described as leader of the *Gewissei*, which could be relevant as Bede states the West Saxons were originally known by a similar name. The *Gewisse* may be derived from the Old English word for 'reliable' or 'sure'. The ASC has *Giwis* as a great grandfather of Cerdic the first king of the West Saxons. After Constantine dies, Vortigern arranges for Constans to take power then has him assassinated. Vortigern is once more portrayed as the bad and foolish king. The infants, Aurelius and Uther, are whisked off to Armorica to protect them from the murderous king. Hengest and Horsa arrive and this time are given land near Lincoln. We learn Hengest's daughter's name, Renwein, and the same tale of being gifted Kent. Octa and Ebissa arrive and are settled in the North, this time with an unlikely 300 ships. We meet the Saint Germanus of the HB rather than that from Constantius of Lyon.

As in the HB Vortigern is deposed and Vortimer fights four successful battles before being poisoned by his new mother in law, Renwein. Hengest returns with 300,000 men and Vortigern regains the throne. A peace conference is called near Salisbury at which the Saxons treacherously slay 460 nobles. Vortigern is captured and forced to cede London, York, Lincoln and Winchester. Geoffrey then copies the story of Emrys Ambrosius from the *Historia*, but renames him Merlinus.

Aurelius and Uther come of age, so we must assume at least fifteen years have passed. They return and lay siege to, then burn, Vortigern in his castle. Ambrosius takes the fight to the Saxons defeating them at the battles of Maisbeli and Kaerconan. Hengest is executed and Octa and Ebissa are given Bernicia in Northumberland. Ambrosius rules for four years, but we shall leave the story at this point.

The whole tale is unreliable and cannot be trusted as history. The only date he gives is the death of Arthur in 542. In my previous book, *King Arthur Man or Myth*, I compared the timelines from the various sources and it would appear that Geoffrey follows the AC in dating Arthur c. 500–540 and Badon c. 516-20. The most we can say is that Geoffrey roughly follows the narrative for Vortigern and Hengest in the HB. He doesn't date Hengest but seems to place his death a generation before Badon. As we shall see, this is in line with the dating from another source.

The Anglo-Saxon Chronicle

The ASC is a late ninth-century document, possibly commissioned by Alfred the Great around 891. A number of manuscripts survive and for the entries below I have referred to Swanton's translation unless stated.[13] It dates the appeal to Romans to 443 and the rejection is blamed on the fact 'the Romans were at war with Attila, king of the Huns'. In fact this war was c. 450 so it is possible the date is an error. The Britons send an appeal to 'the princes of the Angle race' in that same year. It is interesting that once again the Angles are singled out rather than the Saxons or Jutes. The copyist records the following for the reign of Martianus and Valentinian (449–456): 'In their days Hengest and Horsa, invited by Votigern, king of the Britons sought out Britain.' They land at Ebba's Creek (Thanet, Kent) and are given land in the south east in return for fighting the Picts. Bede's description of three tribes is repeated. Their numbers increase but there is no mention of a revolt: 'They then sent them greater support. Then came the men from three powers of Germany; the Old Saxons, the Angles, and the Jutes.'

In the same passage we read the following: 'Their leaders were two brothers, Hengest and Horsa; who were the sons of Wihtgils; Wihtgils was the son of Witta, Witta of Wecta, Wecta of Woden. From this Woden arose all our royal kindred, and that of the Southumbrians also.' One could interpret this as Hengest and Horsa led all the Old Saxons, the Angles, and the Jutes. It must be noted that the genealogies of most of the Anglo-Saxon kingdoms trace back to Woden, a subject we will return to later.

The ASC does not describe any revolt or massacre at a peace conference. Instead we get a series of events, most notably battles. The entries for the fifth and sixth centuries cannot not be verified, however it is noteworthy that those involving Hengest are similar to those in the HB. One could divide the battles into three groups. The first involves Hengest in Kent. The second group concerns the arrival in Sussex of Ælle, Bede's first Bretwalda. The third group of battles concerns events in what was to become Wessex. They could all be considered foundation myths and use common motifs such as a small number of ships (often three), brothers, or a father and son, with alliterative names, such as Cerdic and Cynric or Hengest and Horsa.

Our concern here is with Kent and the entries are as follows:

> 455 Hengest fights Vortigern at *Agelesford* (Aylesford, Kent?), Horsa is killed. Hengest and his son Aesc 'succeeds to the Kingdom' (Kent?)

> 456 Hengest wins victory, killing 4,000, at *Crecganford* (Crayford, Kent?) The Britons flee to their stronghold at London and 'abandon Kent'.

> 465 Hengest and Aesc fought the Welsh at Wipped's Creek (unidentified) and twelve Welsh chieftains were killed, along with 'one of their thegns' called Wipped.

> 473 Hengest and Aesc fought the Welsh an they 'fled from the English like fire'.

> 488 Hengest dies and is succeed by Aesc who rules for twenty-four years.

The first two battles seem synonymous with those in the HB. Here only Horsa falls, whereas the HB records Vortimer's brother Cateyrn's, or Catigern's, death too. That text has battles moving from west to east and implies the Britons are victorious. However, Vortimer is only clearly stated as the winner after the third battle on the list, the others are simply described as 'keen' battles. The ASC, on the other hand, have the first two battles going east to west with a victory to Hengest. We recall

Gildas saying victories went first 'to our countrymen now to their enemies'.[14] While the HB implies British victories from west to east, the ASC records Anglo-Saxon victories going east to west. Whatever the case, Hengest returns after Vortimer's death.

There is no revolt or massacre, but the entry for 465 is interesting as it does not claim a victory. It has been suggested *Wippedsfleot* is Ebbsfleet in east Kent. This could make it one of Vortimer's final battles which drove Hengest out, although it seems far too late. It is interesting that twelve Welsh chieftains and one thane are killed but there is no mention of other casualties. Perhaps it is synonymous with the massacre at the peace conference in the HB, where 300 nobles were murdered. Whatever the case, the HB implies these events occurred before the death of St Patrick (c. 457 or 493) and the ASC gives us a timeframe for Hengest in Britain of 449–488.

Table 1: Battles in Kent in the *Anglo-Saxon Chronicle* and *Historia Brittonum*.

Battle	Vortimer's battles from the Historia Brittonum	Hengest's battles from the Anglo-Saxon Chronicles
1	First battle at *flumen Derguentid* (River Darent, near Dartford).	455 Hengest and Horsa fought Vortigern at *Agelesford* (Aylesford), Horsa was killed.
2	At a ford called Episford in their language. Horsa and Vortigern's son, Cateyrn, fell.	457 Hengest and Aesc fought the Britons at *Crecganford* (Crayford), and killed 4,000 men. Britons abandoned Kent and fled to their stronghold of London. The River Cray feeds into the Darent a mile to north.
3	In open country by the inscribed stone on the shore of the Gallic sea. Barbarians defeated.' *They fled to their keels and were drowned.*'	465 Hengest and Aesc fight the Welsh near *Wippedesfleot* (Wipped's Creek) killing 12 chieftains and a thegn called Wipped. Possibly Ebbsfleet, east Kent.
4	Unstated	473 Hengest and Aesc fought the Welsh and seized countless war loot. The Welsh fled like fire.

The map below shows the coastline and roads in fifth-century Kent. What is noticeable is that unlike today, much of the Romney Marsh area in the south was under water or impenetrable marshland. Further west the forested area of the Weald also have made travel difficult. The closest ports to Gaul by which travellers and goods entered Britain were Rutupiae (Richborough), Portus Dubrae (Dover) and

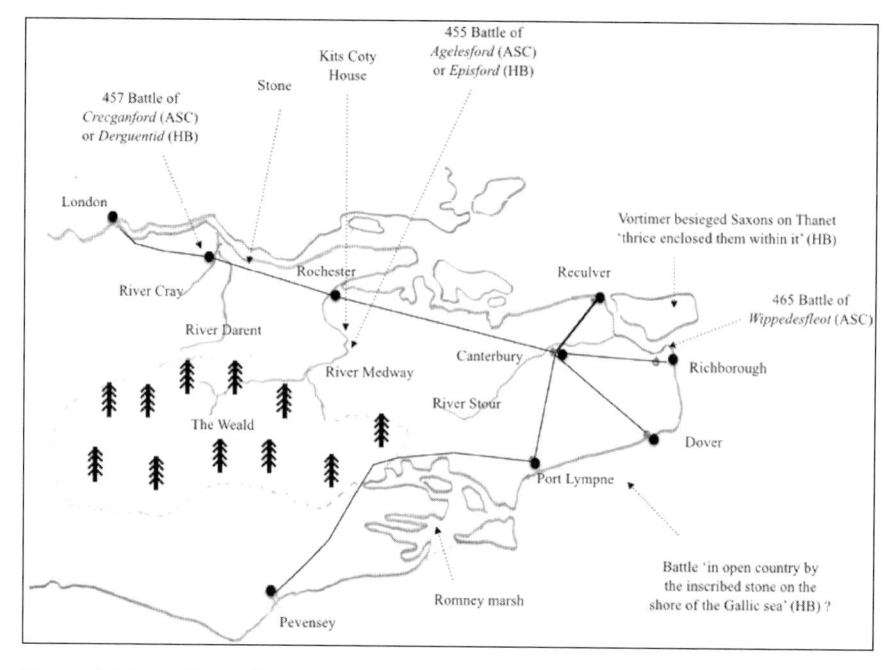

Figure 8. Map of battle locations of the HB and ASC.

Portus Lemanis (Lymne). All these ports were connected by road to Londinium via Watling Street, which passed through Canterbury and Rochester. Further west it passed across the rivers Darent and Cray, on which modern Dartford and Crayford sit. This would be a logical place to make a stand and, as the Cray flows into the Darent, they are easily conflated. One other way out of, or in to, Kent is across the River Medway further south from Rochester. Thus Aylesford is another likely place for a battle.

Bede states that: 'Horsa was afterwards slain in battle by the Britons, and a monument, bearing his name, is still in existence in the eastern parts of Kent.'[15] The HB states the fourth battle he fought, was near 'the stone on the shore of the Gallic sea, where the Saxons being defeated, fled to their ships'. Some have argued this is the 'stone of Titulus', thought to be Stone in Kent.[16] Stone is a few miles east of Crayford on the north Kent coast. However, it's difficult to describe this as on the 'shore of the Gallic sea' as it's in the Thames estuary. Another local legend places the final resting place of Vortimer's brother, Catigern, at Kit's Coty House, a neolithic tomb near Maidstone in Kent. This is a few miles north of Aylesford where supposedly Horsa also was killed in the battle at *Agelesford* or *Episford*. One of Arthur's battles was called *cat coit Celidon*, the battle of Celidon Wood. One can speculate that either Catigern's name or the battle was remembered and associated with the area. This is, of course, speculation and is only included out of interest rather than a serious suggestion. We can see all these locations on map eight.

44

The battle dates in the ASC are interesting as they fall in line with Bede and date Hengest as arriving at fighting age in the 440s, fighting battles between 455–73 and dying in 488. The HB has a confusing and contradictory number of dates but is it possible to have Hengest arriving c. 428 and living into his seventies. We must consider that the more reliable GC states something significant occurred in 440 to make a chronicler consider the Saxons had taken power in the former province. What then does the archaeological evidence say?

Archaeological evidence and literary sources

Kent has a good claim to be the first Anglo-Saxon Kingdom and evidence suggests migration was the prime factor in its formation.[17] The kingdom of Kent was richer and more densely populated than any other in Britain in the sixth or seventh centuries.[18] It was the first to convert to Christianity and the first to have written English law codes from Æthelbert in the early seventh century.[19] Interestingly, we see a marked difference between East and West Kent. Archaeological evidence supports the theory that Jutes were present in East Kent and Saxons in West Kent and that the Jutes had links with the Franks in northern Gaul. The case for Jutish origin is supported by pottery and other artefacts.[20] Additionally, while Frankish material is found all over the south it is more prominent in Jutish areas.[21]

In the second half of the fifth century, Germanic material culture became dominant and was associated with Roman sites of continued occupation.[22] The greatest evidence for continued fifth – and sixth-century activity came from Canterbury.[23] Recent evidence from DNA studies suggests immigration levels of up to 20 per cent linked with populations from Friesland.[24]

Procopius writing c. 553 gives the following information from a Frankish mission to Constantinople. Procopius goes on to state that the king of the Franks claimed he ruled in Britain. This, of course, is at the very least a gross exaggeration. However, it could demonstrate that his influence extended across the Channel.

> Three very populous nations inhabit the Island of Brittia, and one king is set over each of them. And the names of these nations are Angles, Frisians, and Britons who have the same name as the island.
> Procopius, History of the Wars 8.20.6-10

It is noteworthy that the Angles accompanying the Franks did not mention Saxons or Jutes. These Angles of the mid-sixth century may have considered Saxons synonymous with Frisians or even themselves. Other Germanic settlers who had been in Britain since Roman times may have been considered Britons by incoming Angles. The important point here is that Kent would have been the area most likely to maintain communication links with the Franks. However, in the mid-fifth century

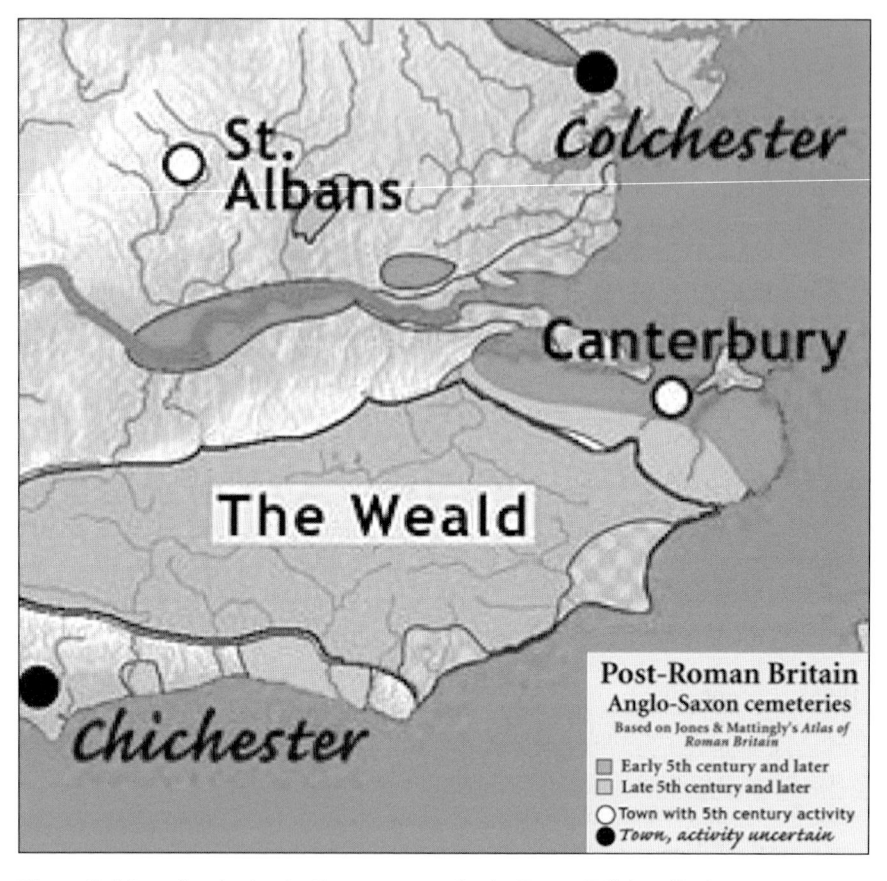

Figure 9. Map of early Anglo-Saxon cemeteries in Kent. (Wikimedia Commons)

in Hengest's time the Romans were still in power in Gaul. The turning point was the death of Aetius in 455, which was followed by a succession of Emperors until the fall of the Western Empire in 476. A short-lived Roman kingdom of Soissons survived in the north until 486 when Clovis I, king of the Franks, began expanding his rule. It would seem that the likely dates for Hengest are before the Franks gained dominance.

Half a century after Procopius met the Franks and Angles in Constantinople, Frankish links were sill influential enough to encourage a marriage alliance between Bertha, a Frankish princess, and Æthelberht of Kent. It was during his reign that Pope Gregory the Great sent Saint Augustine in 597. Gregory of Tours has much to say on this matter and called Æthelberht's father the king of Kent. Bede names his father as Eormenric and the implication from Gregory is that he was still king at the time of Æthelberht's marriage around the 580s. These are the first historically attested kings, although the genealogies from various sources stretch back to Hengest and beyond to Woden.

The First Kingdom

The name of Kent seems to have persisted from a pre-Roman tribal area to the *Cantiaci*, as Caesar called them. Canterbury was called *Durovernum Cantiacorum* in Roman times. Possibly deriving from 'stronghold by the alder grove of the Cantiaci', or 'the walled town of the Cantiaci by the alder marsh'. It was first noted by the Roman historian Ptolemy in the second century and became the capital of the *civitas* of the *Cantiaci*. The name evolved through *Cantware* or *Centrice* in the Anglo-Saxon period to the modern Kent. It is likely the kingdom grew out of the former Romano-British *civitas*.[25] There is also support for a political divide between west and east Kent.[26] It is unique in having had two bishoprics at Canterbury and Rochester. So we have evidence for early settlement, continuation of administrative boundaries and a distinction between east and west Kent.

Given the earlier evidence on this last point it would appear Hengest initially gained authority over East Kent. In terms of dating we have a number of options. The first is to take the arrival date of 428 from the HB and place the revolt around 440 in line with the GC. The second is to take Bede's date of 449 for the arrival and have Hengest fighting in c. 450–70 and dying in 488 in line with the ASC. Alternatively we can attempt to reconcile these sources by accepting the various events in the HB. I would suggest the following timeline is one possibility:

Table 2: Timeline for Hengest.

Date	Event	Source
428	Hengest and Horsa arrive and are settled in Thanet.	HB
430s	Mercenaries help Britons defeat Picts and Scots.	Gildas, HB
440	Vortigern marries Hengest's daughter and cedes Kent. Hengest takes dominant military role. Chronicler is southern Gaul learns of Saxon dominance.	HB GC
440s	Vortimer fights against mercenaries. Request to Aetius for aid denied Horsa killed.	HB Gildas HB and ASC
449	Hengest returns, Vortigern regains power, new treaty agreed	Bede
450s	Revolt	Gildas, Bede Battles in ASC
488	Hengest dies	ASC

Readers may find this an implausibly long life span for the fifth century. An 18-year-old Hengest arriving in 428 would be 63 at his last battle in 473 according to the ASC, and would die aged 78. Not impossible, but perhaps unlikely. The problem we have is the sources seem to pull us in two directions as we shall see when we discuss Vortigern later. First, though, we will turn to the genealogies of Kent.

The Early Anglo-Saxon Kings

Genealogies of the kings of Kent

The first historically attested king of Kent is Æthelberht at the end of the sixth century, who Bede names as his fourth Bretwalda. As we have several different genealogies that go back to the earliest kings of Kent we can use them to estimate whether the death of Hengest in 488 in the ASC is reasonable or if an earlier Hengest might be more likely. Taking Bede and Gregory of Tours we can place Æthelberht's father, Eormenric on the throne at the time of the marriage to the Frankish princess c. 580s. The ASC gives the date 565 for the start of Æthelberht's reign. However, his death is dated to 616 and it is likely the entry for 565 in the Anglo-Saxon Chronicle is actually his birth rather than the start of his reign. We can thus be fairly confident that Eormenric is actually the first attested king of Kent and Æthelberht, born in 565, married a Frankish princess c. 585 and came to the throne between 589–593.[27]

The table below shows the genealogies in the various sources. We can see a number of differences but there are also a number of similarities. The ASC doesn't list all the kings but the other sources all give us Eormenric as the father of Æthelberht. The HB and eighth-century Anglian collection place Hengest as Eormenric's great grandfather. Bede has an additional king in the list.

Table 3: Early Kentish Kings.

Historia c. AD 830	Anglo-Saxon chronicles c. AD 900	Bede AD 731	Anglian collection Eighth century
Hengest and Horsa	Hengest and Horsa 455 Hengest and Æsc succeed to kingdom	Hengest and Horsa 449	Hengest
Octha	Æsc 488 succeeds to kingdom of Kent and rules twenty-four years	Oisc	Ocga
Ossa	512?	Oeric Oisc	Oese
		Octa	
Eormenric		Eormenric	Eormenric
Æthelberht	Æthelberht 565 rules for fifty-three years	Æthelberht 596 Pope Gregory sends St Augustine	Æpelberht

Bede names Hengest's son as Oisc and states he was the founder of the royal house as the descendants were known as the *Oiscingas*. The implication here is that

Oisc was the first 'king', perhaps copying events across the Channel as Clovis I expanded his kingdom.

> This Ethelbert was the son of Irminric, whose father was Octa, whose father was Oeric, surnamed Oisc, from whom the kings of Kent are wont to be called Oiscings. His father was Hengist, who, being invited by Vortigern, first came into Britain, with his son Oisc, as has been said above.
>
> Bede, book 2.5

If we take Bede's king list and make a generous assumption of twenty-five years per generation, we can estimate Hengest's floruit working backwards:

Æthelberht c. 565–616
Eormenric c. 540–590
Octa c. 515–565
Oeric c. 490–540
Oisc c. 465–515
Hengest c. 440–490

We would thus have to extend Hengest a further ten years back to have him at fighting age in c. 449. In reality, lifespans and the reigns of kings were much shorter. The ten kings after Æthelberht reigned for a total of seventy-three years. The eight kings starting from Alfred the Great reigned for ninety-two years. This makes an early Hengest very unlikely and thus we must conclude Bede is more likely correct in dating him as arriving in 449 and the ASC in placing his death in 488. This gives a more realistic age at death of approximately late fifties, still above the average for the time.

For those interested in the legend of King Arthur this is vital in terms of dating as the HB states the following:

> On Hengest's death, his son, Octha came down from the north of Britain to the Kingdom of the Kentishmen, and from him are sprung the kings of the kentishmen. Then Arthur fought against them in those days, together with the kings of the British; but he was their dux bellorum.

It is not clear whether our hero is fighting Octha in Kent, any forces remaining in the north or the Saxons in general. Of course it may be more correct to say Angles or Jutes, but even here we cannot be sure. As we shall see later the most likely locations for Arthur's twelve battles are not in Kent at all. What the literary sources suggest is that some sort of revolt caused part of the former diocese to break away from Romano-British control. The leaders of the initial band of mercenaries are named Hengest and Horsa. However the 'kings of the Kentishmen' come from the descendants of Octha. Bede also makes it clear it is Hengest's son Oisc who gives the name of Oiscings to the kings of Kent which suggests Hengest was never regarded as a king.

The 'unhappy partition'

Gildas tells us a fire 'spread from sea to sea' lasting 'until it burned almost the entire surface of the island and was licking the western ocean with its fierce red tongue'. The clear implication is that the whole island is involved as 'all the major towns are laid low'. But then we hear 'after a time, when the cruel plunderers had gone home'. We are left to wonder where exactly? Back to the east of the island presumably. But the 'unhappy partition' has resulted in Verulamium at least being inaccessible. The graves of '*Aaron et Iulium Legionum urbes cives*' are unknown regardless of whether they were indeed from Caerleon. Bede states the rebellion involved 'every part of the island' but then they returned 'home', presumably to their settled areas. The HB gives us a far more detailed description. After the massacre at the peace conference Vortigern is forced to cede Essex, Sussex and Middlesex and 'other districts' to Hengest, who presumably retains Kent as well. This strongly suggests the entire south-east, or former province of Maxima Caesariensis, was taken over.

To consider the extent of any boundary it is useful to look at what was Roman Britain's largest city, Londinium. The archaeological record suggests London was deserted by 500 and not reoccupied until Alfred the Great in 886. Some historians suggest London was actually abandoned early in the fifth century.[28] Indeed, no evidence of Anglo-Saxons have been found within the city walls for the fifth century.[29] What then of the ASC entry for 457 after the battle of Crecganford when the Britons: 'forsook the land of Kent and fled to their stronghold at London'? There is evidence for Romano British activity within London up to 450 as well as Anglo-Saxon settlements outside and around London after the same time.[30] Lundenwic grew up a mile to the west of the city walls. Indication of continued communication comes from the use of Easter dates in the British church computed in Rome in the time of Pope Leo around 454. However, later changes appear to have not got through, suggesting sometime after this, contact was lost.[31]

At its height, London had a population of between 30,000–60,000 people. By the fifth century urban life had deteriorated drastically. The five kilometres of Roman walls around London would have required 2,700 men to defend.[32] This would require a substantially higher population to support such a force. With the break down of the economy, lack of coinage and a much reduced city population it may have been impossible to defend. On balance, I would suggest a much-reduced London could easily have survived as a 'stronghold' past the mid-fifth century. There is nothing unreasonable about the Anglo-Saxon Chronicle entry for 457. The subsequent rebellion or war may have resulted in it being abandoned completely.

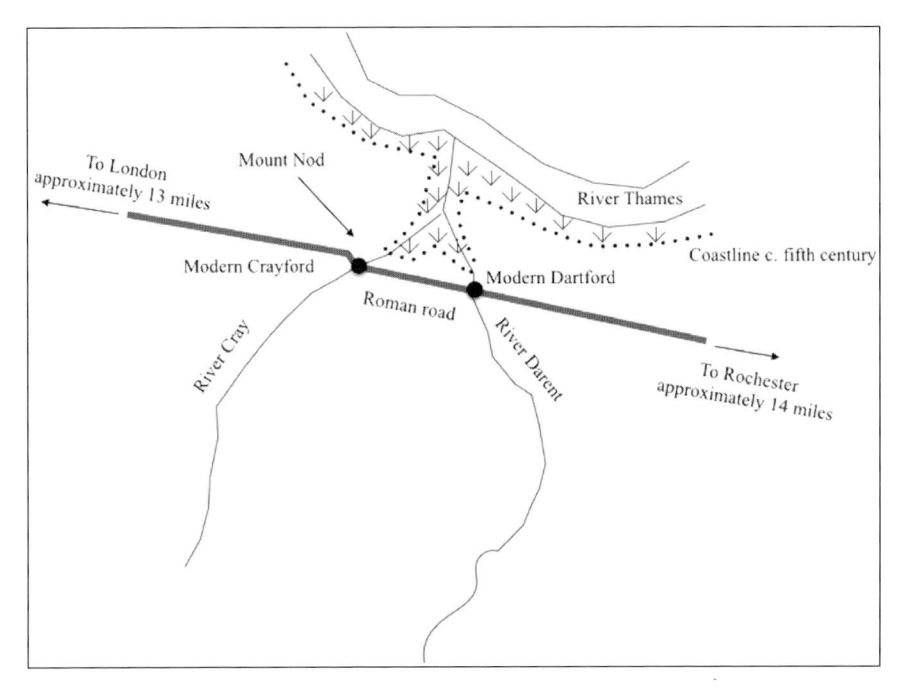

Figure 10. Map of the Battle of Crecganford 457.

The fact Gildas cannot access Verulamium, a day's ride to the north west from the former diocese capital, suggests this is what happened. The next we hear of London is a bishopric established in 604, and Bede describing it as an important market.[33]

We can see in figure 10 what a strategic location Crecganford would have been. The main Roman road from the coast crossed the Medway at Rochester. Fourteen miles to the west and one looks down from East Hill in Dartford into the Darent Valley. Up river to the south lies Lullingstone Villa and a wealthy, productive area. To the west lies West Hill and a couple of miles further on the crossing at Crayford, from which it is just a day's march from London. One can see the Cray meets the Darent a mile to the north where the Crayford Marches would likely have been impenetrable in the fifth century. Local tradition places the site of the battle on the west bank of the Cray, up Crayford Hill and to the right on 'Mount Nod'. This appears to be an old name for the upper part of Iron Mill Lane as it comes up to St Paulinus Church, which stands opposite. I can't find any evidence for this and there has been no archaeological finds indicating a battle in the area for this period. However, it is intriguing to think that somewhere in this area, perhaps under the church itself, lies a mass grave of hundreds, if not thousands, of warriors.

Figure eleven gives us a rough estimate of the 'partition' referred to by Gildas. I would suggest the following phases: Hengest settles in Thanet in East Kent; Hengest gains control of East Kent or civitas of the Cantii; war with Vortimer results in

The Early Anglo-Saxon Kings

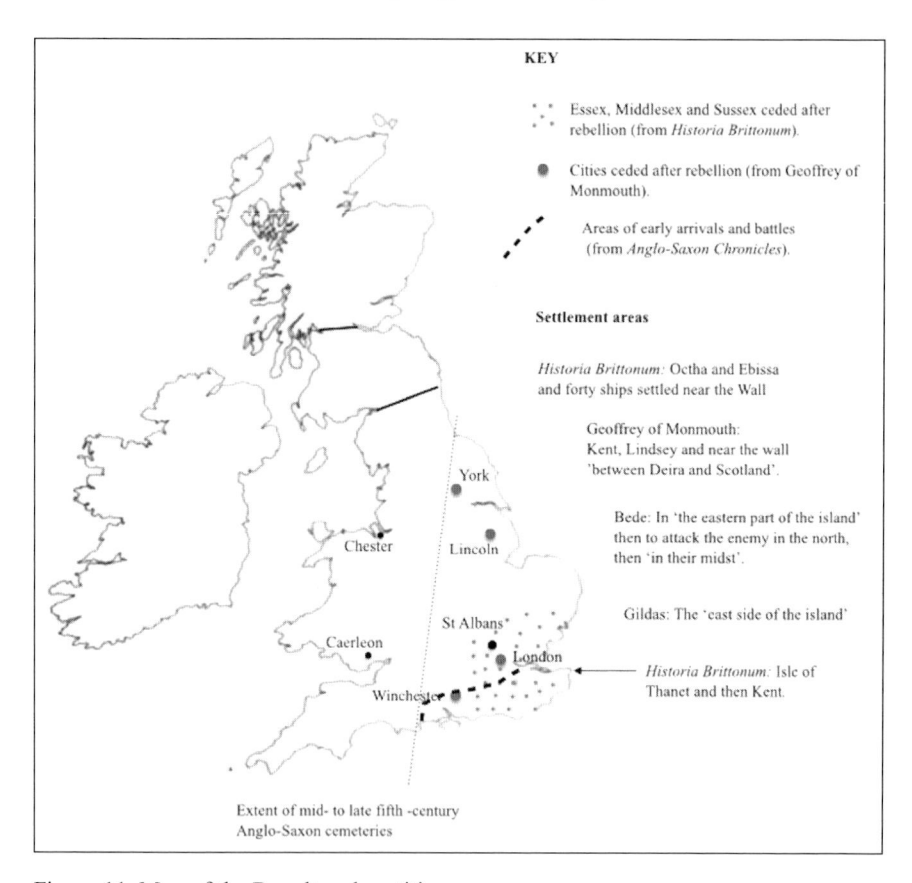

```
                              KEY

                        . *. *   Essex, Middlesex and Sussex ceded after
                        . * .    rebellion (from Historia Brittonum).

                          ●      Cities ceded after rebellion (from Geoffrey of
                                 Monmouth).

                         ...     Areas of early arrivals and battles
                                 (from Anglo-Saxon Chronicles).

                        Settlement areas

                        Historia Brittonum: Octha and Ebissa
                        and forty ships settled near the Wall

                        Geoffrey of Monmouth:
                        Kent, Lindsey and near the wall
                        'between Deira and Scotland'.

                        Bede: In 'the eastern part of the island'
                        then to attack the enemy in the north,
                        then 'in their midst'.

                        Gildas: The 'east side of the island'

                        Historia Brittonum: Isle of
                        Thanet and then Kent.

              Extent of mid- to late fifth-century
              Anglo-Saxon cemeteries
```

Figure 11. Map of the Revolt and partition.

fluctuating boundary the maximum extent of which included West Kent; finally a breaking away of the south-eastern province of Maxima Caesariensis. The resultant war with Ambrosius (and possibly Arthur) had little effect on this boundary as Gildas could still not access Verulamium and other sites.

The name

Hengest and Horsa mean stallion and horseman respectively and one suggestion is that they were originally deities. Horse imagery in the migration period is found in Britain, Scandinavia and northern Europe. Even into modern times, in parts of Germany the gable-end posts of houses were still known by the names *Hengst* and *Horst*.[34] However, they could equally be titles, nicknames or even given names. In the Kent genealogies they appear four generations after Woden.

Horse culture was important to the early Anglo-Saxons and we see evidence of horse deities, funerary rites and iconography.[35] There are hundreds of horse

52

cremations dated to the fifth and sixth centuries. There was a tradition of 'brother gods' or 'divine twins' such as the Roman Castor and Pollux or Norse Baldur and Höðr. Tacitus relates an interesting fact about the Germanic Nahanarvali.

> Among these last is shown a grove of immemorial sanctity. A priest in female attire has the charge of it. But the deities are described in Roman language as Castor and Pollux. Such, indeed, are the attributes of the divinity, the name being Alcis. They have no images, or, indeed, any vestige of foreign superstition, but it is as brothers and as youths that the deities are worshipped.
>
> Tacitus, Germania, Chapter 43

We see here an early tradition of this replicated in later Norse mythology. It is possible the Old English tradition had similar themes. We are thus left with a number of options.

- Hengest and Horsa were mythical figures which were attributed to the later king lists to add legitimacy.
- The two leaders were given these names as titles or epithets but their real names are lost.
- These were their actual names regardless of whether there were also mythical figures with similar names.

Bede was perhaps correct to be cautious when he said the first leaders 'are said to have been' Hengest and Horsa. However, I am persuaded by J.R.R. Tolkien's argument that we should treat them as historical. What is clear from the literary sources is that the first mercenary leaders, whatever their names, were inextricably linked to the British leader Vortigern.

Vortigern

Concerning this name there are many versions and much discussion about its meaning. The excellent *Vortigern Studies* website has a comprehensive list of the various versions.[36]

The earliest copies of Gildas refer simply to *superbo tyranno*, often translated as 'proud tyrant'. Later versions from surviving twelfth – and thirteenth-century manuscripts give a name to him: *superbo tyranno Vortigerno* or *Gurthigerno Brittanorum duce*. However, the earliest reference is from Bede: *Vurtigern, Uurtigern* or *Vertigernus*. The Pillar of Elise, which we will come to soon, names him *Guarthigirn*, which is closer to the later Welsh *Gwrtheyrn*. The Irish equivalent is *Foirtchern* and we have a Saint Guirthiern. The earliest form of the name is *Uuertigernus*.

One claim is this is not a name but a title, leading some to suggest 'high-king' and 'supreme ruler'. A more accurate translation, however, might be 'overlord', a compound of ver/wor/wer, meaning 'over', and -tigern, meaning 'lord'. Welsh sources add the epithet *Gwrtheyrn Gwrteneu* – Vortigern the Thin, which suggests two things. First, at some point it became a name. Second, this particular Vortigern could be distinguished by his relative size. Perhaps there had been a more rotund Vortigern. We do not see a version of Vortigern being used as a title for another figure in Irish, Welsh or Gaulish sources. Robert Vermaat, from *Vortigern Studies*, suggests his actual name was Vitalinus, a name which features in the genealogy of Vortigern in the HB.[37] Chadwick argues there is 'no reasonable doubt that Guorthigirn (Vortigern) is historical'.[38] It is therefore possible that it began as a title and evolved into a personal name.

The word *tigernos* is found in aristocratic names in Britain and Gaul: Cattegirn, Bivatigirnus, Tigernmaglus, Ritigern and Kentigern. In Brittany the title *machtiern* meant 'fine' or 'great' lord, and in Old Irish *macthigern* also meant 'overlord'. Snyder, in *An Age of Tyrants*, argues that these Celtic words for 'lord' reflect how provincial people would refer to the local *decurion* or *curiale*.[39] In Breton charters the word *tigernos* referred to a local lord or a king and was often equated with the Latin *tyrannus*.[40] These positions were often hereditary in Roman times. This might give us a clue as to how kingship evolved. Zosimus states it was the civitates that were freed from barbarian attacks in c. 408 and it was to these same civitates Emperor Honorius sent letters.

A Roman town senate, *ordo*, consisted of up to 100 representatives from the local community. *Decurions* and *curiales* sat on town councils, *aediles* were responsible for public buildings and services, and *quaestors* were in charge of finance and magistrates. There is strong evidence linking *decurions* to the word 'tyrant' in the fifth century.[41] Salvian writing at the time complains there are as many *tyranni* as *curiales* in municipalities, but interestingly they 'glory in this name of *tyrannus*'. In fifth-century Gaul the title tyrant may not have had the negative connotations associated with it by Gildas and others. But we get the impression that these figures were increasing their power, and some, such as Salvian, saw them as illegitimate, tyrannical.

If centralised power weakened within the diocese of Britain, it would be only natural for local structures at *civitas* level to fill the gap. Urban life may have deteriorated in the first half of the fifth century, but as we have seen, some towns did continue along with the increased reoccupation of hill forts. A *decurion* wishing his son to take his place could no longer rely on Roman convention. Perhaps it is no surprise Gildas places the appearance of kings a generation after the end of Roman Britain. It is therefore likely that many of the *tyranni* were *decurions* or local elite, and that some of these figures formed the origin of royal dynasties. It is also likely a local ruler, whether civic, tribal or military, might have been known as a lord in the local vernacular. The *superbus tyrannus* Gildas uses may well be a pun similar to his insults for the five tyrant kings.

Unlike his son Vortimer, Vortigern is not portrayed as a warrior. He is more like a *vicarius* or provincial governor. The use of 'tyrant' by Gildas merely copies other Roman historians when they described Constantine III or Magnus Maximus when describing someone who, in their view, is an illegitimate ruler. Church writers such as Gildas, however, seem to add a moral failing to the phrase. The kings are tyrants because of their behaviour, not by the mere fact of being kings.

His rule, or that of the council he leads, appears to have covered much of the former province as he is able to post mercenaries in the east and the north, by Hadrian's Wall. However, he is also linked to Powys through Welsh genealogies. Powys grew out of the former *civitas* of the Cornovii, whose capital at Wroxeter shows strong evidence of continuation of use into the fifth century. In the HB he is said to be a descendant of Gloiu, the alleged founder of Gloucester.[42]

One version of a possible genealogy is found on The Pillar of Eliseg in Denbighshire, North Wales, erected by Cyngen ap Cadell, king of Powys, who died in 855. It was to honour his great grandfather Elisedd ap Gwylog, and an accepted translation of the inscription includes the following: 'Britu son of Vortigern, whom Germanus blessed, and whom Sevira bore to him, daughter of Maximus the king, who killed the king of the Romans.' A number of different genealogies for Powys exist and while they differ significantly, neither Vortigern nor his sons appear.[43] Interestingly the HB does name a son blessed by the saint. However, in that version the child is the product of incest with his own daughter. The HB names four sons:

> the eldest was Vortimer, … the second was Categirn who was slain in the same battle with Horsa; the third was Pascent, who reigned in the two provinces Builth and Guorthegirnaim … the fourth was Faustus, born of an incestuous marriage with his daughter, who was brought up and educated by St Germanus. He built a large monastery on the banks of the river Renis, called after his name, and which remains to the present period.

Faustus of Riez was a historical figure and we know from the letters of Sidonius Appolinaris he was indeed British.[44] It is possible this is the same Britu on the Pillar of Eliseg and that Germanus renamed him Faustus. However, here his mother is Sevira, daughter of the former Emperor. We thus seem to have two traditions here. The first in which Vortigern is revered as an ancestor of the kings of Powys and linked to Magnus Maximus. The second is the Vortigern of the HB, reviled and hated and blamed for the catastrophe of inviting the Saxons. It is possible the incest story was a slur, and we recall the text also gives us an alternative foundation story for Powys when St Germanus deposes the wicked king Benli.

We have seen the various dates in the HB for the coming of the Saxons, 375, 428 and 449. If Vortigern married the daughter of Magnus Maximus this could equate to the earliest date as Sevira must have been born prior to 388 when her father died. If Vortigern was the same age as his wife, then perhaps we could construct a timeline that fits. Born in c. 385, crowned as king of Powys in 425, received the first mercenaries in 428 and met St Germanus the following year. By 440 he would have been 55 years of age. If Bede's dates are correct then he would be in his seventies during the revolt or massacre at the peace conference.

The problems with the dating has caused some scholars to suggest two or more Vortigerns and the reference to *Gwrtheyrn Gwrteneu*, Vortigern the Thin, could support that. Whatever the case, Vortigern seems to hold power across the whole of the former diocese. His role appears similar to a *vicarius* or civil governor; he is able to allocate land and positions in the south east, first Thanet and then Kent, but also in the far north near Hadrian's Wall. But he is also connected to areas in Wales.

The text also tells us some interesting things about Ambrosius Aurelianus. He is from South Wales and is a young boy when Vortigern is an adult. The author is clearly referring to the same Ambrosius as Gildas, but has nothing to say about his later exploits, save a battle something akin to a civil war against Vitalinus at Guoloppum twelve years from the reign of Vortigern. This is possibly Wallop in Hampshire. Interestingly, a ninth-century record names Amesbury in Wiltshire Ambresbyrig, possibly 'the burgh of Ambrosius', and it was certainly a *villa regalis*, or 'royal vill', later used by the kings of Wessex.[45] It's recorded as Amblesberie in the Domesday Book. There are other sites in the south such as Ambrosden in Oxfordshire and Amberley in both Gluouscetershire and Herefordshire. This is all speculative, but would point to Britannia Prima as a likely location for Ambrosius, Vortigern, Gildas and the battle of Badon.

In summary we can be reasonably confident the Vortigern of the HB was a historical figure. The narrative of the HB is confused and the dates contradictory. One interpretation would place his floruit c. 380–440s and have him die before or just after the second visit of St Germanus. This might pull the date of both Hengest and Ambrosius back as well. If one accepts Bede and the ASC then we can suggest Vortigern may have survived into the 460s and perhaps St Garmon has been confused with St Germanus. This would allow an Ambrosius 'in the time of Zeno', and fall in line with the ASC entry for Hengest's death in 488.

Summary

The story of Hengest and Horsa has been seen by many historians as having 'little historical validity'.[46] However, something significant occurred in Britain in the mid-fifth century. Archaeology shows a marked increase in Germanic material culture and burials in the south and east beginning c. 425 and accelerating after c. 450. The literary sources are a little confused and contradictory, especially concerning the date. The HB gives us a reasonable narrative that reconciles these apparent contradictions, although we cannot trust it's validity. Nevertheless, archaeological evidence for this 'first kingdom' is in line with the earliest sources. An early East Kent Jutish region with Frankish material absorbed a West Kent area which had a heavy concentration of Saxon material culture.[47]

At the same time, other Germanic peoples appeared to have settled in increasing numbers, especially in the east between the Thames and the Humber. Notably, Saxons down the Thames Valley and Angles in Lincolnshire and East

Anglia. Bede names the first leaders Hengest and Horsa. Whether these were their real names or not, some scholars accept it at face value. Evans, in *The Life and Times of Hengest*, describes him as 'a real historical figure, a mid-fifth-century outlaw-adventurer'.[48] J.R.R. Tolkien provides a very credible timeline which puts Hengest's floruit as c. 425–488 and the establishment of the Kingdom of Kent in 490 with Oesc as the founder.[49]

In some ways it is academic what the names of the leaders of the mercenaries or Germanic peoples were. They may well have been nicknames. Hengest is never described as a king. He is a warrior and adventurer. Spanning the generation between Vortigern and Ambrosius, his was a world of mead halls and a warrior culture very different from the Romano-British of the south east of the former diocese. However, it is not Hengest who Bede describes as one of his seven kings who held sovereignty over the 'southern provinces'. This distinction he gives to our next warrior leader, Ælle of the South Saxons.

Chapter Three

Ælle, the First Bretwalda

> Indeed, now they are troubled,
> the thoughts of my heart,
> that I myself should strive with
> the high streams,
> the tossing of salt waves
> the wish of my heart urges
> all the time
> my spirit to go forth,
> that I, far from here,
> should seek the homeland
> of a foreign people
>
> *The Seafarer*, Anglo-Saxon poem,
> The Exeter book, late tenth century.

The first 'Bretwalda'

Bede introduces the concept of Bretwalda when describing Æthelberht as 'the third of the English kings who ruled over all the southern provinces that are divided from the northern by the river Humber and the borders contiguous to it'.[1] The first he names as Ælle of Sussex, king of the South Saxons. Before we discuss Ælle we will briefly look at what Bede means by 'sovereignty'. We have seen Bede uses the word *imperium* rather than Bretwalda. It is unlikely this was an official title but rather a description of the political and military fact at the time. Below we see the list of kings that Bede states held this *imperium*. His reasons for leaving out Mercian kings such as Penda are more likely political rather than an aversion to a pagan king. After all he includes Ælle and Ceawlin, both almost certainly pagan.

- Ælle of Sussex (c. 488–514)
- Ceawlin of Wessex (c. 560–592, died 593)
- Æthelberht of Kent (c. 590–616)
- Rædwald of East Anglia (c. 600–24)
- Edwin of Deira (616–33)
- Oswald of Northumbria (633–42)
- Oswiu of Northumbria (642–70)

Ælle, the First Bretwalda

The ASC introduces the word Bretwalda, wide-ruler, in the ninth century ASC. It adds Egbert, king of Wessex (825–39), to Bede's list under the year 827: 'Egbert conquered the Mercian kingdom, and all that is south of the Humber, being the eighth king who was 'wide ruler' of all the British dominions. And the first who had so great a rule was Ella, king of the South-Saxons'.

The ASC adds Alfred alongside Egbert, both ninth century kings of Wessex, to Bede's list. In the year 886 'the whole English nation turned to him', and at his death in 901 he was described as 'king over all the English nation'. Kings of Mercia such as Penda and Offa could also lay claim to the title, but perhaps a West Saxon copyist couldn't bring themselves to acknowledge this of their northern neighbours. Swanton describes the phrase as a 'poetic rather than political assertion'.[2] Perhaps 'influence' is a better word. What sort of 'overlordship' might Ælle have had in the late fifth century? It is unlikely to refer to just the Sussex area where he landed. Although this first Bretwalda only warrants three entries in the ASC:

> 477: 'Here Ælle and his three sons, Cymen and Wlencing and Cissa, came to the land of Britain with three ships at a place called Cymen's Shore, and there killed many Welsh and drop some to flight into the wood which is named *Andredes leag*.'

> 485: 'Here Ælle fought the Welsh near the margin of *Mearcred's Burn*.'

> 491: 'Here Ælle and Cissa besieged *Anderitum* and killed all who lived in there; there was not even one Briton left there.'

Echoes of this three sons can be heard in local place-names. Firstly the landing at *Cymenes-ora*, the shore of Cymen. This is thought to be at the southern tip of the Selsey peninsula by the Owers banks.[3] The second, Chichester, is suggested to have derived from the their son, Cissa, and can be seen in an earlier form of the town's name, *Cissan-ceaster*.[4] The iron-age hillfort at Cissbury, north of Worthing, might also echo his name. Lancing, some claim, derived from Wlencing.

Andredes leag, was the forest north of the fort at Anderitum (Pevensey) also known as The Weald. Anderitum is certainly the Roman Shore fort at Pevensey.

Henry of Huntingdon in the twelfth century states Cissa succeeded his father in c. 514 but gives us little more information. Richard of Wendover, writing a century after Henry, gave Cissa's death in 590 which seems improbable given his arrival in 477 with his father. Perhaps two different persons of the same name have been mixed up. Or possibly the arrival date is much later than the ASC claims.

The location of Mearcred's Burn, Mearc Raedsburn or Mearcraedes Burnan is unknown. It may have been fought at a boundary stream. One suggestion is Slonk Hill to the north east of Shoreham.[5] The Northbourne stream ran from the foot of Slonk Hill to the River Adur which was a broad estuary in the fifth century. The Roman road, now the Old Shoreham Road, crossed the river at this point and may have been of strategic value. However, there is a tradition it is much further east near the villages of Penhurst and Ashburnham in East Sussex to the north east of the Roman Shore Fort at Pevensey. An earthwork connects the villages. In the twelfth century Henry of Huntingdon claimed the battle was inconclusive which the ASC implies by not claiming a victory.

The Sussex Archaeological society conducted a study on this area in the early twentieth century.[6] Town Creep near Penhurst is to the north east of Pevensey. The argument is that Mercred was Brittonic and thus the first part of the place-name, Mecredsburn or Mecred burnanstede, evolved into Mercreed and then Mercreep, with the Mer – later being dropped and later replaced by 'Town'. Between Creep Wood and Sprays Wood flows a branch of the River Ashburn and nearby is 'Tent-Hill'. A tradition survived in this area into the nineteenth century which claimed the nearby earthwork was besieged and destroyed by the Saxons. Roger of Wendover, a thirteenth-century writer, claimed the Britons were led by Aurelianus Ambrosius. We note he uses Geoffrey of Monmouth's corruption of the name of the man lauded by Gildas.

The battle at Anderitum can be confidently located at the former Roman Shore fort at Pevensey. The fort measured approximately 300m by 150m with over 750m of walls. This would require about 640 men to defend at one man per 1.2m. It was located on a narrow spit and surrounded on three sides by sea in the fifth century. The walls themselves are 8m high and up to 4.2m in width.[7] There were at least thirteen semi-circular bastions placed irregularly round the defences. On visiting it becomes apparent just how large the interior is and how formidable the walls are. With adequate defending forces it would be difficult for an attacking force.

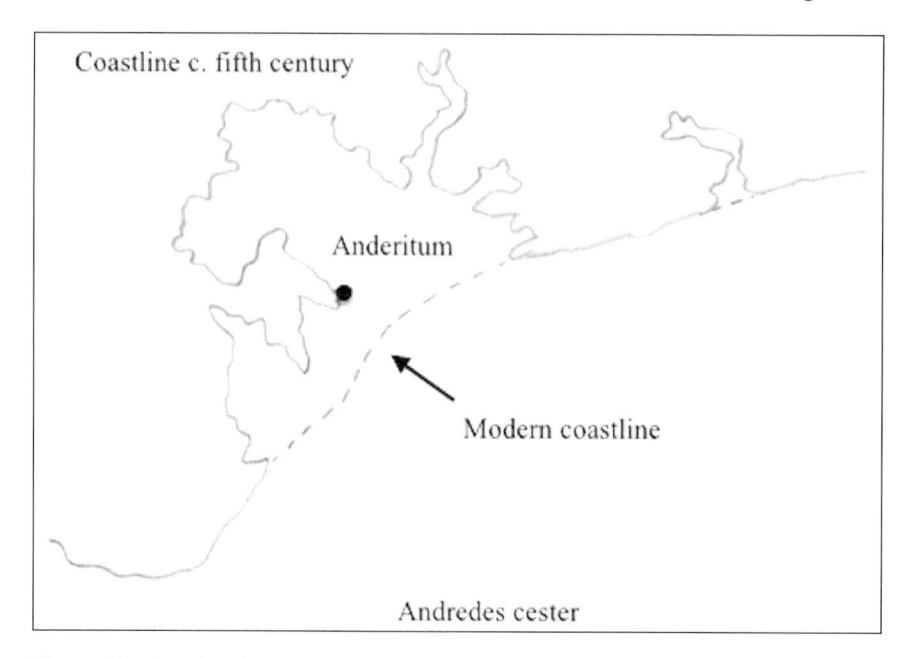

Figure 12. Map showing coastline around Anderitum c. 491.

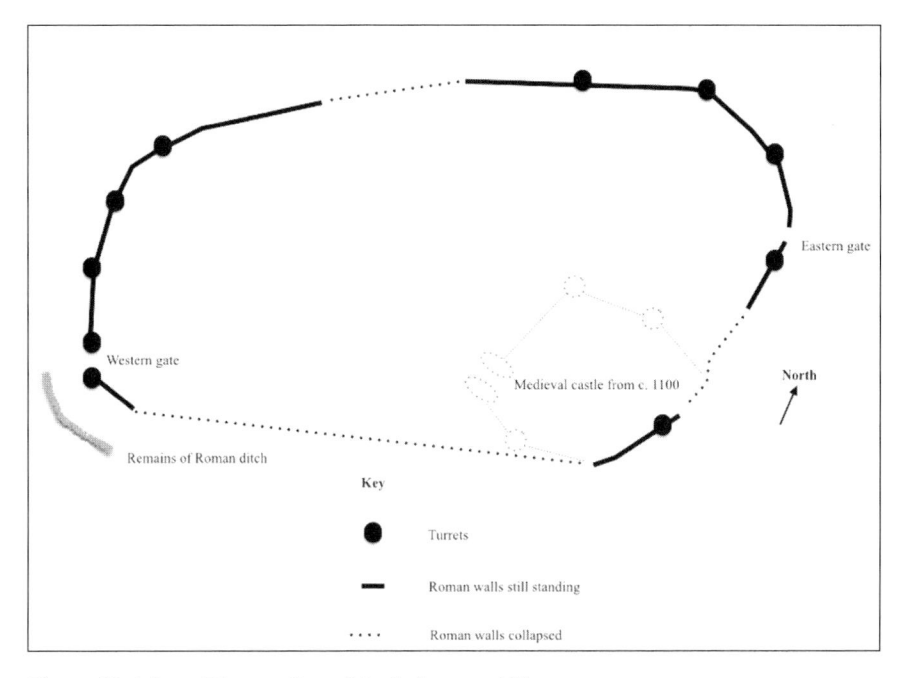

Figure 13. Map of Roman fort of Anderitum c. 491.

The most likely method might be a long siege or subterfuge. The ASC seems clear: The word used is besieged. The phrase 'killed all who lived there' is also interesting. A Roman fort was garrisoned by soldiers, but with Roman authority gone it is possible people utilised these places for protection similar to the reoccupation of hill-forts. If it was a fort garrisoned solely by soldiers then one might expect different wording. We could, of course, be reading too much into this as it might be a casual literary device written centuries after the event. However, it is possible that decades after Roman rule ended people were living in the fort at Pevensey. If so, perhaps we can only speculate as to how many and if there were any soldiers to man the walls at all.

We can see on the next map the events appear to occur from west to east in what was formerly the *civitas* of the Regni. We recall the archaeological evidence for Germanic material was patchy along the south coast and the area was relatively isolated due to the forested area to the north. This might make settlement easier to understand, but not the description of the earliest leader as 'overlord' or 'bretwalda'.

There is no further mention of South Saxon kings until the middle of the seventh century. Archaeology does indeed show early evidence of Saxon settlement along the south coast between Chichester and Pevensey. The border of the *civitas* may have been the River Meon to the west of Portsmouth some twenty miles to the north west of where Ælle likely landed. The borders of an early Sussex kingdom likely stretched from the territory of the *Meonware* in the West to the River Cuckmere in the East.[8] There are hints that the initial settlement involved the Eastern half centred

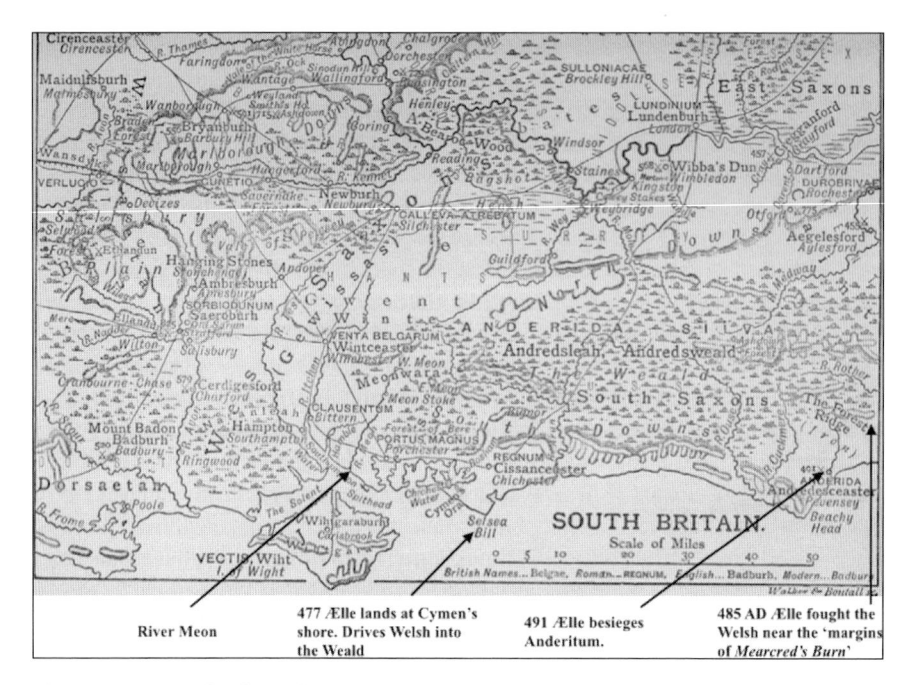

Figure 14. Map of Ælle and the South Saxons. (Wikimedia Commons)

at Pevensey and that later, the Western half incorporating the former *civitas* capital at Chichester was consumed.[9] Highdown Hill rises 260ft to the north of Worthing and is thought to be the burial-place of the kings of Sussex.[10]

At the top is a small fort with a double rampart and ditch with views of the sea two miles to the south and Cissbury Ring Hillfort less than four miles to the north-east. Since the late nineteenth century a number of excavations have been carried out; 150 inhumations and twenty-eight cremations were recorded.[11] A number of interesting facts present themselves:[12] Most of the burials are on a Christian west–east axis. The grave goods suggest Germanic people settled in the area in the fifth century. Grave goods, often prohibited in Christian burials, are similar to those listed in continental law codes for 'men's goods' and 'women's goods'. Belt buckles, spear heads and shield bosses, along with an all-purpose knife. Shields were about 2ft in diameter. Only two swords were found, pattern welded and of good quality. An Anglo-type spear was also found similar to a type common in Frankish cemeteries and the Rhineland. Women's graves often contained brooches, usually a matching pair worn at the shoulders. Belt buckles and small knives were also found. A number of glass objects were also found which appear to have been made in northern France, Belgium and the Rhineland.[13] One specimen is a fine goblet with Greek inscription dated to c. 400 which is thought to have originated in Alexandria in Egypt.

The finds at Highdown have led to some possibly significant conclusions:[14] the earliest graves from Highdown and Alfriston, twenty-four miles to the east, suggest a mid-fifth century date. The earliest settlements suggest, as in other areas, marginal land was allocated by a local British authority. The large number of late Roman and sub-Roman objects found suggests trade or assimilation in the earliest period. There is no evidence that the native population of Sussex were destroyed or driven out. It is possible Ælle arrived a generation earlier, but if he arrived when the ASC states, in 477, then the area already had Germanic settlers or mercenaries. Whether they would have been receptive to this new warlord is another matter.

We have seen how the establishment of an early Kentish kingdom was likely based on the *civitas* of the *Canti*. Further north the *civitas* of the *Trinovantes* also seems to have evolved into the later kingdom of Essex.[15] Recent analysis shows a lack of early Germanic material culture around major urban sites such as London, St Albans, Rochester, Canterbury and Colchester.[16] In the Thames basin material and burials are largely confined to coastal areas and waterways.[17] Rippon finds evidence for early Anglo-Saxon settlement confined to 'the fringes' of *Catuvellauni* and *Trinovantes* areas.[18] The site at Mucking, Essex, places settlers as early c. 400. Inhabitants appear to have been confined to a small area, possibly a grant of land peripheral to existing Romano-British communities.[19] The first areas of settlement were sparsely populated and formed tribal, and later *civitas*, boundaries, such as fens, woodland, high ground and rivers.[20] We get a similar picture across much of the south and east including Sussex. The distribution of cemeteries and *Grubenhauser* (sunken houses) in the Northern Thames Basin in the mid-fifth century suggests 'immigration may have occurred within the context of Romano-British socio-political control'.[21]

In the fifth and sixth centuries Sussex was 'virtually cut off' from England by the forest, river estuaries and marshland.[22] Place name and archaeological evidence suggests early presence was confined to the coast and river estuaries. How, then, could Bede describe Ælle as holding imperium? In general Sussex seems to have followed the same pattern for the southern and eastern provinces of the diocese. An increase in Germanic material in these areas in the early fifth century indicates settlement on unoccupied land or positioning of mercenary forces to protect strategically important areas. However, if we take the dating of the ASC at face value Ælle and his sons arrive a generation or more after the arrival of Hengest and his subsequent rebellion. If we accept Bede's dates and the narrative in Gildas, then Ælle is a contemporary of Ambrosius Aurelianus. The former active in 477–91, and the latter 'in the time of Zeno', 474–91. This date has caused some to speculate Ælle was the Saxon leader at Badon, which Bede dates to c. 493. A heavy defeat might explain the absence of further mention and the apparent gap in the archaeological record suggesting a hiatus in further expansion.

Halsall, in *Worlds of Arthur*, suggests it is more likely he preceded Ceawlin of Wessex, Bede's second 'overlord'.[23] However, Gildas does state the Britons had experienced a time free from external wars, if not internal ones. It may be he is referring to just one province which is likely to be Britannia Prima. On balance I would suggest the most likely solution is as follows: the events of the mid-fifth century caused the south eastern province, *Maxima Caesariensis*, to break away, either wholly or in part, from the former diocese. The western and northern provinces remained essentially Romano-British. The eastern province containing Lincoln and Leicester is a little more difficult to ascertain. The later borders of the emerging Kingdoms, both Brittonic and Anglo-Saxon, suggest these kingdoms were loosely based on the boundaries of former *civitates*. The important question is, did any provincial structure survive?

If we could answer yes, this might explain how one person could hold *imperium* over a large area or group of peoples. The HB suggests that Hengest eventually took control over Middlesex, Essex and Sussex. The ASC has our first Bretwalda arriving during Hengest's lifetime. Yet three years after Hengest's death, Ælle besieges *Anderitum* and 'killed all who lived in there'. We get a clear indication from this that significant pockets of Roman-British still lived in the area. We are reminded there is significant evidence for continuation of both population and land use. In addition DNA studies do not support any large invasion of Anglo-Saxons and displacement of the indigenous Romano-British.

Another clue comes from the ASC. In 823 the West Saxons conquer what they later describe as the 'East Kingdom', which included Kent, Sussex, Essex and Surrey.[24] Admittedly this is three centuries later, but it is at least curious the same territories are mentioned in the HB. For Ælle's 'overlordship' to mean anything it would have to have included at least authority over the surviving *civitates*, or even provincial structure in the south east. This would have included the majority Romano-British population as well as the range of Germanic and other settlers. The ASC suggests this was not an entirely peaceful process. Bede, writing two and half centuries later, gives him sovereignty over the English south of the Humber. This would include the former province of *Flavia Caesariensis* whose capital was at Lincoln. Yet we have seen two important pieces of information: first, there is evidence of a surviving British authority into the sixth century centred at Lincoln; second, the archaeological evidence suggests Angles, not Saxons, were the dominant influence in terms of material culture and burial practices.

We cannot assume the Germanic settlers were a homogenous group any more than the Romano-British. Rather what we seem to have is fragmenting political, military and provincial structures at the same time as increasing immigration from a range of different Germanic peoples. This is occurring after a major deterioration in economic and urban life. Yet at the same time we see significant evidence for continuation of population and land use as well as the survival of former *civitas* boundaries. Into this situation we have a warlord arriving with a small force of warriors who much later is regarded as holding *imperium*.

Figure 15 shows one possible scenario. The dotted line encompassing the South Saxons, Kent and East Saxons indicates the minimum area that was likely under his rule. If Bede is correct, this authority stretched to the Humber and in effect covered the two eastern former Roman provinces. Whether there was any surviving administrative structure is another matter. However, as we shall see in the next section, in Gaul these structures did indeed survive under barbarian rule. To the west, Britannia Prima may well have survived into the late fifth century at it perhaps in this context we should view Ælle's imperium and the battle of Badon.

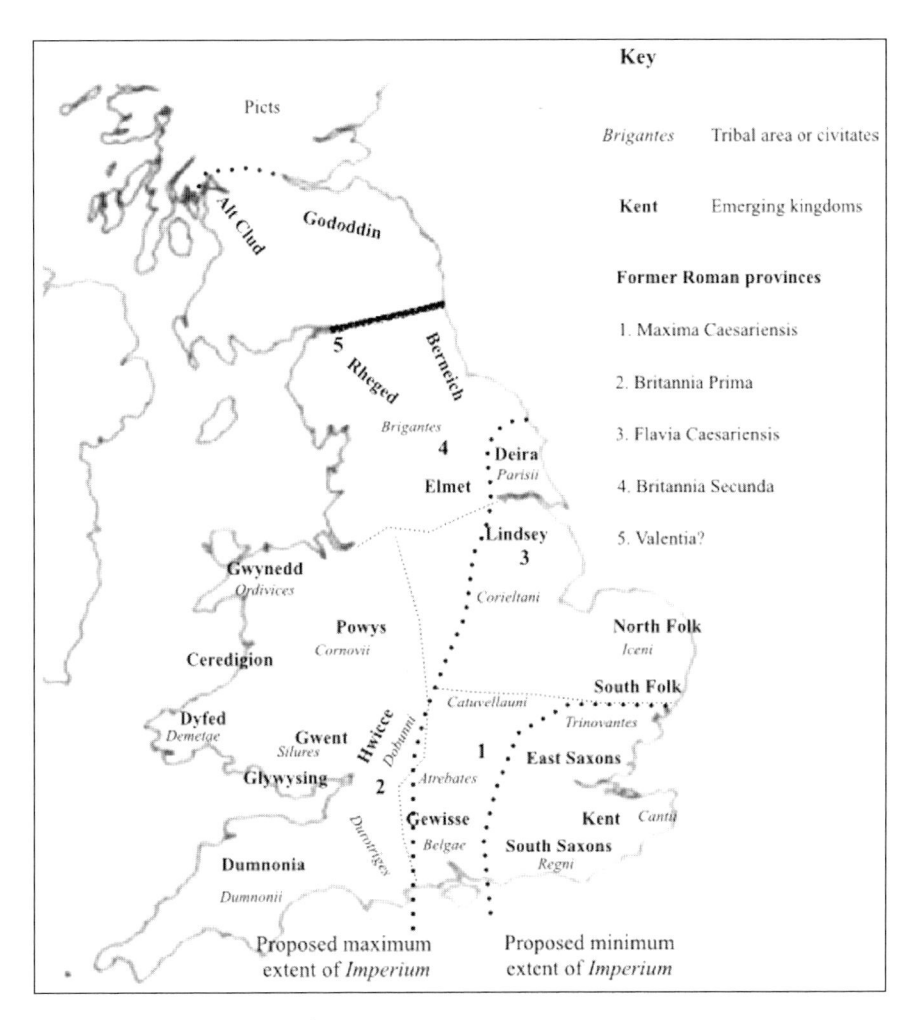

Figure 15. Map showing Ælle's *imperium*.

We hear no further of the kings of Sussex until 607 when Ceolwulf of Wessex fights against the South Saxons. The next reference in the ASC is for 661 when Wulfhere, Penda's son, leads the Mercians 'as far as Ashdown'. Wulfhere follows this by giving the Isle of Wight to Æthelwold, king of the South Saxons, and receiving him at baptism. This conversion is also recorded in the AC for 665: 'The first celebration of Easter among the Saxons.' Interestingly, it also records, 'the second battle of Badon, Morgan dies'. Who Morgan was and what, if any, connection there was is unknown. It's worth noting the reference to Badon and wonder if there is a link to Wulfhere's raid in the ASC 'as far as Ashdown' dated to 661. If this reference to a second Badon refers to the same location rather than a similar victory over the same enemy then it is one of the few clues for the likely location of the famous battle. We will cover this further in a later chapter. Before we discuss the changing cultural identity of the south and east of Britain it is worth looking at events in Gaul.

Fifth-century Gaul

After the fall of Constantine III in 411, the first half of the fifth century was dominated by the increasing presence of Germanic tribes. Franks had been present in the north for many decades. The major incursion over the frozen Rhine in 407 resulted in Burgundians being settled in the south east of Gaul, Alemanni in the east and the Visigoths in Aquataine in the south west. In the first quarter of the fifth century Constantius, *the magister militum* and later Emperor, had defeated Constantine and regained control over much of the diocese. Sozomen, writing at the time, reported the province 'returning it's allegiance'. It is possible the reference to the break with Roman rule could in part be connected to the *bacaudae*, a colloquial term meaning bandit, synonymous with rebel.[25] Peasant freeholders may have been likely recruits, however contemporary reports suggest they came from the lesser aristocracy to whom 'the oppressed flee'.[26] This is an important point to remember when we discuss changing cultural identity, as at this point contemporary writers make no distinction these *bacaudae* and barbarians.

Drinkwater suggests the burdens of heavy taxation, economic contraction, arrival of significant barbarian peoples and warfare caused social unrest.[27] By 431 tax revenues had dropped by an estimated 50 per cent.[28] Social mobility which 'energised the imperial administration in the fourth century dried up'.[29] It is at least possible that whatever regime now existed in Britain may have been regarded as *bacaudae* by some in Rome. Perhaps some in Britain viewed themselves the same way.

In Gaul Constantius had stabilised the province for the time being. The next significant figure is the likely person to whom Gildas claimed the Britons appealed. Aetius was made the *Magister Militum* in Gaul in 425. For the next thirty years he maintained Rome's power, mainly by playing off the various Germanic tribes and the careful use of *foederate* troops, including Huns. The Roman war with the Huns drew in various peoples on both sides and culminated in a Roman victory at the Battle of the Catalaunian Plains in 451. The Hunnic threat ended with the death of Attila in 453. It is intriguing to imagine a delegation from Britain arriving in Gaul to request military aid for the senior Roman military official just as the Hunnic threat intensified.

Unfortunately for the Western Empire, Aetius was murdered in 454 and Rome was sacked by the Vandals a year later. At this point the ASC claims Hengest was fighting battles in Kent against the Britons and Bede is saying a rebellion of mercenaries is sweeping across the island. In Gaul local power blocks appeared 'with remarkable speed'.[30] Power structures emerged by the late 450s centred on the royal courts of 'barbarian' strongmen such as the Goths at Bordeaux. The Roman Empire of the West had been a 'federation of regions'. Fault lines widened between regional elites and the central imperial government and this was perhaps even more the case in Britain where tribal identities may have re-emerged.[31]

The Western Empire descended into a succession of nine emperors which ended in 476 when the General Odoacer deposed the last Western Roman Emperor, Romulus. We are concerned with events just before that and what might have caused a Saxon leader to head for Britain in 477. Gaul had already started to fragment after the death of Aetius. In the early 460s an area of northern Gaul had broken away as the Kingdom of Soisson, ruled by the Roman General Aegidius (a possible alternative for the Agitius of Gildas). He had served under Aetius and was also *Magister Militum* of Gaul. The final disappearance of Roman authority from Gaul occurs in this period.[32]

In the 460s we see evidence of Saxons in the Loire Valley and raiders and settlers on the coast.[33]

This comes from both the archaeological and literary record. Gregory of Tours describes a 'great war' between Romans and Saxons. The Saxons are 'cut down and pursued'. Frankish allies of the Romans capture islands in the Loire formerly held by the Saxons. Gregory then tells us of another war, this time between Goths and Britons. By this he likely means Britons who had settled in Armorica and north of the Loire. The Britons are defeated at Bourg-de-Deol in central Gaul and are expelled from Bourges near the Loire River.

Jordanes, in the *The Origin and Deeds of the Goths*, describes the same war. The Emperor Anthemius (467–72) made one last attempt to exert Roman authority in Gaul against increasingly powerful Germanic tribes. A letter was sent requesting aid from a 'King Riotimus of the Brittones' to fight the Visigoth king, Euric. Riotimus arrives with 12,000 men 'by way of the ocean'. This could mean across the channel from Britain or from Armorica, down the west coast of Gaul and into the River Loire. He is met by the Goths before he can meet up with his Roman Allies and is defeated never to be heard of again. It is possible this force came from Britain and the name Riotimus is in fact a title, meaning great or high king.

Here we have evidence of Saxons being displaced from the Loire Valley in the mid-460s. A little later the Franks and Goths expand their zones of influence. A Saxon warrior or adventurer a decade later might view Britain as a better choice. These events supply a reason, independent of British sources, for migration of Germanic peoples away from Gaul and towards Britain.[34] At the same time we have a record of Britons fighting in Gaul in the 460s. It is possible Riotimus was a contemporary of Ambrosius Aurelianus, although Bede places him perhaps a little later. If we accept Jordanes's account of an army of 12,000, this leads to some interesting thoughts. If they arrived from Britain this would suggest the situation was stable enough to allow 12,000 troops to be organised, equipped, trained and transported to Gaul. If they came from modern Brittany, why were they not made available for their fellow countrymen across the Channel?

This might make us doubt our timeline as it would point to a stable Britain in c. 470 and any revolt of mercenaries after that date. It would make Aegidius the more likely recipient of any appeal and mean Gildas simply assumed it was Aetius and mis-applied 'thrice consul'. Professor Dumville accepts the appeal was to Aetius but places the hiring of the *foederati* to the 480s.[35] This allows a perhaps more likely length of time for the events listed in Gildas. It would suggest the provincial and diocese structure survived much later than thought. However, it leaves the GC entry for 440 requiring some explanation. It also shortens the time for the acculturation and adoption of English for much of the indigenous population in the south east. Dumville, like Bede, places Badon at approximately 500. On balance, I would accept the GC entry for 440 and Bede's assertion that Ambrosius fought a war against the incomers in the last quarter of the fifth century.

In Gaul events were moving fast. In 465 Aegidius had been succeeded by his son, Syragius, in Soissons. Within ten years of the end of the Western Empire in 476, the Franks had conquered the kingdom as they expanded their dominance under Clovis I. After the capture of Soissons the Roman/Breton border now became a Frankish/Breton one. Clovis went on to defeat the Thuringians in 491, the Goths in 507 and the Alemanni in 508. The relationship in the sixth century between Britons and Franks was said to be one of peace and there may have been a treaty around 497.[36] However, Procpius writing a hundred years later describes the Armoricans fighting off the Franks, so that they were forced to make them 'their companions and relations by marriage'.[37]

This might give the impression that barbarian peoples were displacing the population and taking over swathes of territory. In fact there was no 'sharp break' between Roman and Germanic administrations.[38] As the Western Empire fragmented it caused political vacuums.[39] However, the barbarian migrations of the fifth century were the product rather than the cause of this. The Roman state had become inefficient and corrupt.[40] With the loss of the Rhine frontier and military control the Germanic tribes filled the void. When the Romans moved the prefecture headquarters from Trier in central Gaul to Arles near Marseille power shifted further south. Some in society welcomed the new order. With Roman authority removed, Gaul fragmented into separate states.[41]

A 'climate of violence' spread across Spain and Gaul in the fifth century.[42] One of the reasons was the prevalence of raiding as part of the culture of many Germanic peoples. St Patrick writes of Roman Gallic Christians ransoming baited captives from the Franks and others. The age of the absentee landowner was over and replaced by those with 'power on they spot'.[43] Some local landowners built defences and we see one example in Dardanus, former Prefect of Gaul, who fortified a local town in the Alps.[44] It would seem that early Germanic kingship was inexorably linked with tribute and this appears to be the case in Britain as well with Æthelberht of Kent.[45]

Events in Gaul may aid us in considering what was occurring in Britain just a short journey north. Clovis retained the Belgic provincial organisation after he conquered Soissons in 486. In general the administrative structure in Gaul survived well into the fifth century, even in areas under barbarian control.[46] For example, as late as 469 there was a certain Evantius, of the rank of *praeses*, responsible for maintaining the road between the Visigoth capital at Toulouse and Clermont.[47]

There was still a resident Count at Triers in the 470s and Christianity still thrived. It wasn't just local elites who rose to power, bishops became virtually monarchal in fifth-century Gallic cities.[48] We can see not only how structures and roles were maintained, but also a smooth transition to new management positively supported by the church. Gallic bishops wrote to Clovis after he conquered Soissons and advised him, having 'undertaken the administration of *Belgica Secunda*'.[49]

If a similar chain of events occurred in Britain, despite political and military upheavals, then we can consider a number of intriguing possibilities: provincial and *civitas* organisation survived even in areas under 'barbarian' authority; offices and roles such as *praeses, comes* or *praefectus* were retained; some roads were maintained; and Christianity survived even in areas under barbarian control. A number of examples of Roman terminology survived in Britain.[50] In Offa's court in the c. 780s a certain Brorda was styled *patricius*, *princeps* or *dux*. In the seventh century we hear of Blæcca, *praefectus* of Lincoln. Two other examples from King Ecgfrith's Northumbria are Osfrith, *praefectus* of *Inbroninis* (possibly Fenwick) and Tydlin, *praefectus* of Dunbar. Waga of Carlisle is described as a *praepositus*. In Kent we hear of a Raedfrith, Ealdhun and Aethelnoth, termed *praefecti*, a word closely related to royal *gerefa* or reeves. If the Romano-Gallic population survived and prospered under Frankish and Gothic authority, one wonders what the response of the Romano-Britons was? Once again we must remind ourselves this is not a homogenous group. The view of the situation might be affected by one's social, cultural or economic position within society as well as one's ethnicity, which itself might be complex.

Cultural identity

We noted in chapter one that *civitates* were largely based on pre-Roman tribal areas. These affiliations may have remained a factor into post-Roman Britain.[51] Sidonius Apollinaris writing c. 471, refers to a Briton as *Regiensem*, identifying him as a citizen of the Regni.[52] The importance of the *civitas* was central to cultural identity in the fifth century.[53] The *patria*, or hometown, held a significant loyalty for a leading Roman.[54] We see this in inscriptions in south-west Wales: 'Here lies Paulinus, guardian of the faith and always lover of his homeland.' We recall Vorteporix bore the Roman title *protector*. We see here that both a religious and military leader were seen as important roles. What we see in Gaul is the emergence of a division between the two.[55] Bishops wielded 'soft pastoral power'. Those bishops that did act like petty lords were the exception rather than the rule.

In Britain distinctive types of villas and socio-economic material culture suggest tribal differences persisted throughout the Roman period.[56] This tribal, or *civitas*, identity is one of many within a wider sense of Roman identity that was fostered throughout the empire. Two major events added to this: first, the *Edict of Caracalla* in 212 expanding citizenship; second, Christianity was adopted as the official religion by Constantine in the early fourth century. The Edict of 212 removed the distinction between *cives*, citizens, and *populi*, natives. Now everyone was a citizen, in theory at least. Ethnic identity can be complex and often socially constructed.[57] One of the features of Roman identity was its multi-ethnicity and Roman law as its defining feature.[58]

At the beginning of the fifth century most people in Gaul and Britain still saw themselves as Roman. However, within a few generations the descendants of these same people saw themselves very differently. Attitudes towards the barbarians also changed. The influx of a large numbers of different tribal groups with a diverse range of cultures had a significant affect on the Western Empire in the fifth century. These 'barbarians' were not a homogenous group. The Vandals in Africa were described as a 'huge mob of diverse savage enemies' which included Alans, a 'mixed company of Goths', and others of 'diverse backgrounds'.[59] In the fourth century barbarians had been seen as those outside the law and civilised behaviour. Roman attitudes were generally negative and the term was used pejoratively to mean uncultured, unreliable, and undesirable. There was even an imperial law laying out punishments of exile and confiscation for the wearing of barbarian breeches.[60] The Emperor Gratian was criticised for preferring the company and dress of 'barbarian comradeship'. Mixed marriages were discouraged, sometimes by law, although there were important exceptions, such as the marriage of the Gothic king Athaulf and the empress Galla Placidia in 414.[61] A marriage criticised by the Byzantine Chronicler Philostorgius as a 'union of iron and clay'. Similar attitudes and language was used with the rebel *bacaudae*.

Despite these attitudes contemporary reports from Gaul give us some idea how cultural identity evolved. They report a decline in culture and 'Latin learning' during the fifth century.[62] The importance of literature was 'second only to a blood tie' for aristocratic Romans. This was one distinctive difference with barbarian culture.[63] Every major Gallic city had a literary circle while barbarians did not take part in such 'literary activities'. Society was hierarchical and 'everyone knew their place' in a system of obligations and favours.[64] However, the prevalence of rebel *bacaudae* suggests this social order was under strain exacerbated by the influx of considerable barbaric tribes from the beginning of the fifth century.

Birth and merit had been the two primary routes into the senatorial order.[65] But by the mid-fifth century there was a growing disinclination to hold state office. During the reign of Petronius Maximus in 455, over 1,000 Gauls refused to hold imperial offices.[66] This was at the same time as the imperial administration was contracting and the number of offices reduced significantly.[67] Aristocratic Romans were not only withdrawing from political life, but from whole regions. The elite had already begun to withdraw from the Rhine region at the end of the fourth century as the threat from barbarian raids increased.[68] Further departures occurred from south-west Gaul with the arrival of the Goths in Aquitaine in 412.[69] Ties between the Gallic and Italian aristocracy loosened and became remote.[70] The elite Romano-Gallic aristocrats concentrated on a 'quest for local influence' rather than advancement through the empire.[71] If this was occurring in Gaul in the mid-fifth century, we can suggest that a similar process was already the situation to the north.

In fact, if we recall the 'Rescript of Honorius', this break occurred much earlier. The visits of St Germanus show that some communication and links persisted, but not enough to allow Aetius to respond positively to any request for help. If Romano-Britons hadn't given up hope for a return to Roman authority in 410, they likely did by the mid-fifth century. We should certainly consider potential generational differences. As the older generation passed away, those in power increasingly had never known Roman rule.

If the ties that held the Western Roman aristocrats started to fracture, what then of the mass of people? Salvian of Marseilles, writing in the mid-fifth century, claimed the Romans under barbarian rule desired to never again 'pass under Roman authority'.[72] He also reports that many 'even those of not obscure birth' chose to live among the barbarians, flee to the Goths or, notably, the *bacaudae*, to avoid Roman 'iniquity and cruelty'. Importantly, this view is especially common among the 'Roman plebs' or free Roman citizens, which is exactly how many people in the Romanised parts of Britain would have seen themselves. It is not clear exactly who or what the Bacaudae were.[73] Arguments range from peasants to local landowners. The word is Celtic, from *baga*, 'warrior'. They were Romans and usually described as 'public enemies' or 'rebels'. The central government often employed barbaric troops to quell this unrest.

Freeborn Roman citizens found themselves branded as *bacaudae* and subject to 'vicious campaigns of repression'.[74] Salvian himself had fled from Barbarian raids in the Rhineland. Now he witnessed Roman citizens fleeing to the barbarians to escape Roman authority and taxes 'the *Romana respublica* is now dead ... strangled, as if by thugs, with the bonds of taxes'.[75] The blame, according to Salvian, lay with local elites such as town councillors, *principales*. He even described the process;[76] high taxation led to impoverishment, this in turn led poor farmers to hand the titles of their farms to the rich and eventually become little more than slaves working on, what was once, their own land.

A law by the Emperor Majorian in 458 gives further clues. It mentions the flight of inhabitants of cities to avoid 'the injuries caused by the tax collectors'. Paulinus of Pella, c. 414, reported that 'many are flourishing through the favour of the Goths'.[77] He also relates how the town of Bazas, south west Gaul, was affected by violence where a 'servile faction mixed with the insane fury of a few young men and even freeborn men which was armed in particular for the slaughter of the nobility'.[78] One fifth-century playwright was able to include the line: 'It is in fact common knowledge and manifestly clear that all lords are wicked.'[79] An anonymous fourth-century author wrote about the distribution of gold: 'the houses of the powerful were stuffed and their splendour enhanced by the destruction of the poor'.[80] It would seem from this evidence that social unrest was a significant problem. Aside from open rebellion by *bacaudae*, many free citizens were finding Roman authority oppressive. Salvian wrote that the Roman order hung on by a thread: 'dead or at least drawing its last breath'.[81]

One of the groups that angered the Pelagian author of the treatise, *De divitiis* (On Riches) c. 408–414, was not the great landowners but the *iudices*, provincial governors acting as judges.[82] Pelagian writings focused on the corruption of government by wealth. At the same time the Roman elite were turning away from public office. Many saw the church as a viable alternative. After the death of Aetius important military positions became dominated by Germanic officers, such as Ricimer and Odoacer. As Roman rule waned the various Germanic tribes flexed their muscles. Senior Roman figures became very comfortable plotting with these same barbarians against Roman rule, such as Agrippinus with the Burgundians and Arvandus with the Goths. Barbarian rulers also changed their attitudes. Athaulf, king of the Visigoths, is reported to have first wanted to obliterate the Roman Empire and replace it with a Gothic version.[83] The difficulty of ruling a fractious people convinced him to defend the Roman name by Gothic arms, helped by his Roman wife Galla Placidia. Similarly, Anglo-Saxon Kings from the fifth to eighth centuries often claimed to be heirs of Rome and could still be 'regarded as culturally late Roman'.[84] As power shifted away from Roman rule in the second half of the fifth century, Barbarian rulers made efforts to protect Roman subjects and aristocrats.[85]

Various barbarian Law Codes started to emerge, such as the Laws of Theoderic (453–466) and his son Euric (c. 476) which tried to preserve the status of Romans and Goths back to the time of the initial settlement in 418. One example decreed 'ancient boundaries are to stand'. Land held for more than fifteen years could be kept if voluntarily given in the first place. Land taken by force could be recovered within thirty years through the courts. The Burgundian Law code of the early sixth century commanded that 'Romans be judged under Roman Laws', discouraging the transfer of Roman matters to Burgundian advocates.[86] Social laws also applied, such as a prohibition against mixed marriages. The late fourth-century Theodosian Code referred to this and was repeated in the Burgundian Code. For example, a Roman girl who married without her parents' consent could have none of their property. In 506 the Council of Agde, south-west Gaul, declared mixed marriages with heretics as improper. What these examples might demonstrate is how common mixed marriage was. Since the marriage of the Gothic King Athaulf and the Roman Empress Placidia in 414, Germanic names within Roman families increased.[87] Perhaps the concept of Ambrosius Aurelianus having a brother called Uther and the latter naming his son Artorius is not so unlikely.

Many of these new law codes were written by the Romans themselves, although now working under barbarian kings.[88] One example from Narbonne concerns Leo, 'counsellor of the most powerful king', Euric of the Visigoths. Importantly the Visigoth king had conceded the language of law was Latin written by a Gallic-Roman.[89] In the Burgundian Code, Romans and Burgundians had roughly equal status, although barbarians were still considered outsiders.[90]

One important cultural change was the increase in the use of violence. In Germanic society there was a legal concept of self help. As the Roman legal machinery deteriorated, factionalism and quarrelling increased, even among the Roman aristocracy. The system of *Wergeld*, formalised in Germanic law codes, began to look like a price worth paying if it settled a dispute quickly and in your favour. Thus an increase in violence, banditry and hostage taking increased.[91]

Many Romans profited from barbarian patronage and by the end of the sixth century, Gallic aristocrats had adopted a new ideology.[92] This process affected the barbarians too, so that it was difficult to tell how much 'barbarian ethnic identity' remained.[93] Roman attitudes towards them had changed and they no longer saw them as outsiders.[94]

Halsall argues ethnicity is multi-layered: fluid, dynamic, performative, cognitive and situational.[95] Roman identity in sixth-century Gaul was 'elastic' and we can see how it changed over the period. One important component was their adherence to Chalcedonian Christianity (adhering to the definitions and resolutions of the Council of Chalcedon, the Fourth Ecumenical Council held in 451).[96] This process affected the Germanic people settled in Gaul as well. However, while Christianity may have added to a sense of common identity, other variables were weakening it. Heavy taxation, corruption, social unrest, increased Germanic settlement and conflict had weakened the fabric that held the Western Empire together. Aside from the *becaudae* and general dissatisfaction in the populace, the elites were also turning away. Fewer and fewer people were willing to take on the burden of public life, and elites became more focused on local matters.

The question is, can we use the example of Gaul to speculate on the situation in Britain? Some historians view the early fifth century as a 'post-colonial period' and 'a number of aspects of Roman economy and material culture appear to be actively rejected, especially in south-eastern England'.[97] Social and cultural identity in post-Roman Britain can be divided among three significant groups:[98] the indigenous elites, Germanic migrants, and the indigenous peasantry. None of these groups were homogenous. Thus we have a number of different overlapping groups, each with multiple layers of cultural identity that are constantly changing. Halsall estimates a change in ethnic or cultural identity to take a 'generation or so'.[99]

Snyder, in *An Age of Tyrants*, makes the point that for Patrick *cives* and *Romani* are closely linked, perhaps indicating he grew up in a more Roman society.[100] This may have been the case in the generation between 410 and the visit of Germanus in 429. Gildas, however, makes a clear distinction and for him *cives* are his fellow Britons and are separate from the *Romani*. What seems to have developed in post-Roman Britain was a sense of *patria*, country or homeland, and *cives*, fellow countrymen. We see this when Gildas berates the five tyrant kings for waging war against their fellow *cives*. Linguistically we start to see words such as *combrogi* and *cymry*, meaning fellow countrymen. It may be that when St Patrick and Gildas used the term *cives,* they were yearning for a greater unity. Gildas especially seems to be talking over the heads of his kings.

At the second council of Tours in 567 it was determined that neither Briton nor Roman would be consecrated bishop without the consent of the metropolitan and provincial leaders. There also seems to be a clear ethnic distinction between Britons and Romans in the eyes of sixth-century Gallic churchmen. When Constantius, writing in 480, speaks of the visit of St Germanus, he uses ethnic linguistic labels: *Brittani, Saxones, Picti*, which he doesn't do when referring to events in Gaul. St Patrick though sees his people as simply *cives*, citizens.

In contrast, Gildas views a marked difference between *Britanni*, 'cowardly in war', and *Romani*, 'our worthy allies'. However, evidence from contemporary inscriptions from Britain suggest people often preferred to identify with local tribal names.[101] Thus we get *Elmetiacos* (Elmet), *Ordous* (Ordovici), *Venedotis cives* (citizen of Gwynedd). This didn't prevent outsiders viewing Britons as a homogenous group. Fifth-century religious figures such as Pelagius, Fastidius and Faustus are all referred to as Britons by their Roman contemporaries. It would appear some Britons took on this label:[102] at Arles a sarcophagus lid from c. 420–60 reads Tolosanus *Britannus Natione*. Bishop Mansuetus at the council of Tours in 461 called himself *episcopus Britanniarum*.

We can make some broad points. First, that a Roman identity persisted but also a local identity often based on the *civitas*. Whether any pre-Roman tribal identity survived is open to debate; it had certainly gone through massive changes. This civic identity may have created a provincial or diocese-wide feeling of *patria* or homeland. Britons were often viewed on the Continent as a homogenous group, often in disparaging terms: the Gallic poet Ausonius c. 382 writes, 'no good man is a Briton'; Namatinaus in 417 describes 'the wild Briton'; and Pelagius is insulted by Zerome and Prosper with the word *Britto*.[103] So a Briton might identify as, for example, *Venedotis cives*, but at the same time feel part of a wider civic Roman community. As the disillusionment with Roman central government and taxes grew, that attachment perhaps moved from the wider Empire to Britannia. But the diocese itself consisted of five provinces which had experienced very different levels of Romanisation and urbanisation. It had also experienced levels of Germanic settlement confined to specific areas.

Sidonius Apollinaris ended his career as Bishop of Clermont. When he tried to prevent it being absorbed in the Gothic kingdom he met with resistance within the town.[104] Some local Romans now viewed their best interests as lying with the Goths rather than the Empire. One of Sidonius's correspondents was Namatius, who served Euric as admiral of the Gothic fleet. Sidnoius's own son led the Clermont militia in support of the Goths in the battle of Vouille in 507. His grandson Arcadius assisted the sons of Clovis in getting rid of their nephews. Within two generations Gaul had changed completely.

It is worth considering what this might mean in practice. Imagine a rural farmhand in late fifth-century lowland Britain. A villa estate in southern Lincolnshire for example. The area had experienced decades of significant migration from various Germanic tribes. The largest group were the Angli, but Saxons, Friesians, Jutes and many others were also represented. Mixed marriages may have been frowned on by some but increased nonetheless. Our farmhand likely had friends or even relatives from various backgrounds. If he descended from indigenous Britons he was a Christian. However there is no guarantee he felt loyalty towards the local bishopric, at Lincoln. Perhaps his family were Pelagians or Arians. His attitude would likely be influenced by multiple factors: his economic situation; his relationship with the local landholder at the villa; the political situation in the *civitas* and wider province; the various layers of cultural identity. Nor is the situation static, he may well change his view and loyalty as the situation changes. Should conflict erupt and he is forced to take sides what decision does he make? Does he support the villa owner or use it as an excuse to help destroy him? Similar decisions arise for *civitas* and church authorities. Does ethnic identity trump economic considerations? Which decision is safer for himself and his family in a dangerous world?

A series of events in North Africa is instructive.[105] The spread of Christianity in the region created a new sense of identity. Specifically the appearance of rural bishops as leaders.[106] In 411 Augustine had placed a monk, Antoninus, as bishop of the hill village of Fussala, south-east of Hippo. Antoninus built a palace and hired a retired soldier to head a force guarding the city walls. He was also able to arrange the release of prisoners arrested by the Count of Africa. All this made him very popular at home, but less so with Augustine who tried to depose him. A power base emerged led by a bishop aided by a local strongman at odds with the very person who had placed him there.

We have seen in the Western Empire of the fifth century Gaul was experiencing significant social unrest, political upheavals and social change. Cultural identities and loyalty were was undergoing enormous changes. Fifth-century Britain may have been far more complex and nuanced than the simple Romano-British versus Anglo-Saxon that is often portrayed. As this chapter concerns Ælle of the South Saxons we will investigate Saxon identity. But first we will turn to the origins of the 'Germans'.

Origins of the Germans

The Greeks differentiated between four main 'barbarian' peoples: the Celts and the Scythians to their north, Persians to the east and Libyans to the south.[107] Pytheas of Marseille in 320 BC was the first Mediterranean observer to a difference between *Keltoi* and *Germanoi*. He described the Germani as amber collectors likely located on the banks of the Baltic who later moved south.[108]

The Germans were also observed as a distinct group in the late second century BC by Poseidonius of Apamea. The Romans first described the Germans as a people in the first century BC.[109] Language gives us some clues as to the origins of what the Romans called the Germanic people. The Proto-Indo-European group of languages originated during the Copper Age on the European steppe north of the Black and Caspian seas. Proto-Germanic developed no later than 500 BC and later split into West, North and East Germanic, with the former later evolving into Old English.[110]

Tacitus, in the first century, states the name 'Germania' had only only recently been applied to the area. The first people to cross the Rhine, the Tungri, were once called 'Germani'. This tribal name came into general use and was then applied to all peoples from across the Rhine. Eventually the Germans themselves adopted it, partly, Tacitus claims, to frighten the Gauls.[111] Other tribal groups include the Marsi, Gambrivii, Suebi and Vandilii, which leads to Tacitus claiming the names are 'both genuine and ancient'.

The Roman view of the Germanic peoples was rather poor. While they were viewed as a tall and blond 'good-looking' people, they had 'abysmal habits':[112] irrational and superstitious; incapable of living to written laws; incapable of loyalty outside their group; possessed a 'death wish'; and appalling personal hygiene. What is important to remember is that a member of the various tribes classed by the Romans as German would not have viewed themselves in that way at all. Rather they would have identified with their tribal name. This was as true in the fourth century as it was when Julius Caesar first crossed the Rhine. They would have called themselves Langobard, Vandal, Goth or Frisian.[113] In Britain a Jute might have felt as different from an Angle as a Briton. A Friesian mercenary whose family had been in Britain for generations might have identified as a Romano-Briton first. Or perhaps a Romano-Cantii, given the importance of *civitas* in fifth-century social identity. Both may have been very confused or insulted to be called Saxon or barbarian by Gildas.

Saxons

The name *Saxones* first appears in Ptolemy's *Geography* in AD 150.[114] He located them between the Rivers Ems and Elbe next to the Chauci. In modern terms this is in the region of Schleswig-Holstein, south of Denmark on the Jutland peninsula. Tacitus, writing in the second century, classed the *Anglii* as coming from the *Suebi* tribe originating from modern Germany. By the end of the fourth century AD archaeological evidence shows Saxons moving westwards towards the north-western European coast.[115] By the mid-fifth century Saxons had settled in the Loire valley and the Germanic Roman General Odacer used them to fight against the Goths around 460. Gregory of Tours records a 'great war' between the Romans and Saxons and at the same time Britons were being expelled from Bourges. The Saxons appeared to have lost this war as they are described as being 'cut down and pursued', losing many of their islands in the Loire to the Franks. Sidonius Apollinaris, in the last quarter of the fifth century, writes complaining of Saxon pirates off the Gaulish coast.

Procopius writing in the sixth century described Britain as populated by three 'populous nations', with each ruled by their own king: *Anglii, Frissones,* and *Britonnes*. He learnt this from Angles accompanying a Frankish embassy to Byzantium around 553. The implication is that Angles viewed the Saxons as either Frisians, or perhaps so assimilated into the British population as being indistinct with the Friesians a separate group. Saxons were seen as distinct from Jutes. Tacitus referred to the Jutes as *Eudoses*, while *Eote* is the Anglian name used in the poem *Beowulf*. In the West Saxon dialect it became *Yte* and the New Forest area was called the land of the *Ytene* in later Old English. Indeed Bede states the land opposite the Isle of Wight was named for the Jutes. We can identify their homeland prior to the migration period as follows: Jutes in the north of modern Denmark; Saxons around the Elbe river in Germany and Angles in between in the Schleswig-Holstein region between modern Germany and Denmark and the island of Fyn.

Ælle, the First Bretwalda

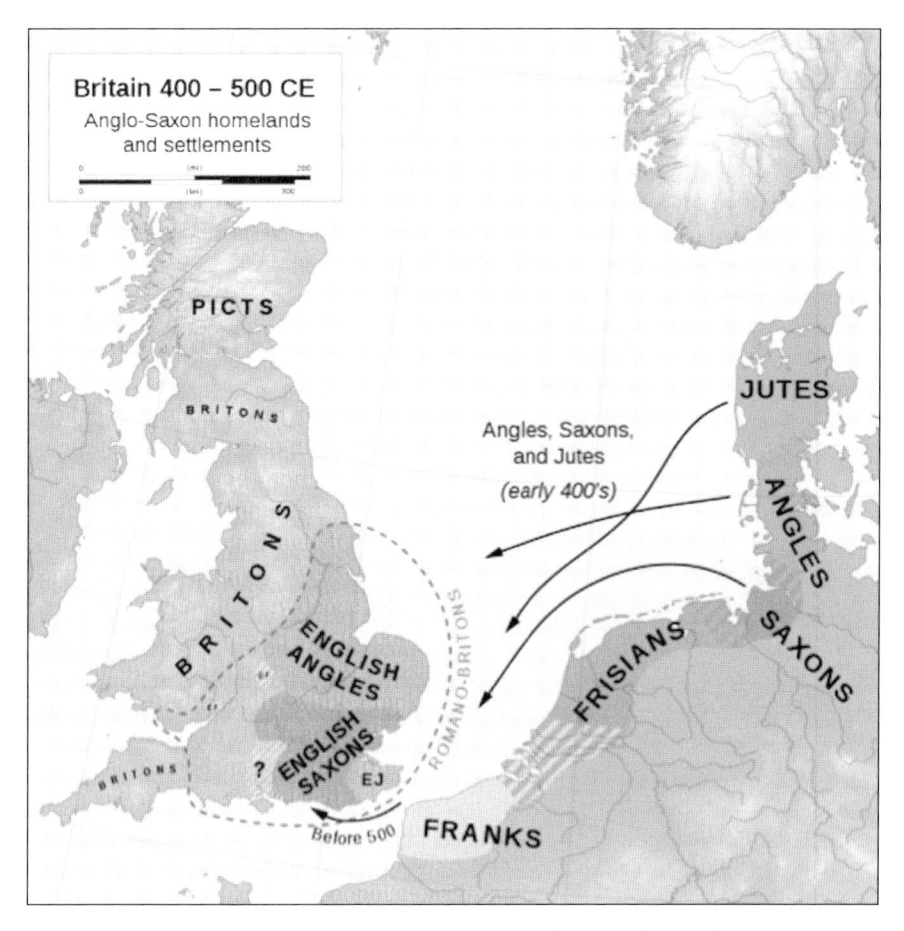

Figure 16. Map showing Saxon, Angle and Jute homelands. (Wikimedia Commons)

What we must remember is the settlement areas do not represent a mass invasion and replacement of the indigenous population. Instead the coloured areas on the map represent where a predominance of burials and material culture from the three groups are found. In the 'Angle' eastern area, for example, the indigenous population remained the majority in many regions. Evidence for a continuation of land use and population is strong. Indeed, we have signs that a Romano-British authority centered on Lincoln persisted into the sixth century. What we have is evidence for a change in material culture which *could* be the result of significant immigration of Germanic people. It could simply be the adoption of practices by the Romano-Britons. However, evidence from burials and recent DNA studies suggest some immigration did take place. At the same time, the literary sources such as Bede list a number of different groups settling in Britain. These groups initially settled in marginal areas such as coastal and river ways. But they also settled near

Romano-British centres of economic activity. What we have is a range of different Germanic peoples settling mainly in the most Romanised part of Britain over a number of decades. At the same time three main groups dominate specific areas. This during a time of political, religious and social upheaval.

The Romans, and Britons, often used Saxon to describe Germanic settlers in general. Celtic speakers also conflated Saxons with Angles and other Germanic people. Hence *Saeson* (Welsh), *Sasanaigh* (Irish) and *Sassenach* (Scottish Gaelic), although in the fifth century it was as likely referring to Angles as Saxons. We see *Saxones* mentioned in the *Laterculus Veronensis* (Verona List) in c. 315, which lists fifty-three barbarian peoples (*Saxones* appear at number six). In the mid-fourth century Julian the apostate, emperor 361–3, describes 'the most warlike of the peoples who live beyond the Rhine and shores of the western sea'.[116] Interestingly, he states both the Franks and Saxons supported the usurper Magnentius ten years before because of their 'ties of kinship'. Magnentius had the support of the provinces of Britannia, Hispania and Gaul and this might suggest Frankish and Saxon allies were at least present between 350–3.

Ammianus Marcellinus tells of 'constant raids' in Britain in 364 involving Saxons, Scots, Picts and Attacotti. We then hear of a major incursion in 367. This 'barbarian conspiracy' may have in fact been a carefully orchestrated internal uprising. However, he goes onto to describe a major Saxon raid in 370 on an unspecified part of the Roman border. Their defeat led to a contingent of young men being handed over for military service. It is unknown where they were posted or even if they arrived. The surviving raiders were allowed home but were ambushed and slaughtered by the Romans en route. Unfortunately we are not told where exactly *home* was.

The fourth-century poet Claudius Claudianus was the first writer since Ptolemy to specifically disassociate Saxons from the Franks.[117] They are described as raiders from the sea and associated with Britain: the Saxons come 'whatever wind might blow'; 'With the Saxon tamed the sea is calmer'; and 'the Orkneys dripped with slaughtered Saxon'. Another contemporary writer, Orosius, places them 'among the coasts and inaccessible swamps of the ocean, fearsome for the courage and mobility'.[118]

An early fifth-century document, the *Notitia Dignitatum*, uses the phrase *Comes Litoris Saxonici per Britanniam* (count of the Saxon shore in Britain). This was a series of fortifications in the south and east from the Solent to the Wash. It was matched by similar defence systems commanded by the *dux* of Armorica and Belgica Secunda on the other side of the channel. Some of the Saxon Shore forts show early abandonment (Lympne, Reculver, Caister and Burgh) as do many of the Yorkshire signal stations.[119] Richborough in Kent is recorded as the base for the *Legio II Augusta* in the *Notitia Dignitatum* and thus may be one of the last sites garrisoned in late Roman Britain. Only Portchester in Hampshire shows occupations well into the fifth century and a later Saxon presence. It is possible the name reflects Germanic *foederati* troops or immigrant settlements. Interestingly, there is no example of any Roman defensive system anywhere being named after an enemy.[120]

Alternatively, it may refer to a coastal area designed to defend *against* Saxon raids. Saxons are mentioned only once in the Notitia. An *ala Saxonum* are listed alongside an *ala Francorum* and *ala Alamannorum*. Another interesting example concerns a group of captured Saxons destined for the arena in the later fourth century. The frustrated Roman statesman Symmachus (died 402) complained that twenty-nine of his potential gladiators had broken each other's necks with their bare hands.

Sidonius Apollinaris in fifth-century Gaul describes Saxon pirates in the North Sea as 'the most ferocious of enemies'. He also states that Julius Caesar triumphed over Scots, Picts and Saxons in his campaign in Britain.[121] Could it be that he assumed Saxons were in Britain five centuries earlier because that was the case in his day? And perhaps had been throughout much of the fifth century?

Sidonius describes the Saxons at the court of the Gothic king, Euric, in Bordeaux:[122]

> we see the blue-eyed Saxon, lord of the sea but fearful of the land. The razor blade, content no more to hold it's usual course round the head's extremity, drives back the hairline, with clean strokes shearing the skin, thus making the head look smaller and the face longer.

Salvian of Marseilles, a contemporary of Apollinaris, describes the Saxons as 'savage in their cruelty but admirable for their chastity'. His view was that God allowed the barbarians to triumph because they were more pious and less sinful than the Romans.[123]

Gregory of Tours (538–594) also made reference to Saxons. The first involves the General Odoacer leading Saxons successfully in the capture of Angers. The Frankish king Childeric pushes them out and there is subsequently a Roman-Saxon war, suggesting some betrayal. The Saxons were defeated and the Franks captured several islands. The importance of this event is that it no longer portrays Saxons as raiders. Instead they are settled in the Loire valley and, at one point at least, fighting with and under the Romans. In the sixth century we hear of Saxons being allowed to settle within Sigibert's Austrasian kingdom in return for military aid and a promise of allegiance. This adoption of the Roman federate system is similar to the one described by Gildas for Britain the previous century.

Procopius is told by the Anglo-Frankish embassy in c. 553 that 'so great apparently is the multitude' of people in Britain that large groups are migrating to Frankish lands. This could be a garbled reference to Britons migrating to Armorica, but more likely refers to Saxons being given land by the Frankish king Theuderic I. Legend names their leader as Hadugato. He is first mentioned in the *Translatio sancti Alexandri* by Rudolf of Fuldac, 863–5. In the eleventh-century *Deeds of the Bishops of the Church of Hamburg of Adam of Bremen*, these Saxons arrived from Britain and are given land by the Franks in return for aid in the war against the Thuringians c. 531.

Later in the the sixth century Alboin, the king of the Lombards (560–572), requested help from Sigibert's Saxons and they were allowed to send 20,000 men.

They had been accompanied by their wives and children but returned when they were 'not allowed to live under their own laws' by the Lombards.[124] Vernantius Fortunatus (c. 540–610) was a good friend of Gregory of Tours. He was raised in Italy but moved to Merovingian Gaul to earn a living as a poet in the Frankish kingdoms. He praised Sigibert, king of Austrasia (561–75) as a conqueror of both Thuringians and Saxons. He apparently personally led his men 'on foot before the lines'.[125] Another dedication was to Lupus, a Gallo-Roman general serving Sigibert, who fought against Danes and Saxons. Chilperic, king of Neustria, is said to 'inspire fear in the Goth, the Basque, the Dane, the Jute, the Saxon and the Briton'.[126] His dedication to the Bishop of Nantes includes a description of Saxons as 'a hard people … living like animals'. Isidore of Seville (died 636) states that they derived their name from the fact they were a 'hard and strong race of men, that surpasses all other pirates'. Saxon settlement in the Bayeux region of northern Gaul is twice mentioned by Gregory of Tours.[127] The *Saxones Baiocassini* were also used by the Franks to fight against, and reinforce, Breton armies. In the sixth century the Frankish king of Austrasia claimed he he ruled over Visigoths, Thuringians and Saxons.

What is noticeable is that in the fourth century Amminaus regards the Saxons as aliens, outsiders and raiders. By the sixth century Gregory regards them as part of the Merovingian world, even if they are not always loyal. For instance, a certain 'Childeric the Saxon' was made a *dux* of a *civitas*. Is this an echo of Hengest being awarded Kent by Vortigern? There is much archaeological evidence of Saxon presence in northern Gaul, especially on the coastal area between Boulogne and Calais extending to the Somme in the south.[128] In the seventh century a Saxon *dux* Bertoald rebelled. Clothar II personally cut off his head in a duel and then repeats this punishment with every Saxon male taller than his sword (approximately 80–90cm).[129] By the time of Charlemagne the *Lex Saxonum* issued in c. 802 was *pro universis Saxonebus*, 'for all the Saxons'. By then at least they are viewed as one people. Interestingly, they swear an oath on their weapons which is attested in many barbarian law codes.[130]

In ninth-century Gaul, a monk, Rudolf, attempted the first written history of the Saxons to compare with Gregory of Tour's *History of the Franks*. He appears to have copied much from Tacitus's description of peoples of Germania, although Tacitus never mentioned Saxons at all. Among their traits and customs Rudolf lists:[131] the 'best laws for the punishment of criminals'; a rigid social order of nobles, freemen, freedmen and slaves; intermarriage with other tribes discouraged and within orders forbidden; worshipped false divinities like Mercury; consecrated trees and groves; practised divination using twigs and the pattern of bird flights; and practiced human sacrifice. Sidonius claimed they killed one in ten captives chosen by lot, *per aquales et crucialrias poenas*. Either crucified or through 'tortuous drowning'. Ennovius of Pavia (died 521) claimed the Franks and Saxons burned their victims. In the eighth century, Charlemagne legislated against the pagan custom of human sacrifice.

If Germanic immigrants in Britain retained a 'rigid social order' and discouraged marriage with the indigenous population this might go some way to support the notion of an apartheid type system.

Two centuries later in Britain there was a still sense of kindred with their continental cousins.[132] Bede referred to the tribes of Germany from whom the Angles and Saxons sprung. Saint Boniface, a contemporary of Bede, describes continental Saxons as 'of the same blood and bone', and refers to his native Wessex as *transmarina Saxonia*. A bishop of Leicester refers to them as 'our people'. The term *saxones* can be interpreted in one of two ways.[133] First, as a series fragmented autonomous sub groups. Second, as a generic term for coastal raiders. Yet we cannot know how indigenous Britons in southern and eastern Britain viewed their new neighbours. They may not have shared the description Gildas gives of 'barbarians'. Perhaps they simply shrugged their shoulders and carried on ploughing their fields as they and their fathers had done under, often absentee, Roman landowners.

Kingship

In the *Finnsburg Fragment* Hengest is referred to as the leader of the remaining warriors after Hnæf is killed. The HB never refers to him as a king, instead giving that title to his descendants. Bede uses the word commanders, chieftains or leaders to describe Hengest and his brother, Horsa. However, the seven rulers whom Bede describes as holding sovereignty 'over all the southern province' are described as kings. Thus Bede, writing in the early eighth century, appears to view Ælle as a king. What does this mean in a fifth-century context?

Three main early terms for Germanic king are known:[134] the earliest *piudans*; *truhtin* which may have originated as a leader of a war-band; and *kuning* which evolved from a petty king, or *regulas* to refer to large scale kingship. Tacitus provides an interesting distinction between a king and a war leader:

> They choose their kings for their noble birth, their commanders for their valour. The power even of the kings is not absolute or arbitrary. The commanders rely on example rather than on the authority of their rank – on the admiration they win by showing conspicuous energy and courage and by pressing forward in front of their own troops.
> Tacitus, Germania, Chapter 7

Centuries later Bede states that the continental Saxons 'knew no kings'.[135] Although he goes onto say they have many chiefs. This could simply be semantics, as petty kings were known among the Alemanni, Franks and Anglo-Saxons. In 626 the Anglo-Saxon Chronicle records that Edwin of Northumbria invaded Wessex where he 'felled five kings there'. This was in response to an assassination attempt by Cwichelm, king of the West Saxons. It is noteworthy because it is Cynegils who is recorded as king for this period. Cwichelm and Cynegils are recorded as fighting in 614 and 628, while the latter is not mentioned in Edwin's campaign.. Thus it would appear there was not only a duel kingship in Wessex but several under kings, five of whom were killed. Kent also appears to have been divided between East and

West Kent. From Bede and surviving charters it is clear that it was common for two kings to rule together even if one was dominant.[136] This division appears to have been a political one, possibly based on Roman administrative districts. Kent is unique in possessing two bishoprics shortly after the conversion period, post 597.

On the Continent the early Franks also 'lacked a strong monarchical tradition', allowing the Roman *dux* Aegidius to govern them in the mid-fifth century while their king, Childeric, was in exile.[137] Gregory of Tours implies that Aegidius and Childeric were at some point allies fighting against Saxons in the 460s. It is an interesting fact that their sons were eventually to be at war a generation later. Clovis I defeated Syagrius and annexed the Kingdom of Soissons into the expanding Frankish kingdom. A number of contemporary accounts give some insight into the evolving nature of kingship among Germanic tribes.

First we recall Gallic bishops advised Clovis to 'undertake the administration of *Belgica Secunda*' after his defeat of Syagrius'.[138] Following his victory against the Goths at the battle of Vouille in 507, the Eastern Emperor Anastasius I granted Clovis the consulship in 508. While the latter title may have been superficial it did not prevent Clovis accepting it. Kings in Britain and across Western Europe, even centuries later such as Charlemagne, king of the Franks (768–814), were keen to accept the trappings of Roman prestige. Second, we have an account of the battle of Vouille between the Franks and the Goths which may have been contemporary with Ælle across the channel. Whether this shows the expectation that kings lead from the front or was specific to Clovis is not known: 'some of the soldiers hurled their javelins from a distance, others fought hand to hand'.[139] During the battle two Goths attacked the Frankish king, Clovis, with spears. He was saved by 'the leather corselet … and sheer speed of his horse', although he was injured enough to be described as 'very near to death'.[140]

Last, we have an interesting tale from Gregory of Tours.[141] Clovis and this army gathered in Soissons to distribute the booty after the death of Syagrius. The troops took the treasure and 'placed it in a heap before them'. In the heap was a particular jug or ewer of 'great size and wondrous workmanship' that had been taken from the church. Clovis had separately agreed to return it. However, he had to ask permission of his troops if it was included 'in his share'. This is not the picture of an omnipotent king but of a war leader, first among equals but bound by a common understanding. Gregory claims they all agreed except one, who struck the ewer with his axe. Clovis had to accept this; however, the act was neither forgotten or forgiven. If this distribution occurred at the end of the campaign season then Clovis spent some months before he exacted revenge as Gregory tells us it was 'at the end of the year' when Clovis gathered his troops. The pretext was an inspection during which he came face to face with the 'feckless fellow'. Clovis castigated him for the state of his arms and threw the man's axe to the floor. When he stooped to retrieve it Clovis raised his own battle axe and split his skull with it. The troops were 'filled with might dread', but no response is recorded. This incident may well be context specific for those individuals at that point. However, it does suggest there were some constraints on rulers. Circumventing social rules about sharing booty was clearly taboo even for a king. Even if the same king could kill a warrior in front of the troops and suffer no repercussions.

When Clovis died he left a largely Frankish-dominated Gaul under the control of four of his sons, each of whom was a king of one part of the former Roman provinces in Gaul. We can compare these kings with the nature of their grandfather, Childeric's rule as a king of the Salian Franks within a crumbling Western Roman Empire. What does this suggest for Ælle in Britain? The ASC gives us the common foundation story of a leader arriving with three ships. Taken at face value this suggests a war leader with about a hundred warriors. All the sources place his arrival after Hengest, and some historians, such as Halsall, suggest it is more likely his floruit is sixth century rather than fifth. The ASC claims he fought three battles against the Britons and that the last one involved the storming of the Saxon Shore fort at Pevensey, killing all the defenders. Yet by any measure this is after Kent and much of the south east has been lost to Roman-British authority.

If reliable this would suggest a number of things: Hengest's area of authority did not stretch south of the Weald; the south-east province had broken away and fragmented, leaving pockets of Romano-British 'polities'; or Ælle carved out his domain from Kentish control which the ASC simply referred to as Britons or Welsh. The distribution of battles and early settlement does suggest Sussex was based on the former Roman *civitas* of the *Regnenses*. However, for Ælle to be described as holding sovereignty or *imperium*, or as a Bretwalda, his influence must have extended far beyond this small coastal strip. It would certainly have meant authority over the south east and the areas Gildas describes as inaccessible. Interesting that Ælle has this distinction but Oisc does not. The first Kentish Bretwalda is Æthelberht at the end of the sixth century. The HB has Arthur fighting a series of battles but there is no mention of Ælle. If we accept the date, the little we are told in the ASC and by Bede, then I would suggest this first Bretwalda is more a warrior than a king.

Table four highlights the discrepancy between the foundation myths and the attested kings. The four kings highlighted are the ASC and Bede's first four Bretwaldas. Unsurprisingly, the three earliest alleged founders of dynasties were in the south-east. It is interesting that we have no early kings of East Anglia, given that was one of the earliest regions with significant settlement. Of course this could simply mean an earlier dynasty was replaced by the *Wuffingas*, as Wuffa's descendants are known. Mercia is also a puzzle. On one hand in the Trent valley, Lincolnshire and the East Midlands there is a large amount of early Germanic material culture and burial material. Yet we also have evidence for the survival of a Romano-British polity centred on Lincoln into the sixth century. Additionally, the ASC records the West Saxons pushing north from the Thames Valley and fighting Britons.

We do get some battles between the West Saxons and other Anglo-Saxon kingdoms: in 568 Ceawlin fought against Æthelberht of Kent; in 597 Ceolwulf is said to have fought against the *Anglecyn*, although whether this refers specifically to those in what became Mercia is not clear; and in 607 Ceolwulf fought against the South Saxons. It is not until 628 we have a definite example of a West Saxon-Mercia conflict, when the West Saxon kings Cynegils and Cwichelm are said to have fought Penda at Cirencester. The battle appears to have been indecisive as they 'came to an agreement'. What this suggests is that until 597, and possibly as late as 628, the expansion of the Gewissae, or West Saxons, was at the expense of the Britons. The implication is that much of what later became Mercia was under 'British' authority much later than is commonly thought. It is possible this mirrors the situation in Lincolnshire where the evidence suggests a Brittonic polity survived until the mid-sixth century.

Table 4: Earliest Anglo-Saxon kings.

Kingdom	First alleged founder of dynasty or arrival.	First alleged king	First confirmed historical king
Kent	Hengest 449	Octa 488	Æthelbert 589–616
South Saxons	Ælle 477	Ælle	Æthelwealh 660
Wessex	Cerdic 495 (or 532)	Cerdic and Cynric 501 (or 538)	Ceawlin 560 (or 580)
Deira	Soemel	Soemel (5 generations before Aelle)	Ælle 560–600
Bernicia	Oesa (grandfather of Ida)	Ida 547	Æthelfrith 592–616
Essex	Sledd	Sledd	Sabert c. 600
East Anglia	Wehha (father of Wuffa)	Wuffa 571	Raedwald 599–624
Mercia	Icel (grandfather of Creoda)	Creoda 585	Penda 626

The appearance of 'princely graves' from the sixth century suggests an increase in inequality which might suggest larger polities were evolving out of a number of smaller authorities. It has been suggested the development of 'ranked societies' forms a 'transition period' between a fragmented political situation and the formation of early kingdoms.[142]

Ælle, and other Anglo-Saxon kings, were not arriving into a vacuum. The Britons were also appointing kings as Gildas tells us: 'kings were anointed, not in God's name but as being crueller than the rest' (DEB 21.4). However, the appearance of kings is not proof of the complete disappearance of all provincial structures. We have seen how local elites and town *decurions* may have formed the basis of royal dynasties. Anglo-Saxon dynasties may have evolved through intermarriage. We recall Hengest being granted Kent in return for Vortigern marrying his daughter.

Many of the Wessex kings have distinctly Brittonic names, not least the founder Cerdic. Alternatively they may simply have taken over, pushing the previous rulers to one side.

Henry of Huntingdon in the twelfth century was the first to describe the Heptarchy, or seven kingdoms (Kent, Sussex, Essex, Wessex, East Anglia, Mercia and Northumbria). It is unlikely that Ælle in the fifth century viewed his world in same way. The earlier seventh-century Tribal Hidage lists thirty-four peoples. Bede also describes 'peoples', *gentes*, *nationes*, and *populi*, and the word *provincia* rather than *regnum* to describe kingdoms.[143] This more fragmented, complex, political situation was likely closer to the truth. West Saxon charters often used term *rex Saxonum*, only referring to king of the *West* Saxons from the mid-eighth century.[144]

This suggests there was a large number of different groups and sub-kings. There were likely shifting loyalties and alliances. The provincial structure started to fragment in the mid-fifth century. Large recognisable kingdoms had emerged after the mid-sixth century. The process, speed and nature of the fragmentation of the old and formation of the new between 450–550 is hidden from us. But we have seen some clues from Gaul as to how this may have played out in Britain.

All the later Anglo-Saxon royal houses claimed to be descended from Germanic gods. In fact all claimed Woden as an ancestor, except the East Saxons who traced their line back to Seaxnet. We have seen that post-Roman Britain was largely Christian with a significant Romano-British identity. This identity appears to have evolved but was still seen as distinctive by Gildas in the sixth century. Yet Christianity survived and flourished in the west at least. In the east the various Germanic settlers brought with them a different cultural identity but also a new religion.

The Germanic gods

We should not view Germanic religion as homogenous. Nor should we see a clear line of evolution between the traditions described by Tacitus in the first century and the later Viking traditions in the middle ages.[145] The 'heathen tradition' was a folk religion which promoted a communal identity and exclusivity. This was at odds with a 'universalist' religion like Christianity which actively sort converts. There may well have been some themes that were more consistent and widespread than others. But importantly there was no single Germanic religion. Tacitus describes their 'traditional songs', which form the 'only record of the past'.[146] The Germans celebrated the god, Tuisto, described as 'earth-born'. His son Mannus was 'the fountain-head of their race' and had three sons. From these sons came three groups of tribes: the Ingaevones, by the sea; the Herminones, in the interior; and rest called the Istaevones. These gave rise to other tribes, including the Tungri. The Suebi, and later the Angles and Saxons thus derive from these alleged tribal groups.

The Early Anglo-Saxon Kings

In his book *The Elder Gods*, Stephen Pollington lists a number of common themes present in shamanic cultures and early Anglo-Saxon England: [147]

- A belief in the existence of parallel worlds where powerful beings exist.
- The gateway between these worlds involves climbing a high peak or tree.
- A separable soul can journey between these worlds, inhabit animals' bodies or be re-incarnated.
- Belief in spirit journeys and their benefits.
- Belief in spirit helpers from other worlds appearing in animal guise.

Catholic Christianity had been installed by Emperor Theodosius (379–95) as the only legitimate imperial religion. At the same time Arianism also spread and became a 'badge of Gothic identity'.[148] The Gallo-Roman church was Catholic in belief and the Franks perhaps viewed this as a means to acquire prestige, but also as a counter to the growing influence of their Arian Gothic neighbours. Gregory of Tours records that the Franks, despite adopting Catholic Christianity, continued to worship agrarian deities. The sixth-century Gallic church seemed more concerned with adherence to ritual observances than eradicating heathen practices. What might this tell us of Saxon and Angle attitudes?

Pollington suggests that heathen tradition may have been more tolerant and open.[149] Germanic religion focused on the tribe and was more accepting of the present world as it was. Christianity rejected the present world and focused more on the rewards in the next. The Germanic traditions were polytheistic and local. Christianity, however, was a proselytising religion eager to convert in a way that likely baffled many Germanic peoples. Ultimately it was success that swayed it. The link between Roman Christianity and the authority of the Roman Empire was attractive. In addition, the early church allowed itself to be moulded to fit Germanic customs. As well as embracing many of the agrarian festivals, it also adopted the heroic military ideal.

In Kent, when Æthelbert died in 616 his son Eadbald rejected Christianity. Around the same time when the East Saxon King Saeberht died his three sons threw the Bishop out of London. This demonstrates that the initial conversions may have added a thin veneer of Christianity onto the former pagan elites. It tells us little of the religious beliefs of the bulk of the population, or their cultural identity or ethnicity.

In East Anglia Rædwald had returned to paganism and it was his successor, Eorpwald, who made the kingdom officially Christian in c. 628. We then see evidence of Christianity increasing its influence. In Northumbria Edwin converted in 627, and in Kent Eorcenberht succeeded Eadbald in 640. Bede tells us he was the first king to command that pagan idols were destroyed. What this suggests is a period of flux in the first quarter of the sixth century. Ultimately Christianity became the dominant religion, but there was noting inevitable about its victory. It was perhaps the death of Penda of Mercia in 655 which signalled the beginning of the end for paganism. It is worth noting that Kent received its Christianity from

Catholic Francia, whereas Northumbria and Mercia received theirs from the Celtic missionaries. The Synod of Whitby in 664 turned the church towards Rome.

Yet we see evidence of the old Anglo-Saxon paganism persisting. The law code of Æthelbert makes no reference to religious observances. However, by the eighth century we see punishments appear for infringements against ecclesiastic rulings.[150] The last Anglo-Saxon kingdom to accept Christianity was Sussex in 686. In c. 700 Guthlac refers to a certain Cissa as 'living among heathen people' in the *Vita sancti Guthlaci*, written by Felix soon after Guthlac's death. In 743 the school of Boniface of Mainz compiled evidence of 'pagan' practice. There are similar references to heathen ideas and practices in England in the seventh to eighth centuries.[151] Cnut's eleventh-century legal code specifically outlawed such practices. As late as 959 we read in the ecclesiastical canons of King Edgar that on feast days people should refrain from 'heathen songs and devils' games'.[152] In a sermon in 1014, attributed to Archbishop Wulfstan of York, we read of 'everywhere despisers of divine laws and Christian customs'.[153] He doesn't directly mention pagans but references 'wiccans and valkyries'.

There was a persistence of pre-Christian traditions which suggests a total replacement of pagan beliefs by Christianity was the exception rather than the rule.[154] One example is the significance of a sacred tree or wood. Tacitus states the Germani of his time did not use temples but rather 'sacred groves'. In the eighth century Boniface records something similar. He destroys a 'Holy tree' near Hesse, Germany, known as 'Jupiter's Oak'. Early Anglo-Saxon Christian tradition depict Christ as a warrior and Satan as more of a rival chieftain than evil incarnate.[155] Poems such as *Heliand*, *Guthlac* and *The Dream of the Rood* make appeals to this heroic theme.

However, back in the fifth and sixth centuries it is very likely that Germanic settlers would have been pagans. It is possible some may have been Christian and if so, perhaps Arian as well as Catholic. But given the earliest attested Anglo-Saxon kings were pagan, we can be confident Ælle and his sons were also pagan. The conversion of the Anglo-Saxons took several decades from c. 600 and some practices continued. What then of the Christian population of the south east? Did Christianity all but die out in the 150 years between the *adventus saxonum* and the arrival of Augustine? The evidence from Lincoln suggests some survival, but what the bulk of the rural population believed in Kent, for example, is unfortunately unknown. Let us now turn to, what Stephen Pollington calls, *The Elder Gods*.

Tiw

One of the earliest chief god is thought to be *Tiw*, equivalent to the Greek Zeus and Roman Jupiter. It derives from *deiwos*, 'shiner', or 'shining sky'. From this we get *teiwar-fadar*, 'sky-father'. The word *teiwa* appears to have become the general word for god. Old English *Tīwesdæg*, meaning 'day of Tīw', gives us Tuesday. This is also the day attributed to Mars, as in French *Mardi*. Mars was the god of war and aggression and the principal god in some German tribes such as the Tencteri and

Hermundures. In later Norse mythology, Tyr helps bind the wolf Fenrir and loses his hand in the process. Place names associated with Tiw include: Tuesday, Surrey; Tyesmere, Worcestershire; and Tishoe, Surrey; It is possible the story of Tyr and Fenrir is replicated on the Sutton Hoo purse lid.[156] In addition, various examples of on eye being depicted differently may have parallels in the Woden cult. A bracteate (a type of thin medal) was found in Sweden and dated to the sixth century.[157] It depicts a long, heated figure with his hand seized in the jaws of a beast. In his other hand is a yarn winder. It may be an early depiction of the tale of Tyr and Fenrir. We have evidence of trade links between Scandinavia and eastern England in the fifth and sixth centuries and it is likely the god Tiw formed part of the tradition of some peoples who had settled in Britain at that time.

Woden

The name derives from the Germanic *wodenaz*, lord of frenzy, rage or excitement.[158] The earliest known tale of Woden comes from Paul the Deacon's History of the Lombards in the eighth century. He tells how both the Vandals and Lombards were at war and approached Woden and his wife Frea to request help in their struggle. Interestingly he claims: 'Wotan, who they called Godan ... is the same one as is called Mercurius among the Romans and is worshipped as a god among all the peoples of Germania, who is understood to have lived not in those times nor in Germani, but in Greece long before.'[159]

Woden gives us the fourth day of the week, *Wednesdaeg*, 'day of Woden'. He can be linked to the Roman god Mercury and the French for Wednesday, *mecredi*. Mercury is linked to knowledge, cunning, stealth, deceitfulness, writing, elegant speech and messages. All these aspects are found in Odin and we have some evidence similar traditions were present in the Old English Woden.[160] Elfric, a West Saxon of the tenth century, talks of Mercurius, a 'deceitful man', who the heathen worship as a god and is also known as *Odon*.

In Scandinavia in the migration period Odin was thought to possess various 'powers':[161] shape-shifting; control of the elements; knowledge of writing and spells; and control of the dead. Place name evidence in England is widespread: Wednesbury and Wednesfield, Staffordshire; Woodnesborough, Kent; Wenslow and Wensley, Bedfordshire; and Adam's Grave, formerly *Wodnesbeorh*, in Wiltshire. Woden also features in several king lists. It has been suggested this was in fact a very human king rather than a god.[162]

Thunor

The god þunor was the defender of the warrior or farmer. This included the vast majority of the populace in Anglo-Saxon society. He was seen as equivalent to the

Roman Jupiter, the thunder-wielder. His name gives us *þunresdaeg*, or Thursday. When the Saxons were forced to renounce their gods, the three to be forsworn were 'Woden, þunor and Seaxneat'.[163] Place names gives us Thundersley, Essex, Thursday in Surrey, Thundridge, Hertfordshire and Thunderlow in Kent. Interestingly, they are all in the south and south-east, with none in Anglian areas.

Frige

The OE Frige, *Frigu*, or Norse *Freyja*, was associated with sexuality, magic, fecundity and violent death. The name is also linked to the Norse goddess Frigg, associated with childbirth and wealth and power over the household. It hints at a combination of 'wise and caring mother' and 'sexually available maiden'.[164] It forms the basis of *Frigedaeg*, Friday, and the Roman *dies veneris*, day of Venus. Various palcenaoes linked to her are Frobury and Froyle in Hampshire, and Fretherne in Gloucestershire.

Lesser gods

Ægel: Linked to archery. Possibly to place names such as Ægelesprep, possibly Aylesford or Aylesbury.

Æsc: Æsc, or ash tree, may have decried from *Ansiz* or the Gothic *Ansis*. The Anglo-Saxon Chronicle names Æsc as Hengest's son and could be the basis for Bede's Oisc. Later Norse legends name Askr as one of two beings created by the gods out of pieces of wood, the other being Embla (possibly 'Elm tree')

Bældæg: The OE Bealdor means warrior, prince, lord or nobleman. He features in the genealogies of Wessex and Bernicia as the son of Woden, eight or nine generations before the first kings of those kingdoms respectively. In the Roman period there is evidence he was linked to Hercules but also to virility and fertility. The later figure of Baldur is linked to warrior initiation rites.

Genealogies

Figure 17 shows the genealogies of the Anglo-Saxon kingdoms from various sources such as the HB, Bede and Anglian collection. I have put the first attested kings in bold. There is a level of consistency in terms of number of generations from Woden although Kent appears to be an outlier. If this Woden was in fact a person rather than the Germanic deity, then most of the genealogies are placing him twelve generations before the first attested kings emerge in the last quarter of the

The Early Anglo-Saxon Kings

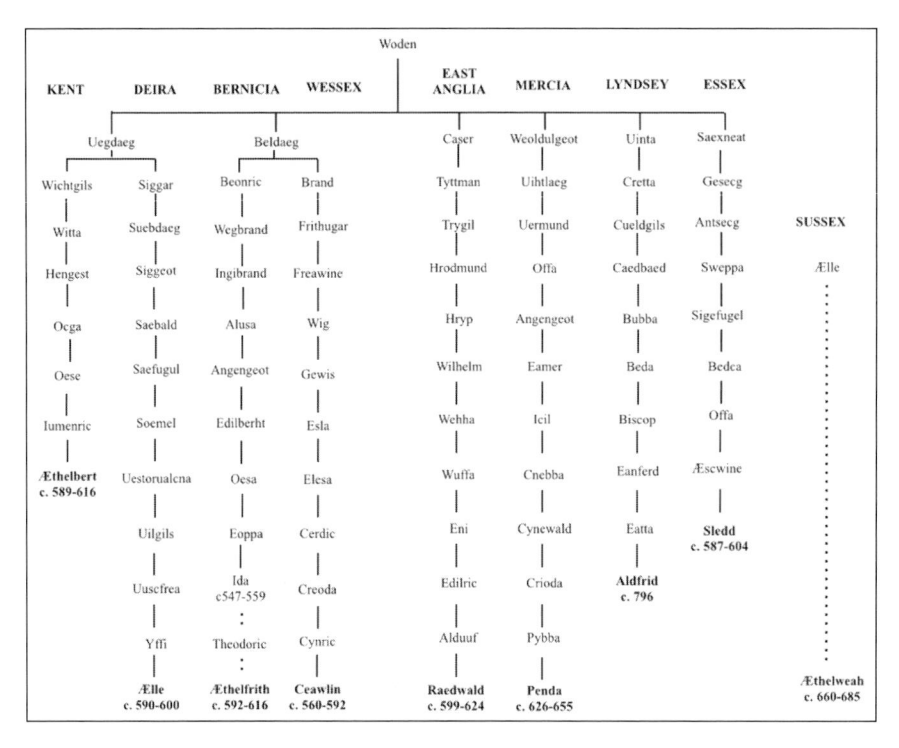

KENT	DEIRA	BERNICIA	WESSEX	EAST ANGLIA	MERCIA	LYNDSEY	ESSEX	
				Woden				
Uegdaeg		Beldaeg		Caser	Weoldulgeot	Uinta	Saexneat	
Wichtgils	Siggar	Beonric	Brand	Tyttman	Uihtlaeg	Cretta	Gesecg	
Witta	Suebdaeg	Wegbrand	Frithugar	Trygil	Uermund	Cueldgils	Antsecg	SUSSEX
Hengest	Siggeot	Ingibrand	Freawine	Hrodmund	Offa	Caedbaed	Sweppa	Ælle
Ocga	Saebald	Alusa	Wig	Hryp	Angengeot	Bubba	Sigefugel	
Oese	Saefugul	Angengeot	Gewis	Wilhelm	Eamer	Beda	Bedca	
Iumenric	Soemel	Edilberht	Esla	Wehha	Icil	Biscop	Offa	
Æthelbert c. 589-616	Uestorualcna	Oesa	Elesa	Wuffa	Cnebba	Eanferd	Æscwine	
	Uilgils	Eoppa	Cerdic	Eni	Cynewald	Eatta	Sledd c. 587-604	
	Uuscfrea	Ida c547-559	Creoda	Edilric	Crioda	Aldfrid c. 796		
	Yffi	Theodoric	Cynric	Alduuf	Pybba			
		Ælle c. 590-600	Æthelfrith c. 592-616	Ceawlin c. 560-592	Raedwald c. 599-624	Penda c. 626-655		Æthelweah c. 660-685

Figure 17. The Anglo-Saxon genealogies.

sixth century. This would place a human Woden c. 300. Of course we cannot trust these late genealogies and there's no proof a real warrior lies behind the ancestral figure. What it does show is a willingness to adopt a similar tradition across a number of different Germanic groups and early kingdoms.

Summary

While there is some dispute as to the dating and historicity of Ælle we can make some observations. He appears to have arrived after the Western Roman Empire finally collapsed in 476. If his date is accurate, he arrived a decade after Saxons were pushed out of the Loire Valley in Gaul by the Romans and Franks. The later expansion of Frankish territory under Clovis would have likely made Britain an easier target for any prospective warlord or adventurer. He may have been a contemporary with Riothamus in Gaul and Ambrosius Aurelianus in Britain. It is likely he arrived after Hengest had gained control of at least the *civitas* of the *Cantii* and possibly a much wider area within the former province of *Maxima Caesariensis*.

He would have been confronted with a fragmenting provincial and *civitas* structure. For many, this political and social turmoil must have been devastating.

For an ambitious young warrior with a war-band the chaos would have presented an opportunity. Just over 200 years later he is remembered by Bede as the first who held *imperium* south of the Humber. For this to be true he would have had to have found support from further afield: Kent, East Anglia and Lincolnshire. Two generations after Ælle's battles in the ASC, Gildas is lamenting the 'unhappy partition' with the barbarians. We also have two 'gaps' that seem to coincide with Gildas's forty-four years of relative stability and 'freedom from external wars'. First, the archaeological record suggests expansion of Germanic material culture and burial practices stopped. Second, there is a gap between the first two of ASC's and Bede's Bretwalda's. Yet Gildas claims he cannot access certain sites, one being St Albans. Fifty years after Gildas we have a number of attested kings of emerging kingdoms.

If this is correct then we can tentatively suggest the following scenario: the war described by Gildas and Bede, led by Ambrosius Aurelianus, was against nascent Anglo-Saxon-led kingdoms of the south and east, most notably Kent and Sussex. Or perhaps the fragmenting *civitates* along the border between the former provinces as they contracted. After Hengest's death Ælle rose to dominance of a disparate group of peoples and former *civitates*. The war culminated in the battle of Badon, dated by Bede to c. 493. If we accept Bede's date for Ambrosius Aurelianus, 474–91, and the ASC's dates for Ælle, 477–91, then it is logical they would have been contemporaries. We will discuss this war and the battle of Badon in particular in chapter five. We will also investigate other figures and battles such as Arthur and Urien and the battles of Lindisfarne and Catraeth. Before we do that we must first look at the nature of weapons and warfare of the time.

Chapter Four

Weapons and Warfare of the Fifth and Sixth Centuries

In the crumbling Western Roman Empire a number of military related changes had taken place by the fifth century.[1] The Roman *scutum* shield and *gladius* sword were long gone. Shields were now round or oval. The longer *spatha* sword, approximately 75–100cm, was better suited to hacking over the top of a shield wall or using from horseback. As swords lengthened spears became shorter, which improved their performance as a handheld offensive weapon rather than in a defensive formation such as the Greek Phalanxes of the past. At 190cm, the *spiculum* was slightly shorter than the *pilum*, which it replaced. It was better at thrusting while still retaining penetrative force when thrown. The *lancea*, a lightweight throwing spear, became more common. Shorter javelins were used too, such as *plumbatae*, lead-weighted darts, five of which could be carried in the rear of a shield.

The Roman legions became smaller in size to increase mobility. Thus mobile forces of 1,000 to 1,200 replaced the large 5,000-strong legions of the past. Estimates of unit sizes are difficult as research shows that the strength on paper might not reflect the reality and may have to be reduced by a third.[2] While the legions became smaller and more mobile, they also became more reactive. The late Roman Empire employed a 'strength in depth' philosophy with the smaller legions set back from the frontier which was garrisoned by *limitanei* ('the soldiers in frontier districts'). The tactics on the battlefield became less aggressive and more defensive. More often than not the Romans employed a close order defensive formation and waited to receive the enemy attack.[3]

Another major change was the significant number of Germanic recruits in the legions of the fourth and fifth centuries. In fact, late Roman armies often adopted the '*barritus*', a Germanic war cry.[4] This could be compared to the battle against the Saxons and Picts c. 429 when St Germanus ordering the Britons to shout 'Alleluia!' three times. Cavalry also became more important and the units larger, increasing to 600.[5] Although once again this may reflect a paper strength only.[6] By the mid-fifth century, in what remained of the Western Empire, the *alae* of the *limitanei*, border forces, had reduced from twenty *turmae* (thirty men each) to just ten.[7] If we compare the fifth-century Roman army to its first-century equivalent, the percentage of cavalry units had almost doubled from 20 to 35 per cent.[8] We are left to speculate what structures survived in Britain. We do see a hint of this in the famous epic poem *Y Gododdin*, where a cavalry force of 300 attacked the

Deirians at Catraeth. On the other hand, cavalry units in the mid-fifth century were 'crushingly expensive to maintain'.[9] Which is one reason Aetius chose to employ Germanic and Hunnic mercenaries.

Across the Western Empire between 380–420 the Roman field army had lost half its strength.[10] We can see this was even more pronounced in Britain. We can make a rough estimate of the units in Britain from the early fifth-century *Notitia Dignitatum*. The three commands were as follows: count of the Britons, 3,000 cavalry and 2,000 infantry; count of the Saxon Shore, 1,000 cavalry and 3,500 infantry; and the Duke of the Britons based at York with 4,000 cavalry and 15,000 infantry. This gives a paper strength of 20,000 infantry and 8,000 cavalry. If we estimate units were, on average, at two-thirds strength, then we have approximately 18,000 troops. Historians estimate between 12,000–20,000 by the end of the fourth century, compared to a force of perhaps 50,000 in the 2nd century.[11] We must, then, consider what troops did Constantine III take to Gaul in 407? What was the effect of the apparent reduction in coin supply and economic collapse in Britain in the fifth century?

A generation later there was still an army of sorts for St Germanus to take command of. We can only speculate what sort of military force Ambrosius Aurelianus was able to muster in the second half of the century. Gildas describes the Britons martial ability in withering terms: 'unwarlike'; 'ignorant in the ways of war'; a 'leaderless and irrational mob'; 'too lazy to fight, too unwieldy to flee'; and they sat about 'day and night rotting away in their folly'. Yet he also lauds Ambrosius Aurelianus and the celebrates the victory at Badon, 'almost the last, though not the least slaughter of the villains'. Additionally, we know the Britons of the west and north did hold back the Anglo-Saxons, in some cases for centuries. It is clear the Romano-Britons retained a significant level of military capability for some time. We will briefly look at Germanic warfare before turning to potential size of armies in that period.

Early Germanic warfare was waged in three main ways:[12] by the kindred in feuds; by war-band in raids; and by the tribe in large-scale wars with other tribes. Tacitus describes Germanic leaders as leading more by example than by exercising their authority.[13] In addition, the concept of loyalty was more important than obedience. One aspect specific to the Germans was the ritual slaughter of prisoners. In 105 BC the Cimbri executed captured Romans, and in AD 58 the defeated Chatti were executed and their material destroyed. The ritual destruction of equipment and horses has been confirmed by archaeological finds.[14] A good example is the destruction of Varus's legions in the Teutoburg Forest in AD 9. We can compare this to the entry in the Anglo-Saxon Chronicle 491 where at Anderitum, not one person was left alive.

There are two distinct points concerning early Germanic warfare;[15] the first is the lack of discipline and inferiority of equipment. There was a relative lack of good quality iron. The second is the 'religious and even irrational' approach to fighting. We will see if these early observations, mostly by the Romans, were relevant in the fifth and sixth centuries. Another aspect of fifth century warfare was that warriors fought within their war-band rather than as a cohesive whole. The battle of Finnsburg includes the phrase 'sixty war bears' when describing a young prince's war-band. The ASC entry for 755 describes a war-band of eighty-four attacking and killing a king of Wessex. The law codes of King Ine (688–725) details that a body of over thirty-five men were designated a *here* or army.[16] We will see how important the war-band became a little later.

Size of armies

Early Germanic tribes numbered on average about 100,000 and these could have supported around 15,000 warriors.[17] Tribal armies of later Germanic peoples were relatively small, approximately 3,000 warriors being the standard size.[18] We have already noted that Roman armies became smaller and large-scale pitched battles became less common. In 357 two Alemannic kings mustered a force of 35,000 from various tribes and sub-kings and this was considered a very large force.[19] Even one of the kings' immediate war-band of 200 was unusual. Far more common an example was in the same year as the Western Caesar Julian spent two months besieging 600 Franks in an abandoned Roman fort in Gaul rather than attacking them. When they surrender they were conscripted into the army and sent to the east.

The Battle of the Catalaunian Plains in 451 saw a Roman force led by General Aetius facing the Hunnic army of Attila. Both sides numbered in the tens of thousands. These large scale battles became rarer. In the sixth century, General Belisarius of the Eastern Roman Empire commanded armies of 16,000 in Africa and 8,000 in Italy. A late sixth-century manual described armies of 5,000 to 15,000, but viewed those nearer the lower end as the norm.[20] Regarding Britain, historians suggest it is unlikely any post-Roman kingdom could raise armies of 10,000 to 20,000, and that a few thousand would have been the norm, with 5,000–6,000 the upper end of the scale.[21] By the end of this section I will attempt to show that although it is unlikely, it is not impossible.

The literary sources portray the various Anglo-Saxon arrivals as small in number. The ASC has Hengest arriving in three ships, as does Ælle. Cerdic arrives with five ships on the south coast, followed by Port and his sons with two ships and later Stuff and Wihtgar with three. The subsequent battles suggest conflicts of just a few hundred men. The HB describes re-enforcements of sixteen and forty ships, implying 500 and 1,200 warriors respectively. This relatively small number of mercenaries would have been spread across a number of locations. The subsequent revolt might not have involved large numbers of troops.

Forts such as Bremenium, north of Hadrian's Wall, at one time garrisoned a unit 500 strong and would be a likely posting if they were fighting Picts. If the army of the Britons had been reduced to the low thousands, then a mercenary force of a few hundred or a thousand would have been of significant help. All this has led many scholars to speculate that battles in fifth – or sixth-century Britain would have involved a few hundred, or at most the low thousands. To put this into context, the

Weapons and Warfare of the Fifth and Sixth Centuries

Battle of Maldon in 991 between Vikings and Anglo-Saxons involved about 3,000 on each side, whereas the Battle of Hastings in 1066 has been estimated as between 7,000–10,000 on both sides. The consensus is that the former represents the upper end of Dark Age battles. Four sources exist for Maldon: a 325-line fragment of a poem, the Anglo-Saxon Chronicle, the Life of St Oswald and the twelfth-century Book of Ely. It describes a Viking army of ninety-three ships, which suggests 2,800 men. The poem implies roughly equal forces. The earlier Tribal Hidage gives Essex 7,000 hides of land which, at one armed man per five hides,[22] would give 1,400 men. If we add the local burgh levies and hearth troops of nobles and the leader, Earl Byrhtnoth, then this gives a good indication of the size of the armies in the early middle ages.

On the other hand the ASC records battles with a large number of casualties. We can estimate very rough numbers from these casualties. A 50 per cent casualty rate after a shield wall breaks might seem reasonable. However, after the Battle of Stamford Bridge in 1066, the defeated Viking army could only man twenty-four out of the original 300 ships.[23] This suggests a casualty rate of 92 per cent. The following examples from the ASC, though unverified, gives us significantly larger armies than might be expected: in 457 Hengest and Aesc killed 4,000 Britons at Creaganford; in 508 Cerdic and Cynric defeat Natanleod, a British king, killing 5,000 at Netley in the modern New Forest; in 614 at Beandun, 2,065 Welsh are killed. In contrast, a battle in 878 in Devon has a half brother of Ivar the Boneless being killed with 800 men plus forty of his own war-band.

At the Siege of Mons Badonicus, Gildas simply states it was 'pretty well the last defeat of the villains and certainly not the least'. Bede says it was 'no small slaughter of the invaders'. The HB gives us some numbers: 'The twelfth battle was on Badon hill and in it 960 men fell in one day, from a single charge of Arthur's, and no-one laid them low save him alone.' Interesting that this number represents two infantry cohorts, on paper at least, or just over thirty ships' crews. It could simply be literary device. Yet if it was a siege and the Britons were victorious, one could speculate a force three times that of the defenders. One likely scenario might be a force of 3,000 overwhelming a hill-fort or makeshift camp. The much later HRB describes 'vast numbers' of the enemy and 'many thousands' being killed, with Arthur personally slaying 470 men in one charge alone.

While literary sources might be exaggerated, archaeology has given us some clues. Danish bog finds unearthed evidence of fifty major battles between the third and fifth centuries.[24] At Illerup, 40 per cent has been excavated and revealed about 350 warriors, five of whom appear to be high ranking, with a further forty of middle rank, based on armour, dress and weapons. A rough estimate once the whole site is investigated comes to about 900 fallen in one battle. These could represent a defeated army disposed of, or the fallen from both sides. The forty well-armed warriors could represent a war-band, with the bulk of the remaining being conscripted farmers. From these figures, estimates of about 1,500 have been made for armies in the regions from which many of the later Germanic settlers to Britain came.

This would support the case for smaller scale conflicts, however I will attempt to show battles similar to the size at Hastings was at least possible. Estimates of the population in the Roman period range from 1 million to as high as 4 million.[25] Climatic changes, plagues, famines, civil wars and raids put downward pressure on population in the fifth century.[26] I will take a relatively low estimate of 1½ million.[27] If we assume half are children and half female, then we have under 400,000 adult males. If we estimate another half might be too old or infirm, then we have just 200,000 men of fighting age spread across the former diocese. I would suggest a reasonably conservative rule of thumb for this period is that 10 per cent of a population might be able and willing to stand in a shield wall. A much smaller percentage would receive training and serve as a regular soldier or local militia.

One could argue that women, the young and the elderly can man ramparts and throw things down upon an attacking enemy. But in terms of fighting battles or any hand-to-hand combat, then a 10 per cent rule of thumb is a reasonable estimate. However, those men who had received training would be far less. The maximum strength of the Roman army in Britain stood at approximately 50,000 in the second century. This would equate to between 1 and 2 per cent of the population. A post-Roman population in Britain of about 2 million might have 200,000 able bodied men. From this number a much smaller group might receive training and be regarded as soldiers or local militia. A city like London, reduced from a high of 60,000 to perhaps a few thousand, might only have a few hundred able-bodied men – yet its 3.2km of walls required 2,700 men to defend.

One vital question is as follows: did sufficient political or military structures survive to enable the maintenance, supply and training of a military force? If so, then for how long? At what point did the defence of some towns become untenable? At what point did central authority and provincial structures breakdown? We will discuss the emergence of war-bands a little later, but we know this new culture was prevalent among Britons and Anglo-Saxons by the end of the sixth century when petty kingdoms were emerging. What we don't know is the exact process and timing of this cultural change. This process may have been inconsistent across time and geography.

With urban life reduced, or disappeared altogether from some towns, what of the bulk of the population in rural areas? The Tribal Hidage gives us some clues. Thought to have been compiled in the seventh century, it lists the 'hides' of thirty-five tribes. The hide should be considered a unit of taxation rather than an exact geographical area. It is thought that later in Anglo-Saxon England it took about five hides to support one armed warrior.[28] We can thus use the list to estimate the number of warriors each area was able to support in the seventh century. All the tribes are south of the Humber and it is worth noting the figures for the major Anglo-Saxon Kingdoms which are highlighted. With the evidence for continuation of land use it is not unreasonable to suggest similar numbers might be supported a hundred years earlier as the first attested Anglo-Saxon kings appear.

Table 5: Estimate of warrior numbers from the Tribal Hidage.

Tribe	Hides	Warriors	Tribe	Hides	Warriors
West Saxena	100,000	20,000	Wigesta	900	180
Myrcna landes	30,000	6,000	Elmedsaetna	600	120
East Engle	30,000	6,000	Suth Gyrwa	600	120
Cantwarena	15,000	3,000	North Gyrwa	600	120
South Saxena	7,000	1,400	West Wixna	600	120
East Saxena	7,000	1,400	Spalda	600	120
Linesfarona	7,000	1,400	Wihtgara	600	120
Wocensaetna	7,000	1,400	Arosaetna	600	120
Westerna	7,000	1,400	Bilmiga	600	120
Hwinca	7,000	1,400	Widerigga	600	120
Noxgaga	5,000	1,000	East Willa	600	120
Cilternasaetna	4,000	800	West Willa	600	120
Hendrica	3,500	700	East Wixna	300	60
Ohtgaga	2,000	400	Faerpinga	300	60
Pecsaetna	1,200	240	Sweordora	300	60
Herefinna	1,200	240	Gifla	300	60
Unecungaga	1,200	240	Hicca	300	60

The table gives a figure of 64,000 warriors, but it is worth noting the West Saxons could field 20,000 warriors. In any conflict a kingdom would not send the entire force. However, it is important to remember these figures represent the number of warriors an area can support, not the total adult male population. This would have been much higher. On average, one hide has been estimated at roughly thirty modern acres, or 120,000 square metres. This equates to about seventeen football fields. But we have noted it is more useful to see it as a taxable unit. In the table above, Kent has 15,000 hides compared to modern Kent which covers double that. It could just be East Kent, but it is more likely a reflection of uninhabited or uneconomical areas.

Some early kingdoms retained the rough boundaries of the former *civitates*. If the provincial structure broke down completely this might leave an individual *civitas* in competition with a neighbour over resources. In this scenario the *civitas* of the Regnenses, or the later South Saxons, might field a similar army with their neighbours to the north, the Trinovantes or later East Saxons.

In summary we can make the following observations: the military forces in Roman Britain had already been depleted by the civil wars of Magnus Maximus and Constantine III. The collapse of the economy, urban life and Roman authority and the ending of the coin supply must have had a severe affect on standards of recruitment, maintenance and training. The literary, archaeological and DNA evidence all point away from a large scale invasion replacing the population. In fact, it suggests relatively small numbers spread over a long period. Interestingly, this is in line with the various foundations myths of three or five ships and Bede's comments about a range of other peoples. A small town with a population of maybe a thousand might only have 100 able-bodied men. A number of towns and villages along a coastal strip or inland river-way might scrape together a larger force in a dispute against their neighbours, especially if any central authority had collapsed that may have imposed order. A small mercenary force of a hundred or more Germanic warriors, arriving in three or five ships, might be enough to tip the balance.

The consensus and evidence thus points to battles being fought by armies in the low thousands, if not hundreds. Battles involving tens of thousands on both sides, such as Catalaunian Plains in 451, are unlikely. On balance, the consensus of low-scale warfare seems reasonable. However, I would suggest there is nothing preventing battles on the scale of Hastings. The population was certainly high enough. Britannia Prima may have retained some cohesive structure until the late fifth century.[29] If so, then an army of 10,000 or even 20,000 is possible. A hundred years later, however, the provincial structure was gone. Instead, we see the Wocensaetna, possibly the 'Wrekin dwellers' near Wroxeter, supporting 1,400 warriors, and to the south a similar number provided by the Hwinca, evolved from the Roman *civitas* of the Dobunni. It is likely the size of armies went down from the mid-fifth century onwards as the diocese fragmented into smaller units.

The question arises, was there an authority willing and able to organise, train and direct the manpower? As we shall see a little later, dyke and hill forts appear to have been built and re-occupied in the fifth century suggesting this was indeed the case. If there is any truth in Ælle holding *imperium*, Ambrosius leading the Britons to victory and the later legends of King Arthur, then it is possible battles on a larger scale took place. I would therefore not be so dismissive of the ASC in describing conflicts which left up to 5,000 dead on the battlefields of Britain.

Weapons and armour

The most common weapons in the fifth and sixth centuries were the spear and shield. Spear shafts and heads came in different sizes and styles. Angular cutting blades, up to 50cm in length, and long shafts suggest they may have been used two-handed, indeed a Pictish relief shows just that.[30] Shorter, barbed-headed spears, known as 'Angons', and the injuries they caused, are described by a sixth-century source.[31] When embedded in flesh, the head cannot be pulled out without terrible pain and serious injury or death. The barb and iron cover near the head are difficult to cut off if it penetrates a shield. The attacker can tread on the shaft pulling the opponent's shield towards the ground. The range of shorter spears or javelins was around 12–15m.[32] To pierce armour a heavy shaft is required and a needle-shaped head similar to a bodkin-type arrow head.

Missile weapons became more important and we see an increase in light troops and mounted archers in the fifth century.[33] Literary and artistic sources regularly depict archery, yet archaeological finds are rare in Britain. Germanic bows were 'longbows' made from a single piece of wood, in contrast to composite Asiatic bows. A good example of these were found in Nydham, Denmark. Forty bows, 6ft in length with shafts 74 to 94cm and leaf-shaped or barbed arrowheads. The maximum range was about 150–200m, but they tended to be effective from about 100m with accuracy at 50–60m.[34] Archers, whether mounted or on foot, would have carried thirty to forty arrows.[35]

Throwing axes, *francesca,* were also popular and despite their name were used by other Germanic tribes with examples found in Britain. Procopius and Gregory of Tours both describe these short-handled axes being thrown prior to a charge. They had a range of 12m. These differed from the normal axes used in day-to-day work, or the longer axe hammer found at Sutton Hoo, with a shaft of 78cm. They are rarely found in graves or mentioned in the sagas for this period.[36] In terms of missiles, an attacking force might expect arrows, spears and finally throwing axes aside from slings and throwing darts.

At close quarters the *seax* was a single-edged blade ranging from 8–31cm. Longer examples of 54–76cm are not found until the later eighth century.[37] Thus a warrior of our period would have had the shorter version, at up to a foot long, carried horizontally on his belt. The blade would not have been suited to piercing mail. Some warriors would have carried a sword, although there is some debate as to how common this was.

Less than one in twenty grave finds contained swords, the majority containing spears;[38] 22 per cent of graves in Kent contained swords, yet only 3 per cent of Anglian graves further north did so.[39] In the West Saxon area of Abingdon in Berkshire, only two swords have been found in eighty-two cremations and 119 burials. Of course there may have been cultural difference and some groups may have been reluctant to dispose of a valuable weapon, but it does suggest the majority of warriors were armed with spears and a *saex*. Nearly all swords of the period were pattern welded, made from several strips of iron, twisted and forge welded. Normal dimensions from the migration period were 85 to 95cm length and 4.5 to 5.5cm wide, similar to the late Roman *spatha* sword.[40] The hand grip was about 10cm with a narrow upper and lower guard, giving very little protection to the hand.

Swords from the mid-fifth to early sixth century often had their grips covered in precious metal similar to the sword of the Frankish King Childeric.[41] Some swords have been found with a ring attached to the pommel or upper guard and literary sources indicate that, for some at least, a cord was used to attach the sword to the wrist, presumably in case it was dropped in battle.[42] Stories of 'ring givers' are often assumed to refer to arm or finger rings, but it is at least plausible this is an alternative interpretation. Swords tended to be worn by a shoulder strap with the belt becoming more popular from the seventh century.[43] Scabbards would have been wooden, leather covered and lined with wool or fur soaked in oil to prevent rust.

The Roman *gladius* was used at close quarters as a stabbing weapon but the long *spathia* type swords of the fifth century were usually employed as a cutting weapon. They were more suited for hacking rather than thrusting.[44] In general, despite television and film portrayals, mail armour offered good protection against cutting or glancing blows.[45] We have contemporary reports of the effects of weapons on unarmoured men. Ammianus Marcellinus refers to swords of the Goths cutting through the head with such force that 'the severed halves hung down on each shoulder'.[46] Skeletal evidence shows horrific injuries with blows severing legs, penetrating and cutting away parts of skulls.[47]

Quality and workmanship made a difference too. A letter written by a secretary of Theodoric the Great (493–526) described swords 'capable even of cutting through armour, which I prize more for their iron than for the gold upon them'.[48] In contrast, in a later Norse saga the warrior *Steinthor* found, when his sword came against a shield, he often had to straighten his sword out with his foot.[49] No doubt *Steinthor* cursed the blacksmith as he fought for his life. So prized were some swords that an example gifted by Offa, king of Mercia, was treasured by the kings of Wessex 200 years later.[50] It was originally a gift from Emperor Charles the Great and of Avar workmanship.

Swords were a high status weapon for the elite and estimated to have cost, in modern terms, a quarter of a million pounds (or a Ferrari sports car).[51] More common swords may not have been quite so expensive. The laws of the Ripurian Franks, c. 500, set the cost of a sword and shield at two *solidus*, but a helmet at six and a mail shirt at twelve.[52] This contrasts with the *wergild*, or 'man price', of a Frank set at 200 *solidus*. Experiments have shown it takes around seventy-four hours to manufacture a pattern welded sword, together with scabbards and fittings.[53] Breaking that down it took approximately forty-three hours to make the blade and a further thirty-two hours to finish the hilt, scabbard and belt fittings.[54] Two weeks' work for a master craftsman, plus maybe an apprentice and materials, makes the Ferrari analogy seem a little exaggerated. Yet one sword left by King Alfred to his son Ethelred, earl of Mercia cost 120 oxen.[55]

In contrast to the Germanic tradition, the Romans tended not to name their swords. Over 200 swords names have been preserved in literary sources although they are all relatively late, with the earliest being in the tenth century from Anglo-Saxon poems.[56] In the Norse sagas many swords had names and a long history in multiple stories, and owned by different warriors.[57] Inscriptions often recorded who made or owned the sword.[58] Examples include: *Sigimer named the sword; Audmundr made me Asleikr owns me; Biorhtelm made me Sigeberiht owns me*; or simply *Leofric made me*.

Later Welsh tradition recalled 'The Thirteen Treasures of Britain'. One of these was *Dyrnwyn* ('white-hilt') owned by Rhydderch Hael. When drawn by a worthy man it would come alight, similar to the character in *Game of Thrones*. The likely earliest Welsh tale of Arthur, the tenth-century *Culhwch and Olwen*, named his sword *Caledfwich,* meaning hard cleft. This possibly derives from the sword *Caladbolg,* from Irish mythology. The HRB Latinised this to Caliburnus, and the French Romances adapted this further to *Caliburc, Escaliborc, Escalibor, Excalibor* and finally *Excalibur.*

In general we can say that most warriors carried a spear rather than a sword. Those that did, carried it by a shoulder strap. There is no reason to doubt the early Germanic warriors named their swords as much as their descendants. Perhaps the Romano-British scoffed at this. Yet the practice in late Welsh poems and sagas suggests the war-band was not the only development copied by the Britons or shared with their Germanic neighbours.

Shields tended to be oval or round and between 60–100cm in height or diameter.[59] Early Anglo-Saxon shields, at 45–65cm diameter, were smaller than their continental counterparts or later Viking shields. They were 6 to 8mm thick and weighed 3 to 5kg. Poems and art often depict a convex shape which might be better for deflecting blows, but all the archaeological finds are of flat shields. Wooden boards, such as lime wood or pine, were glued together and covered in rawhide. The covering was obviously important enough for King Athelstan in the tenth century to prohibit the use of sheepskin on shields.[60] The boss was up to 20cm in height and protected the hand. Contrary to popular belief, it is quite difficult to use the boss as an offensive weapon. It is far more practical to use the edge of the shield as this allows the fighter to maintain distance and adds reach to a 'jab'.

One common technique used by re-enactors is to 'roll' the opponents shield. If you are right handed you would hold your shield in your left hand and in front of you, with your sword in your right. Rather than stepping in to use the boss you can jab out with the edge of your shield. A jab holding the shield horizontally might smash into your opponents nose or push the top of their own shield into their face. This would leave your left side momentarily unguarded. A jab with the shield vertical might be a better option. If you hit your opponent's shield face on his left side this would twist their shield so it was edge towards you and parallel to your own shield. If you then 'rolled' your shield over to your left this would push their shield down so that your shield was now on top. This would also force them off balance, and to lean back and to the right, leaving their sword arm further away from you. Done quickly it would momentarily expose their whole left side and your movement would have you leaning over them with your sword arm hacking down at their exposed flank. Literary sources suggest shields often suffered damage in battle after repeated blows, with one saga describing a sword blow severing a shield in two and embedding itself in the warrior's head.[61]

One common inaccuracy seen in film and television portrayals is when a warrior's armour appears to offer no protection at all. In fact, mail armour gave excellent defence against most weapons, especially cutting blows. In the fifth century, the late Roman army used both *lorica hamata* (ring mail) and *lorica squamata* (scale armour). Lamellar armour could also be made from leather scales, while a sculpted cuirass was generally worn by officers.[62] Ring mail was also used by Germanic warriors and one example was found at Sutton Hoo burial. Another example, from

Vimose in Denmark, included 20,000, 8mm iron rings weighing about 11kg. It extended to the hips and just above the elbows. The rings were in alternate rows of welded and riveted. Rings of softer metal or butted (without rivets), as is sometimes seen in re-enactments or in the movies, could be torn apart by hand and would not withstand a blow. They were heavy and prone to rust and sources mention leather cases for storage.[63] A good quality mail shirt might take many weeks to make and thus were more valuable than a sword.

While they were excellent for defensive purposes they did have the disadvantage of being heavy and tiring over long distances or prolonged use. At the Battle of Stamford Bridge in 1066 the Viking army were caught unprepared without their mail shirts. This was clearly something one would not wear day to day. Yet the Viking were willing and able to stand and fight. This was because other materials offered reasonable protection as well. Deer hide was nearly as strong as mail but lighter and more flexible.[64] Several layers of linen within leather formed a quilted material that would also be surprisingly effective. The *gambeson* quilted leather armour worn in the later medieval period was just an extension of earlier examples. The late Roman *supermalis* worn under armour was simply two layers stuffed with sheep's wool, and some form of under armour would have been essential when wearing metal armour. But a thicker version covered in rawhide would have been a reasonable alternative for the average warrior. A battle re-enactor for that period has found that five layers of linen is enough to stop an arrow, even at close range.[65] In the late Roman army, light units, infantry or cavalry, generally had no armour.[66] In the fifth and sixth centuries chainmail and swords were likely rare for the average warrior.[67] Most fighters would have been armed with a spear and protected by a shield and a leather padded jerkin.

Given the nature of fifth-century warfare, the one item of protection that was a priority after a shield would be a helmet. However, only four helmets have survived in Britain. A usual design would be four or six metal plates held together with riveted bronze bands, with additions such as hinged cheek plates and nose guards. Some had neck guards of plate or mail and a ridge to protect the top of the head. The most common examples on the Continent are known as *spangenhelms*, and two dozen have been found. Some have eye protection as well but the Sutton Hoo helmet takes this one step further, having a full face guard, and shows significant parallels with the description of helmets in epic poems such as *Beowulf*.[68] The ridges of helmets may have been adorned with an animal crest such as boar or a plume.

Regarding cavalry, the Anglo-Saxons do not appear to have fought on horseback to the same extent as other Germanic tribes.[69] At the battles of Maldon, 991, and Hastings, 1066, the army appears to have travelled on horseback but fought on foot. The ASC entry for 1055 records the Herefordshire *fyrd* fleeing before the battle because they had been ordered to fight on horseback 'against their custom'. A largely infantry force might be at a disadvantage against a Romano-British force with mixed cavalry and infantry units. Although cavalry will not charge against a solid mass of infantry, especially one armed with spears. However, it would be wrong to assume from selected examples of infantry battles that they *never* fought on horseback. ASC entries for 672, a defeat against Picts, 894, a victory by Alfred the great, and 937 for the battle of Brunanburh, all imply early Anglo-Saxon armies could, and did, fight on horseback at times.[70] King Oswine in the mid-seventh century gave a royal horse to St Aiden. Although much later, the ASC entry of 896 refers to two 'horse-thegns', and in the tenth century a code of Athelstan demands two mounted men for each plough a landowner possesses.

In the sixth century, Procopius describes Goth, Vandal, Lombard and Frankish armies using cavalry, and Pictish and Irish carvings show mounted warriors. A ninth-century heroic poem describes a cavalry battle as beginning cautiously with thrown spears followed by hand to hand fighting with swords, somewhat similar to infantry battles.[71] At Hastings the Saxons rode to the battle but dismounted to form a shield wall, while the Norman cavalry attacked by riding up and throwing spears before retreating. The shield wall must have been relatively effective as it resisted for many hours. In another example of anti-cavalry tactics in a sixth-century battle, the Thuringians dug pits to protect against Frankish cavalry.[72] Germanic tribes were generally proficient on horseback after coming into contact with eastern warfare, however, in the fifth and sixth centuries, the Franks and Anglo-Saxons still fought mainly on foot.[73]

Additionally, the heroic poetry of the Dark Ages nearly always describes fighting on foot.[74] Procopius describes a Gothic army in 539 as being mainly infantry with swords, axes and shields. The few horsemen, armed with spears, protected the king. Infantry hurled their axes then charged with swords. Franks and Lombards are described as dismounting to fight on foot with shields, lances and swords in a sixth-century manual of war, *Strategicon*, c. 580: 'they fight according to families and not in regular troops … they charge swiftly with much spirit. They do not obey their leaders well. Headstrong, despising strategy, precaution of foresight, they show contempt for every tactical command especially cavalry'.[75] The Franks arms are recorded as: sword, shield, double headed axe and barbed spear. With few wearing helmets, mail or having horses. The leading men alone had long swords and they fought on foot for which they are 'extremely well practised.'[76] Yet the Alamanni were renowned for their 'excellent' cavalry, and most Germanic armies would have had a fifth to a third mounted. Procopius, describing Goths and Vandals, suggests the cavalry did not use missile weapons but instead advanced quickly to use the spear as a thrusting weapon.[77]

On balance, it would appear the Germanic settlers in Britain were familiar with horses but favoured fighting on foot, with the shield wall the most common formation. They would have stood with their family, tribe or war-band rather than in a unit as the late Roman army. Most warriors would have carried spear, *saex* and shield with the elite bearing a sword. Those without mail shirts would have worn leather or quilted material. Armour and shield were effective enough to allow warriors to stand for some considerable time.

We can imagine the following scenario. A standard football pitch is around 100m long by 75m wide. A war-band of five ships full of men would number about 150 and could stand two deep at one end. Four deep if only covering the width of the goalkeeper's box. A similar force of Romano-Britons facing them at the other end might stand their ground in a defensive position. At this range, arrows would begin to have minimal effect. Enough to make you want to retreat out of range or advance quickly. At the halfway line the archers become accurate. As you advance to the edge of the centre circle in the opponents' half, javelins start to rain in, and at the edge of the eighteen yard box they become accurate. In the thirteenth-century *Dialogue of Taliesin and Myrddin* we have the vivid lines concerning the battle of Arfderydd dated 573 in the Annales Cambriae: 'A host of spears fly high, drawing blood. From a host of vigorous warriors. A host, fleeing; a host, wounded. A host, bloody, retreating.'

To continue our football pitch analogy at the penalty spot, anyone carrying a Frankish axe would unleash this too. The longer 9ft spears, held 3ft from the end, would start to touch tips, and as the shield walls drew together warriors would attempt to thrust their spears over the shields or through gaps. How good your shield and armour was might affect how fast or keenly you covered this distance. The shield walls would push and shove while trying to land blows with spear or sword. Warriors in the rear would hurl javelins, darts or sling shot. Cavalry might lurk at the flanks ready to exploit openings. The first shield wall to break would be extremely vulnerable.

The war-band

The Britons and Germanic peoples developed a common military unit: the *comitatus* or war-band, based on Anglo-Saxon hearth-companions and Welsh *teulu* (family).[78] This is marked a difference to the cultural and social norms of the late Roman Empire, which emphasised central authority. The war-band extended kinship groups bound warriors to their lord, who repaid their loyalty with shelter and food. In the sixth century it had become the dominant force. Its very nature required a level of conflict and raiding to sustain itself. By the late sixth century this turned full circle back in to a monetary system based on the taxation of surplus, which required stability and security for farmers and craftsmen. By the seventh century this social and personal structure gave way to one based more on territory. However, in the fifth and sixth century there may have been less emphasis on territory and more on seeking resources and glory.

The principle function of the *comitatus* was warfare and this is reflected in the annals, sagas and poems of the Welsh and Anglo-Saxons. Literary and archaeological evidence indicates war-bands would have numbered less than 100.[79] We have seen the late Roman Field army numbered in the low thousands and successor states, *civitates* or petty kingdoms raised perhaps a thousand men.[80] The Tribal Hidage had a range of tribal groups who could raise as little as a few dozen warriors to the many thousands of the largest kingdoms such as Wessex.

In northern Europe many Germanic tribes had been based on similar power structures. A *canton* was a small number of farms or villages under the authority of one man. While his immediate *comitatus* was relatively small, he could call upon men from the farms and villages he controlled. Hence later we hear of a military official, *thusundifath* (leader of a 1,000). Such a group would have been made up of several units of *comitatus*. A large army might well have a number of kings and sub-kings. We see this in the fourth century from Ammianus: an army of 35,000 was led by two kings followed by five sub-kings and ten princes with a long train of nobles. Penda's army at the battle of Winwaed in 655 was made up of thirty *duces*, or royal commanders. In the HB the famous Arthur fought with 'the kings of the Britons'. Some examples show multiple leaders on both sides, such as the battle of Dyrrham in 577, where three British kings were slain by Cuthwine and Caelwin of Wessex. Many kings depended on family members to take responsibility. In 595, three of Aedan's sons died at the battle of Circhenn. Eight years later he was defeated at Degsastan by Aethelfrith. Aethelfrith's brother, Theobald, was also killed with 'all those he led' suggesting his entire war-band was wiped out.

This structure was very different from the earlier Roman army and led to different strategies. It was less organised and disciplined and the command was along aristocratic lines in a 'thinly spread military elite'.[81] The war-band had become a basic building block, militarily and socially.

We see how important these ties were in the ASC entry for 786 concerning Wessex. Cyneheard and eighty-four warriors ambushed King Cynewulf and killed him. Cyneheard offered his enemy's men mercy but all declined and fought to the death. The following morning Cynewulf's followers heard of their Lord's death and besieged Cyneheard. This time Cyneheard's men were offered life, but again they all fought to the last man. Both war-bands preferred to fight to the death rather than betray their oaths.

In the sixth century, the world of Gildas is already one of kings and warfare. The kings 'are tyrants' and they wage wars, 'civil and unjust'. Their 'military companions' are 'bloody, proud and murderous men'. Aurelius Caninus has an 'unjust thirst for civil war and constant plunder' and Cuneglasus wages war against 'our countrymen'. The kings chase thieves 'all over the country', but reward thieves who 'sit with them at table'. The war-band may have started out based on close family ties. However, by the seventh century, King Oswine of Deira attracted 'noblemen from almost every kingdom'.[82] A generation later Saint Guthlac fought for Æthelred of Mercia as a young man and attracted warriors from 'various races' into his own war-band. The war-band had become more diverse and yet had risen above even kinship groups in terms of social influence. Much of this was based on the lord's ability to distribute gifts such as armour, swords, treasure or gold. Sagas are full of references to 'ring givers'.

Raiding and tribute became vital to sustain this system.[83] In the sixth century we have records of the Saxons paying the Franks tribute of 500 cattle, and the Thuringians paying 500 pigs to the Saxons. Welsh and Irish poems portray a world of constant raiding, cattle rustling and revenge killings. In the Welsh laws of Hywel Dda, the lord kept one third of the treasure and was expected to distribute the remaining two thirds. We see the emergence of dykes and earthworks, and it has been suggested their primary function was to prevent cattle rustling. Aside from booty from raids, a lord required a surplus from their own lands to support a larger retinue of warriors, but also craftsmen such as armourers and jewellers. The evidence suggests a high standard of living for the elites of all groups in Britain.[84] We also have evidence for a higher calorific intake generally, and a marked increase of height over that period, 3cm for men and 2cm for women.[85]

Hostage taking and fostering also became important concepts. For example, Æthelfrith's son Oswald fled to the kingdom of Dal Riata when his father was killed by Edwin, who had also lived in exile. Given this constant upheaval and warfare, boys were encouraged to learn the required skills early. They were given weapons by the age of 14 or 15, and the archaeological record shows young adolescents buried with full-scale weapons and evidence of battle injuries.[86]

By the sixth century the *comitatus* had become the glue holding emerging kingdoms together.[87] These war-bands were relatively small and are reflected in the foundation myths in the ASC of a few dozen warriors often led by pairs of leaders. The loyalty to the war-band became more important even than kinship bonds. As the centralised Roman provincial system broke down the war-band became the primary military unit, but also a significant social and cultural force. At the *civitas* level this may have accelerated to drift towards autonomy and eventual independence as a petty kingdom. At a more local level, this may have involved the re-occupation of hill forts or the building of earthworks to prevent raiding. Whatever the case, the lord's hall overtook the Roman aristocrat's villa as the centre of power.

The hall

The mead or feasting hall became a significant aspect of social and cultural life in fifth – and sixth-century Britain for both the Britons and the Germanic settlers. This 'hall life' was an important support mechanism for war-bands and their lords.[88] Archaeology and literary sources indicate Britons and Anglo-Saxons used similar building techniques, materials and constructions.[89]

Ranging from 25–28ft in length and up to 100ft in width, one example can be seen at Yeavering in Northumbria, a short distance from the River Glen.

In the poem *Beowulf*, the king Hrothgar built a hall, a 'master mead-house ... there towered the hall, high, gabled wide, the hot surge waiting of furious flame'. There the king, 'would all allot that the Lord had sent him ... the rings he dealt, treasure at banquet ... It was of halls the noblest: Heorot he named it.' In the Welsh poem *Y Gododdin,* the 300 warriors sent out from Gododdin were a 'mead-nourished host'. The warriors came from all over Britain: warriors from Eidyn,; Geraint, with the men of Argoed and men of the south; Isag from the 'southern part'; Bubon ... beyond the sea of Iddew (Firth of Forth); and Cydywal leads the men of Gwynedd. The ruler of Gododdin, Mynyddog Mwynfawr, gave the warriors 'wine and mead from gold vessels ... for a year according to honourable custom'.

The court poet became an important feature in culture and society, whether the Welsh bards or Anglo-Saxon *scops*.[90] Gildas seems to refer to these when he criticises the five tyrant kings for listening to 'criminals and raving hucksters'. The clergy too, for preferring 'fabulous stories' from 'worldly men' to the word go God. The HB refers to several poets from the time of Ida and his sons (after 547): 'Then Talhearn Tad Awen was famed in poetry, and Aneirin and Taliesin and Bluchbard and Cian, known as Guenith Guant, were all simultaneously famed in British verse.' Society had developed a militarily aristocratic elite. The main interests of this nobility were warfare, courage and fierceness in war, generosity in peace, a longing for fame and a horror of disgrace.[91]

An acceptance of death became a price worth paying for glory or to avoid shame. The court poet was therefore a man to be respected, since your heroics or shame could be made eternal in song. One such example can be seen in the HB. Penda was defeated by the Northumbrian king, Oswy (Oswiu), at the battle of Winwaed. Only one of his allies survived, Cadfael of Gwynedd. Cadfael and his men had escaped the slaughter his army, 'rising up in the night' before leaving. He was immortalised as 'Cadfael the battle dodger' and included as one of 'The three faithless/disloyal war-bands of the island of Britain' in the Welsh Triads. These traditions and poems and sagas were all part of the culture of the mead hall. It was a way of life sandwiched between the Roman world and the later Anglo-Saxon kingdoms of figures such as Alfred the great. The hall was at its very core and required a surplus of goods, a culture of loyalty, and significant levels of raiding and warfare to sustain it.

Fostering

There was an early tradition of fostering represented in the poem *Beowulf*, where Beowulf himself was fostered at the age of 7. In *Beowulf* we read: 'I was seven-winters old when the jewel-prince took me, High-lord of heroes, at the hands of my father, Hrethel the hero-king had me in keeping, Hrethel took me when I was seven.'

The *Life of St Cuthbert*, written c. AD 700, describes boys of the same age engaging in physical activities, although we cannot take this as evidence of a 'training regime'. 'When he was a child of eight years he excelled all his companions of the same age in activity and playfulness.' Later we read: 'a woman named Kenswith, who is still living, a widow devoted to a religious life, who had brought him up from the age of eight years until the time when he attained his full growth and entered on the service of God.'

An important stage appears to have been when the boy reached 14 or 15 years of age.[92] We hear from the *Life of St Guthlac* that the saint was already part of a warband at the age of 15. From the *Life of St Wilfred*, we find the saint was given arms and horses at the age of 14 before he decided on a different path. As the historical record becomes clearer we will see many examples of young nobles being fostered or forced into exile. Such as when the future Bretwaldas Oswald and Oswiu had to flee Northumbria when Edwin killed their father Æthelfrith in 616 and seized the throne.

Roads, Dykes and Hillforts

The Romans left an extensive network of over 3,000 miles of roads in Britain. A foundation of coarse rubble was covered with compacted sand or gravel forming a camber to remove water to drainage ditches on either side. The width was between 1.45 to 6.45 metres. This allowed passage for the average wagon of the time, drawn by two yoked animals. Bishop, in *The Secret History of the Roman Roads of Britain*, estimates 40 per cent of the 3,000 miles survived into the medieval period.[93] This was perhaps a consequence of the fragmentation of the provincial structure, yet 40 per cent is a considerable proportion.

Regarding construction, it is estimated the 140 miles of Dere Street from York to Corbridge, at a width of five yards, would have taken 4,000 men a month. This equates to nearly two yards of road per man per day. In contrast, modern estimates include one and a half yards per man per day, and the British Royal Engineers estimate of one yard per man per day.[94] Tacitus records pairs of centuries utilised for construction, meaning 160 men would have taken 650 days to construct the same section.[95] One estimate of the initial Roman invasion in the first century calculates 1,000 men would have taken fifteen weeks to construct a temporary road from the Kent coast to the Thames near London.[96] Over a thousand years later, Edward I left details of his road building during the campaign of North Wales in 1274. Thirty miles from Chester to Rhuddlan was cleared in approximately thirty-four days using 1,500–1,800 woodsmen.[97]

Once constructed, road maintenance was essential because plants such as blackthorn could rapidly colonise them. We recall Evantius who, in 469, was responsible for maintaining the road in Visigoth-controlled south-west Gaul.[98] In 1285 the Statute of Winchester requested manorial landowners clear up to 200ft so that there were no 'ditch, underwood or bushes where one could hide with evil intent'.[99] Henry I required that two wagons or sixteen knights could be able to pass side by side. Maintenance required a central authority to organise labour and resources.

It is worth noting that not only were many of the Anglo-Saxon battles associated with Roman roads, but so too were nearly all later battles on English soil.[100] Examples include Stamford Bridge and Hastings, 1066; Stirling Bridge, 1297; Bannockburn, 1314; Bosworth, 1485; Marston Moor, 1644. Most of the battles of the War of the Roses and English Civil wars were fought on or near Roman roads. Examples from the ASC include Crecganford, 456; Salisbury, 552; Cirencester, 628; and Hexham in 633. If the battle of Catraeth refers to Catterick, then that too was on Dere Street between York and Corbridge.

Concerning travel times, a cart travelling from Catterick to Corbridge (a little over fifty miles) might have taken five days.[101] Infantry might take two days, while cavalry could do it in a day. Indeed, in the early fourteenth century Edward III marched from Barnard Castle to Haydon Bridge in a day before retreating, a similar distance from Catterick to Corbridge.[102] The distance from the heart of Gwynedd to Hadrian's Wall is roughly 250 miles, so we can multiply these numbers by five for Cadwallon's campaign in 633. In 1066 Harold marched south to meet William, averaging twenty-one miles a day, undoubtedly using the surviving Roman roads. More impressive is his march north to York and on to Stamford Bridge, which averaged fifty-three miles a day, a remarkable feat.[103] What this demonstrates is that there was nothing preventing armies campaigning from one end of Britain to the other. As there are numerous attested examples from the seventh century onwards, we can only conclude that it was equally possible in the fifth and sixth centuries. We know the manpower was there because we have equally impressive examples of major building projects, and dykes or earthworks started to appear.

Using our earlier estimates, we might calculate the eighteen miles from Gloucester to Cirencester might take 180 men a summer to build, however maintenance was likely less arduous. With Britain fragmenting and power becoming more localised, we can imagine how some routes were maintained while others neglected. A functioning road is a valuable thing; worth defending, but also worth blocking if the danger outweighs any benefits from keeping it open. We start to see such earthworks appear in this period, many cutting across existing roads.[104] Erik Grigg, in *Warfare, Raiding and Defence in Early Medieval Britain*, describes over a hundred such dykes of the period and makes a number of important observations: most examples are too short and in the wrong location to be associated with borders of documented kingdoms;[105] the vast majority appear to be defensive;[106] and they appear largely designed to control raiding.[107] The building of these dykes peaked in the late sixth and early seventh century.[108] Examples include Bokerley Dyke, Hampshire; Wansdyke in the West Country; and several Cambridgeshire dykes.

A large bank, fronted by a ditch was built on a slope and had the following dimensions: average length 10,331m (6.4 miles); median length 3,235m (2.1 miles); height of bank averaged at 1.8m high and 8.3m wide, with 'v' shaped ditches at 2.1m deep and 6.2m wide and angled at 38–40 degrees.[109] Very little material evidence is found but where they cut across existing Roman roads, or later Anglo-Saxon 'herepaths' (literally army paths), we know they are post-Roman.[110] Evidence from Jutland suggests they were topped by palisades and had gateways cut into them. However the absence of these in Britain implies they were used without.[111] They were often built in open grassland with a good line of sight and lined with turf. They appear to have been designed to be seen from, rather than be seen.[112] It is thus likely they were patrolled rather than garrisoned, and set back to give defenders enough time to man the bank.

Examples from northern Europe suggest Germanic settlers may have brought the techniques with them. The Cambridgeshire dykes, for example, face west, defending East Anglia from the west rather than from raiders from the coast. We find no similar earthworks in Brittany, although the orientation of some dykes, such as Wansdyke, suggests Britons did utilise these earthworks. However, the dykes do not match divisions in material culture.[113] Concerning construction, it is estimated that most of

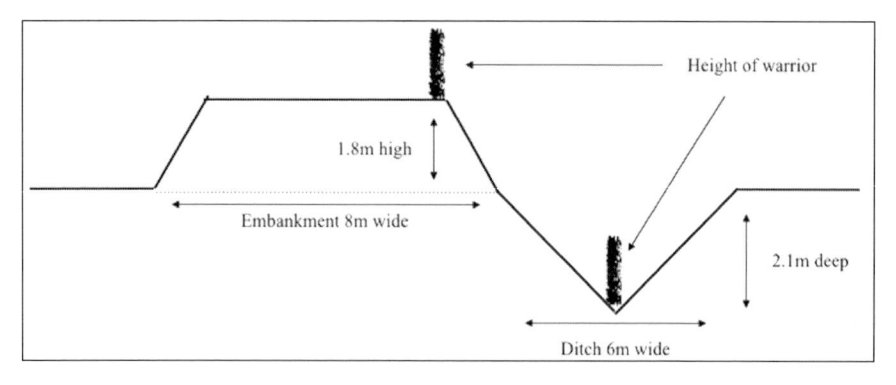

Figure 18. Cross section of earthwork.

these earthworks could have been built by fewer than a hundred men in a single summer season.[114] Grigg finds that most could be built by the inhabitants of a few villages.[115]

Eighth-century Anglo-Saxon sources site obligations for military service, bridge repairs and building fortifications.[116] The later tenth-century Burghal Hidage lays out how many men were required to defend a position, roughly one man for every 4ft. A dyke at Heronbridge, near Chester, would thus need around 500 warriors to defend it. At this site, over 200 males of fighting age were found, half with head injuries and DNA indicating they came from north-east England.[117] It is possible these fell at the battle of Chester in the early seventh century. Æthelfrith, king of Northumbria, had attacked the Welsh of North Wales. Both Bede and the ASC records the battle, the latter for 606:

> Æthelfrith led his army to Chester and there killed a countless number of Welsh; and thus was fulfilled Augustine's prophecy which he spoke: 'If the Welsh do not want peace with us, they shall perish at the hands of the Saxons.' There were also killed 200 priests who had come there in order to pray for the Welsh raiding army. Their chieftain was Scrocmail, who escaped from there as one in fifty.

If the victorious Northumbrians lost 200 men, we can speculate their army was perhaps as low as several hundred and as high as low thousands. Bede claimed Æthelfrith had a 'great army' and that they attacked the priests first, killing 1,200 with only fifty escaping. Evidence of burials indicating warfare is found at other locations. There are over 800 individuals found near six different earthworks with numerous burials dated to the sixth century near the Cambridgeshire dykes.[118]

As society fragmented and became localised, farming practices changed. Cattle grazing became more important. At the same time the war-band was growing in importance and raiding increased, especially for cattle. Earthworks start to appear across Britain. Grigg therefore concludes that the main reason for these early dykes was as protection from raiding, often for cattle, which is a theme of many Irish and Welsh sagas and poems. Nor could one go round if it was flanked by natural features such as rivers, woods or marsh. Raiders unfamiliar with the area might be not aware of how far they needed to travel to get round it and leave themselves open to attack if they tried. Another interesting point Grigg makes is that it takes up to four times the number of attackers to storm a position such as a dyke.

These problems are multiplied when attacking a hill fort. and we see a number of re-occupied hill forts from Cornwall to Strathclyde:[119] Trethurgy and Tintagel in Cornwall; Dinas Powys; Mote of Mark, Dumbarton, and Doon Hill in Scotland; Cadbury castle and Cadbury Congresbury in the South; and Yeavering Bell in the North. At Cadbury we see evidence from one of its ramparts: a dry stone bank filled with Roman masonry, stone, pottery and roofing tiles.[120] Refurbishment of the inner rampart is fifth or sixth century.[121] We can estimate how much labour would be needed in its building; one rampart measures 190m x 160m, giving a perimeter of 700m with a ditch and bank approximately 2m deep and high respectively. Assuming the ditch material was used to form the bank, and the bank was 2m wide, we can estimate 2,800 cubic metres of earth. The British Army calculates that one man can move 0.3 cubic metre of earth in one hour, half the amount in chalk or rocky ground.[122] Therefore, approximately 9,300 man hours are required, and assuming an eight-hour day, nearly 1,200 labour days. Or in other words, a thousand labourers could achieve a reasonable defence in a day or forty labourers would take a month. One estimate for the entire Iron Age Hill Fort construction at Ravensburgh, including timber work, is 200 men in 109 days.[123]

An outer rampart at Cadbury is 10m high and 1.2km in length. We have seen figures for populations and warrior numbers; there was certainly manpower available but what these examples show is that in places, there was an authority to organise and direct those resources. This outer rampart would have taken 1,200 men to defend, and the inner one 700. Given there's not much point building something that can't be defended, we can assume that at one time at least the authority around Cadbury had a considerable military force. It follows that a larger force would be required to storm it.

In summary, this section has shown us a number of interesting points. First, the fifth century saw the building of dykes across Britain and the re-occupation of hill forts in the west and north. These building works could have been carried out by local powers in a relatively short time, certainly in one season. They point to a fragmentation and localisation of power. Many of the earthworks appear to be designed to frustrate raiding and cattle rustling. Roads continued to be used, but many fell into disrepair. Despite this the Roman road network provides clues as to the likely location of early battles. They continued to be important routes for armies for centuries and many famous battles lie alongside them.

Contemporary accounts of battles

In the first century, Tacitus states that only a few Germanic warriors used swords or lances.[124] The spears have 'short narrow heads' and are good for both thrusting and as a missile. The infantry carry several javelins each and can hurl them 'a great distance'. They fight 'either naked or only lightly clad in their cloaks'. Few had armour and only some helmets or 'metal or hide'. The cavalry tactics are interesting: 'Their horses are not distinguished either for beauty or for speed, nor are they trained in Roman fashion to execute various turns. They ride them straight ahead or with a single swing to the right, keeping the wheeling line so perfect that no one drops behind the rest'. Yet the strength lies with their infantry and the fastest and fittest warriors are placed in the van of the army. 'The number of these chosen men is exactly fixed. A hundred are drawn from each district, and "the hundred" is the name they bear at home'.

Two battles involving late Roman armies are worth mentioning. In the first, at Adrianople in 378, Emperor Valens lead 30,000 Roman troops against a Gothic force of around 15,000. Amminaus Macrcellinus described the events:[125] after an eight mile march in the midday sun, the Roman scouts come upon the Goths drawn up behind their wagons in a circular formation. The Roman cavalry on the right wing had advanced the furthest with much of the infantry and the left wing was some way behind. An attempt at negotiations was thwarted by an impulsive shower of arrows from the Roman side. This eventually brought on an attack by the Gothic cavalry that 'routed with great slaughter all that they could come to grips with'. Before the armies came together, arrows and javelins flew, and the lines pushed backwards and forwards 'like the waves of the sea'. The Roman left wing reached the wagons but became exposed and fell back. The Roman infantry were then pressed so close together that a man could 'hardly wield a sword or draw back his arm once he had stretched it out'. Nor was it possible to 'see the enemy's missiles in flight and dodge them.' The Goths poured into the battle and the crush made ordered retreat impossible. We read of helmets and breastplates being split by battle axes, and of severed limbs. The infantry, having shattered their spears, had to 'make do' with their swords. Interesting that the sword here is seen as a 'make do' weapon, secondary to the spear. The end, when it came, was quick. The Romans, 'weak from hunger, parched with thirst and weighed down by the burden of their armour', broke and ran. Roughly two thirds of the Roman forces perished along with Valens.

The second is the battle of the Catalaunian Plains in 451, in which the Roman general Flavius Aetius stopped Attila the Hun and forced his withdrawal. The result of the battle is disputed. Estimates vary from 30,000 to 80,000 on each side and interestingly, Aetius had Saxons as part of his allied force. The general placed the Visigoths on his right wing while he held the left with the Roman forces placing the Alani in the centre. This was due to his mistrust of the Alan king, thus demonstrating the fragility of forming an alliance with many different tribes. Attila, on the other hand, took the centre with his strongest troops and placed his allies on the wings. The 'chequer-board' formation of the republican and imperial legions were a thing of the past. Units were based on tribal affiliation rather than function and training. Both armies attempted to control a piece of high ground in the centre of the plain. The Romans won the race and Jordanes states that Attila urged his men to attack the Romans, who were 'forming in one line with locked shields'.[126] This sounds remarkably like a shield wall. This wall held and the Huns were driven back. Here we have a battle, contemporary with Hengest and Vortigern and a generation before Aelle. The strategy used by the last great Roman general in the West suggests formal disciplined formations were becoming less common.

Later contemporary accounts of battles in Anglo-Saxon England give us a flavour of how Dark Age battles looked and felt. The battle of Burnanburh in 937 tells us that when the battle started there was a 'meeting of spears, the mixing of weapons', and 'they clove through the shield wall and hewed through the linden wood defences with hammered blades'. They 'hewed down the fugitives with blades grindstone sharp'.[127] The ASC records warriors 'shot over shield, taken by spears', then later when the enemy broke the 'West Saxons with elite cavalry ... hacked from behind those who fled battle'.[128] Five kings were 'put to sleep by swords', and the slaughter is described as the greatest ever in Britain of 'people felled by the swords edge'. The Annals of Ulster record that several thousand died on each side and that several kings and nobles also perished:[129] Cellach, son of King Constantine; Owen, king of Strathclyde; Gebeachan, Norse king of the Western Isles; two sons of Sihtric, king of York; Ælfwine and Æthelwine, cousins of Æthelstan; and other ealdormen, and 'a multitude of lesser men'. The kings and nobles of both armies fought and died with their men in a vicious battle of shield-walls. It is possible that casualties were similar until one side broke. It wouldn't even need the whole army to break, just a gap in the shield wall, or a flank turned would suffice. A similar situation is described by Asser in the *Life of Alfred the Great*. The battle of Edington in 878 was fought by a 'close shield wall against the whole army'.

We can see how close Dark Age kings came to death at the battle of Vouille between the Franks and the Goths in 507. We read, 'some of the soldiers hurled their javelins from a distance, others fought hand to hand'.[130] Two Goths saw the Frankish king, Clovis, in the melee and attacked with spears. He was saved by 'the leather corselet ... and sheer speed of his horse', although he was injured and 'very near to death'.[131] No chainmail here, just leather armour. The king is mounted but close to the action.

In 991, ninety Viking ships landed on an island off the Essex coast near Maldon. They were met by the Saxon Earl Byrhtnoth, leading a similarly sized force of 3,000 men. The Vikings demanded gold, like some mafia extortion racket. Instead they are offered 'spears, deadly darts and hard swords'. A small causeway connected the island to the shore, but three of Byrhtnoth's warriors held the narrow bridge against the raiders. The Vikings requested they be allowed to cross to do battle and amazingly the Saxon 'nobleman allowed, due to his overweening pride'. The earl formed his army into a war-wall or war-hedge, then 'hard spears, sharp pointed, their shafts flew'.[132] Spears and arrows fly, but Byrhtnoth is armed with a sword, 'broad and bright edged ... ornamented', as are warriors in the second line when the battle descends into hand-to-hand fighting.[133]

In 1066 King Harold II, the last Anglo-Saxon king of England, fought two battles. The first at Stamford Bridge near York against the combined army of his brother Tostig, and the Norwegian King Harald Hardrada. The invaders had defeated one army and captured York, but Harold had surprised them by marching 200 miles in less than a week. He marched through an undefended York and found an unsuspecting Danish army a few miles to the east spread across both sides of the River Derwent. The Vikings had their helmets and weapons but had left their mail shirts on their ships as the weather was warm and sunny.[134] Those on the western bank fled or were quickly killed. Yet we read a single Norse axeman stood on the bridge and held up the advance while those on the left bank quickly formed up.[135] His end came painfully as a Saxon came under the bridge and 'stabbed him through under the mail-coat'. The English crossed over and made a 'great slaughter', causing the Vikings to flee back to their ships at Riccall a few miles south of York.

Only twenty-four ships out of 300 had sufficient crew for the return journey. The implied casualty rate was over 90 per cent. Both armies are estimated at around 10,000 each, from which we can estimate around 9,000 Danes lay dead. It may have been a 'very stubborn battle' as the Chronicle puts it, but once the shield wall broke the chances of survival were minimal, especially if being pursued by cavalry who 'fiercely attacked them from behind'.

Harold's celebrations were cut short just three days later. William of Normandy landed at Pevensey and set up camp in remains of the old Roman shore fort, the same spot Ælle had besieged and slaughtered the Britons nearly 600 years earlier. Within two weeks Harold had marched the 270 miles south. He stopped at London for just six days and continued on, hoping to repeat the surprise attack the previous month. Leaving London on 11 October, he covered sixty miles in two days. But William knew of his approach, marched from Hastings at dawn the next day and caught his opponent off guard seven miles to the north-west around nine in the morning of 14 October.

As at Maldon seventy-five years earlier, the English rode to the battle but dismounted and left their horses to the rear. They used a formation that would have been as familiar to Aetius in the fifth century as to Alfred the Great in his Viking wars of the ninth. Harold formed his troops into a shield wall along a ridge with forest on each flank. The Normans formed into three lines: archers and crossbowmen in the front; infantry in mail shirts armed with spears and swords in the second; and cavalry in the last line.

Two contemporary accounts survive.[136] Trumpets sounded and the battle began with a 'thick cloud' of arrows, mainly against the English line. The Norman infantry attacked, 'crashing shield against shield'. The defenders threw everything at them: 'javelins, missiles of various kinds, murderous axes and stones tied to sticks'. The English shield wall held firm and the Normans are recorded as making no headway. The cavalry attacked, throwing spears and hacking down with swords, but still the wall held firm. It is worth noting that this wasn't the heavy cavalry charges of later centuries, with lances and supporting high-backed saddles. The Normans were beginning to use cavalry charges, but at Hastings the ground was steep and rough which made this difficult. Instead, the cavalry rode up to the line, discharged their missiles or hacked down quickly with their swords or thrust their spears, wheeled round and made good their escape, protected by their long kite shaped shields.

The reports tell of a lull in the fighting and an interesting interlude. A single mounted Norman rides out between the lines, juggling his sword, and offers a challenge with boasts and insults. One Englishman steps forward and is soon beheaded and the grisly trophy held aloft. The English discipline held. The battle continued and raged all day. We learn that the English were able to penetrate shields and armour, which is a possible reference to the large battle-axes of the house-carls. By all accounts the Normans were struggling against the English wall of wood and spears.

Two events occurred that changed the battle and history. The Norman left flank broke and the some of the English pursued them, sensing victory. Some claimed later this was a ruse and the Normans did use such tactics. However, the whole army began to give way as a rumour that William was dead swept the battlefield. It is worth noting that one small moment can change a battle, that can in turn change history. William removed his helmet, a dangerous thing to do on a medieval battlefield, and urged his men back into the battle. The English on the Norman left were quickly surrounded and the Normans repeated the same tactic to lure more defenders off the ridge.

The defending line began to thin out and weaken. Norman arrows started to have more of an effect. The account of Harold dying from an arrow to the eye is not supported by the contemporary sources and may be a later biblical reference about oath-breakers.[137] Instead, with the battle nearly won, Harold was cut down by four Norman knights. As gaps appeared in the shield wall the tide began to change. With the rumour of Harold's death, the line broke. The battle had lasted all day and only nightfall allowed the English to survivors to escape.

Single combat

We read above about the remarkable event that occurred mid-battle at Hastings. Single combat is a common theme used in many films and books, but just how common was it? One example comes from the sixth-century writer Procopius. A Gothic warrior, Valaris, rode out and challenged the Romans to battle. Paul the Deacon, two centuries later, describes a battle between the Langobards and Assipitti as being settled by two warriors. we read it too in sagas and poems. Menalaus defeats Paris outside the walls of Troy before being killed by Hector, himself later slain by Archilles in single combat. In the Bible, David defeats Goliath with a sling. Geoffrey of Monmouth can't resist the trope in his fantastical *The History of the Kings of Britain*.[138] King Arthur and the Roman tribune Frollo do battle outside the walls of Paris as the populace watch on from the battlements. Arthur receives a blow that reddens his shield and in anger, strikes his opponent with such force that it severs Frollo's helmet and head into two halves. Frollo falls dead with the poetic 'drummed the earth with his heels and breathed his soul into the winds'.

Tactics

We have seen that the shield wall became a common tactic used on battlefields of the fifth century, and this remained the case into the middle ages. One method of countering this was using a wedge, or 'pigs-head' to break the line. This could be countered by forming a 'V' or 'pincer' to enclose in both sides.[139] Saxo, a Danish historian of the twelfth century, describes the wedge as having two warriors in the front, four in the second line, eight in the third and so on doubling each time.[140] The Romans also used similar tactics.

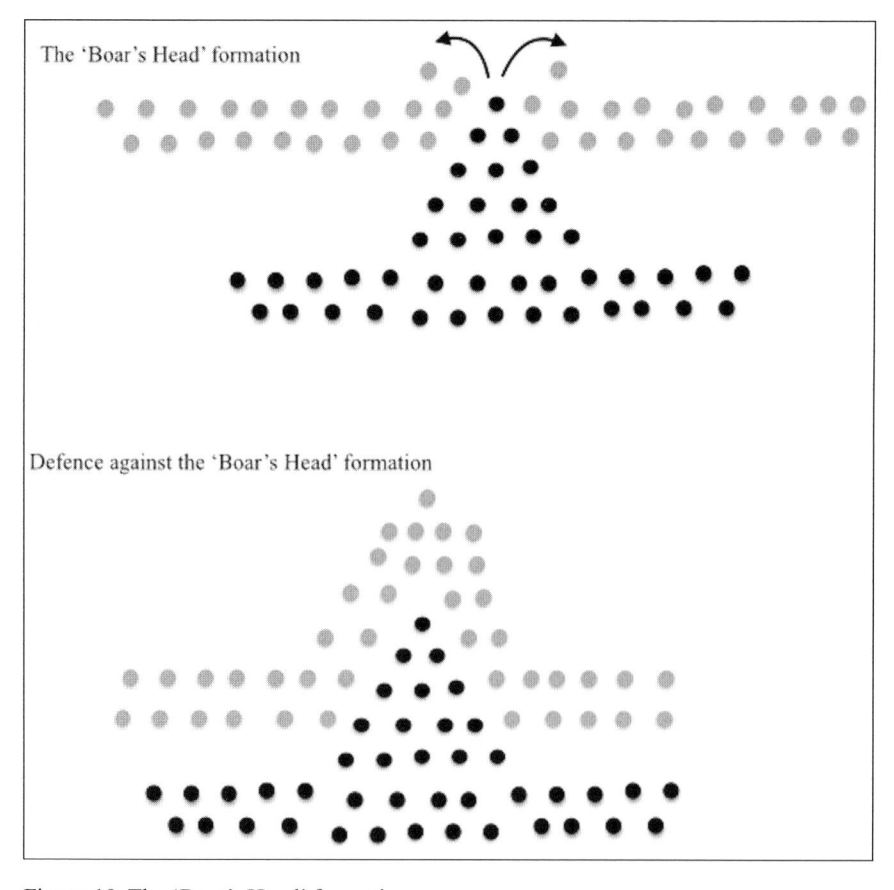

Figure 19. The 'Boar's Head' formation.

It seems reasonable to suggest the battlefields of the fifth and sixth centuries might have looked similar to those Alfred witnessed in the Viking-Saxon wars of the ninth century. We shouldn't assume this to be the case. Shields were smaller and formations perhaps looser, yet we recall the shield wall employed by Aetius against Attila's Hunnic army. What then of the Romano-British? Gildas tells us that the Romans gave advice and left 'manuals on weapons training'.[141] One example might have been a fourth-century text by Vegetius. One piece of advice they may have read was: 'Skill and training are more important than numbers and a large untrained group are vulnerable to slaughter.'[142]

We have already seen how the Roman army in Britain had been depleted and are left to speculate on how much of the training and discipline would have survived. But it is a useful place to start giving us a glimpse of military thinking at the end of the fourth century. The question raised is, did the Britons continue to organise, train and resource a significant defensive force? Despite the collapse of the economy, coin supply and much of urban life, St Germanus did find an army able and willing to fight in 429. We read they are 'in camp' rather than a fort or town. Were they following the advice in Vegetius regarding the building of camps? They should be built near a good supply of water, firewood and fodder and avoid swampy areas and those overlooked by higher ground. He describes various types but they all involve a wide fosse or ditch with an inner embankment.[143] To this temporary defence can then be added ramparts and we are at once reminded of the reoccupation of hill forts and evidence of rebuilding.

Some of the information in Vegetius is out of date by the late fifth century. Recruits using the short Roman *gladius* were taught to strike with the point rather than the edge because a cut seldom killed as the vitals are protected by armour, however 'a stab driven two inches in is fatal'.[144] The *gladius* was suited for the battlefield of the early empire. A solid shield wall, several men deep, is difficult to break. This left over the top of the shield as the easier option for an attacking strike. The later *spatha* sword, being designed more for a cutting blow than a stab, was better suited for this type of warfare. However the spear had greater reach and was the most common weapon of choice for warriors of this period.

In battle Vegetius describes how the light troops should harass the enemy to provoke an attack against the heavy troops who stand 'like a wall of iron', who could 'not flee nor pursue easily'.[145] The light troops can retreat and join archers and others armed with javelins and darts. At the rear are 'carriage ballistas' and 'sling staff men' throwing stones and bolts.[146] If the enemy breaks they are pursued by light troops and cavalry. He describes how an individual infantryman takes up about 3ft, and we are reminded of the Anglo-Saxon *Burghal Hidage* and its estimate of one man per 4ft of defensive work. Vegetius suggests 6ft between each line and thus 10,000 men, in seven lines, could take up a position a mile wide and 42ft deep.[147] Strength in depth was preferable to width and the troops were trained to form a line, wedge or a circle.[148]

Cavalry tended to be used primarily on the flanks or for attacking a fleeing enemy, as at Brunanburh. Vegetius describes a useful tactic:[149] mixing cavalry with

The Early Anglo-Saxon Kings

light troops armed with shields and javelins worked well against a superior cavalry force. Caltrops could also be quickly scattered. This consisted of four spikes, with three on the ground and the remaining one sticking up. Some tactics are common across the centuries and he listed seven common ones below:[150]

1. Rectangular formation with extended front. Should only be used with numerical superiority lest the flanks become enveloped. He describes this as the usual way to do battle in his day.
2. Oblique or angled formation engaging enemies left flank with your stronger right and strongest cavalry to turn flank.
3. Same as 2 but engaging their right flank with your left.

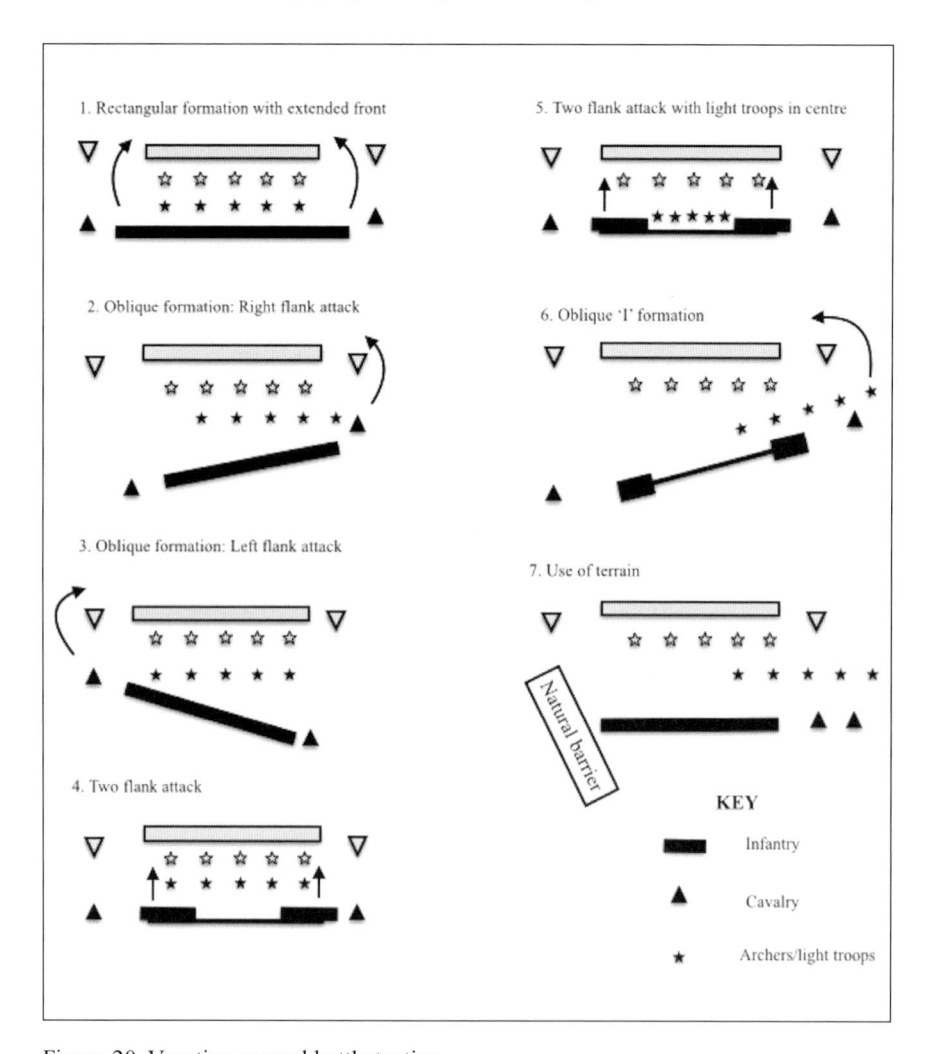

Figure 20. Vegetius general battle tactics.

4. Advance to 400–500 paces then spur on both wings having thinned out your own centre.
5. Same as point 4, above, but place light troops and archers in front of centre to protect from breach.
6. He describes this as the best: a letter 'I' formation, oblique with the right flank attacking first and cavalry and light troops outflanking enemy.
7. Use of terrain: simply by anchoring one flank against mountain, forest or river then placing all light troops and cavalry on the opposite wing.

The late Roman army of the fifth century might have used the following formation:[151] light units of infantry and cavalry, followed by a line of heavy infantry flanked by heavy cavalry. Archers and slingers behind and a reserve force in the rear.

Organisation

We have seen how on the Continent Germanic warriors such as the Franks and Goths fought in kinship groups rather than the disciplined units of the Roman army, trained for a specific function. Instead, Gothic or Saxon armies were made up of several war-bands, often with different layers of sub-kings and nobles. In later Anglo-Saxon England, lordship ties were central to military and social organisation. We see terms such as geoguð (youth) and duguð (proven warrior). The geoguð were young, unmarried warriors, perhaps the sons of duguð. They resided with their lord, receiving food and shelter in return for their service. This became the lord's hearðweru or hirð (household or 'hearth' troops).

These would accompany the king along with his more experienced nobles, the duguð and their retinues. We can see examples of this in ASC, where we read of kings and sub-kings fighting in battles such as Penda, leading thirty royal commanders at Winwaed in 655. The fyrd would therefore be made up of the king's household warriors (gesið) as well as his landed retainers (duguð). We see this reflected in various law codes: King Ine of Wessex (688–726) ruled that any landholding nobleman who neglects military service had to pay 120 shillings and forfeit his land. If he held no land he paid 60 shillings. Peasants were also obliged to serve and were fined 30 shillings if they did not. Contemporary sources show that although the ceorl, as a freeman, had the right to bear arms, he would rarely have joined the king's fyrd. The word fyrd had, by the time of Alfred, acquired a distinctly martial connotation, and had come to mean armed expedition or force.

In the eighth century, King Offa of Mercia laid out 'three necessities' or 'common burdens', and they formed the bedrock of military organisation a century later under Alfred the Great.[152] These included Bridgework, *brycggeweorc*, Fortress work, *burhbot*, alongside army work, *frydfaereld*.

The Domesday Book for Berkshire records:[153] 'If the king sent an army anywhere, only one soldier went from five hides, and four shillings were given him from each hide as subsistence and wages for two months. This money, indeed, was not sent to the king but was given to the soldiers'.

It would seem likely from these sources that the kings and more important noblemen would possess a coat-of-mail and a crested helmet, a sword, shield and spear. Noblemen of middling rank may have possessed a helm, perhaps a sword, and a shield and spear. The lowest ranking warriors would have been equipped with just a shield and spear, and perhaps a secondary weapon such as an axe or seax.

The Burghal Hidage states there is to be four men to defend every *pole*, roughly 5m. Or roughly one man every 4ft. Archaeological evidence from Bath (with 1,275m of wall) and other towns show these estimates are remarkably accurate. It follows from this that the Roman town at Aqua Sulis would have required 1,000 warriors to defend the walls based on the later Anglo-Saxon Burghal Hidage. Population densities were greater in the larger urban areas. Londinium may have had 45,000 at one point, Viroconium 15,000 and Lincoln about half that. Bath, smaller still, would likely have had 3–4,000 citizens. Using our earlier rule of thumb we can see this might only provide 400 men of fighting age. Without a garrison or mercenaries it might be difficult to supply an adequate defence. With a declining urban population it would be all but impossible.

Paul Hill in *The Anglo-Saxons at War 800–1066*, focuses on the later Anglo-Saxon period but suggests that during the migration period the average size of a war-band 'could scarcely have numbered more than a few hundred'.[154] He goes on to state that the later eighth century *fyrds* and *heres* (armies) would have been a similar size. King Ine (689–726) defined the size of an army in his law code: 'We use the term "thieves" if the number of men does not exceed seven, "band of marauders" [or 'war-band'] for a number between seven and thirty-five. Anything beyond this is an "army" [here]'.

The tenth-century Burghal Hidage lists thirty-three strongholds in Alfred's Wessex and gives calculations involving number of men per hide and length of wall. This implies a garrison strength of 27,000 spread across various *burhs*.[155] Analysis of duties imposed by Aethelred II in 1008 describe a helmet and mail coat from every eight hides, and one ship from every 300 hides. This implies an army of 10,000 mail clad warriors and a navy of 267 ships.[156] As those with mail coats were in the minority we can speculate about the numbers of available men across the kingdom as being much higher. A century later, an early eleventh century source records 24,000 mail coats in London.

We cannot assume these sorts of arrangements were in place in the sixth or even fifth centuries. Many of them evolved or were put in place in response to events such as the later Viking attacks. However, it does give us some clues as to how many warriors were considered necessary to defend a fortification. It shows why some towns may have been abandoned. London in particular required a significant garrison to defend its walls. Some towns, such as Cirencester, appear to have abandoned some areas but utilised others such as the amphitheatre. Alfred was able to support the building of *burhs* because he had the resources and organisation. Fifth-century Britain had suffered a major economic shock along with significant de-urbanisation.

Summary

We have seen how warfare evolved in the fifth century. The highly organised large multi-legion sized armies of the Empire were in the past. Instead, armies became a collection of war-bands. These war-bands became the primary social building block as well as military unit. While shields were smaller than the later middle-ages, shield-walls were becoming common on the battlefield. The archaeological, historical and literary evidence suggests that most warriors would have fought on foot armed with shield, spear and knife, protected by leather or quilted material. A smaller percentage would have mail armour, helmets and swords.

We see an increase in building of earthworks and reoccupation of hill forts. However, at the same time the rural settlements were, 'without exception', undefended by walls or earthworks.[157] Blade injuries become more common, yet at the same time remained relatively rare.[158] In the west of Britain we find only two examples for this period, while in Anglo-Saxon areas there are four blade injuries per 300 inhumations for the period, a little over 1 per cent. If we compare this to fourth-century Roman Britain, an individual would have been three times more likely to be wounded by an edged weapon a century or two later. We can compare these rates to modern times, bearing in mind soft tissue injuries would not show up, and blade injuries don't equate to death. The highest murder rate today is 134 per 100,000 in Tijuana in Mexico. This equates to 0.134 per cent.

With political fragmentation came a reduction in army sizes. Yet resources were adequate enough to build substantial earthworks in dykes and hill-forts around Britain. If the poem *Y Gododdin* is to be believed a relatively minor kingdom was able to equip and direct a force of 300 cavalry against another kingdom, which was able to muster seven times their number. The later Tribal Hidage implies that kingdoms such as Essex and Sussex could supply 1,400 warriors, Kent, 3,000 and Wessex 20,000. Yet scholars have suggested the emerging petty kingdoms of the fifth century, many based on former Roman civitates, would have struggled to support more than 1,000 warriors. However, this is assuming the complete collapse of any provincial or military structures. This may not have been the case. In the west, Britannia Prima may have held together up to c. 500.

First, the HB implies that Hengest was ceded most, if not all, of the former province of Maxima Caesariensis. Second, for Bede's description of Ælle as holding imperium to mean anything it would have to mean a similar level and extent of authority. St Patrick still refers to his people as citizens and Christian. Several decades later Gildas seems to be preaching to his audience as though they are also one people despite the presence of several tyrant kings. All this suggests that while the diocese fragmented in the mid-fifth century, some of the five provinces retained some sort of cohesion much later than has been suggested. The war of Ambrosius Aurelianus could be seen in this context. Possibly a provincial level war between west and east. Battles of the size recorded in the ASC would not be unlikely. It is to this conflict we will now turn.

Picture 1. Outer ditch and wall at Richborough Roman Fort, East Kent. (by author)

Picture 2. Exterior wall at Pevensey Roman Fort, East Sussex. Taken by Ælle in 491. (by author)

Weapons and Warfare of the Fifth and Sixth Centuries

Picture 3. Interior of Pevensey Roman Fort, East Sussex. (by author)

Picture 4. Highdown Hill, Sussex. Fifth-century Anglo-Saxon cemetery. (by author)

Picture 5. Outer ditch at Cissbury Hillfort, Sussex. (by author)

Picture 6. Cadbury Castle Hill Fort. (Wikimedia Commons)

Weapons and Warfare of the Fifth and Sixth Centuries

Picture 7. Warriors outside reconstruction of a King's Hall c. 700 in Lejre near Roskilde. (Ivanowich)

Picture 8. A Dark Age lord in reconstruction of hall c. 700 in Lejre near Roskilde, Denmark. (Ivanowich)

Picture 9. Shield bosses, bowls and brooches found at Highdown Hill fifth-century Anglo-Saxon cemetery. (Worthing Museum)

Picture 10. Glassware found at Highdown Hill. (Worthing Museum)

Picture 11. Glassware found at Highdown Hill possibly c. 400 from Egypt. (Worthing Museum)

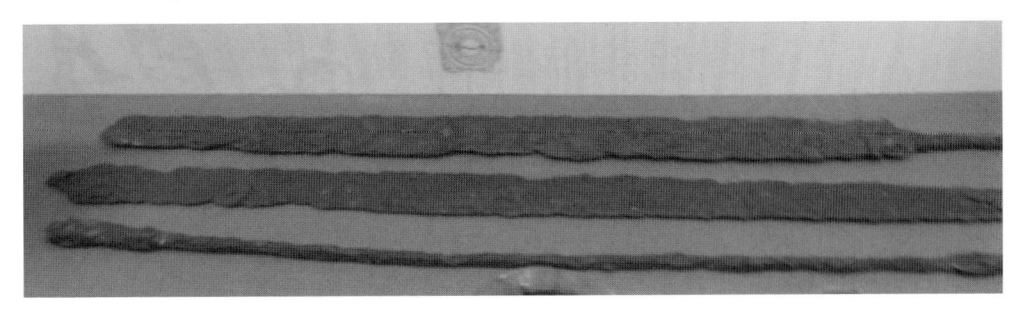

Picture 12. Two swords and spear found at Highdown Hill. (Worthing Museum)

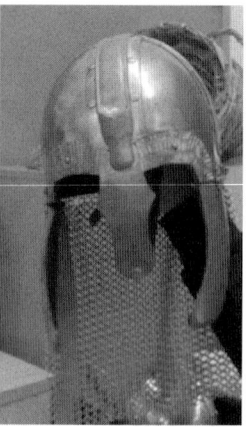

Above left: Picture 13. Quoit military style brooches found at Highdown Hill. (Worthing Museum)

Above right: Picture 14. Replica of Vendel helmet at Worthing Museum. (Worthing Museum)

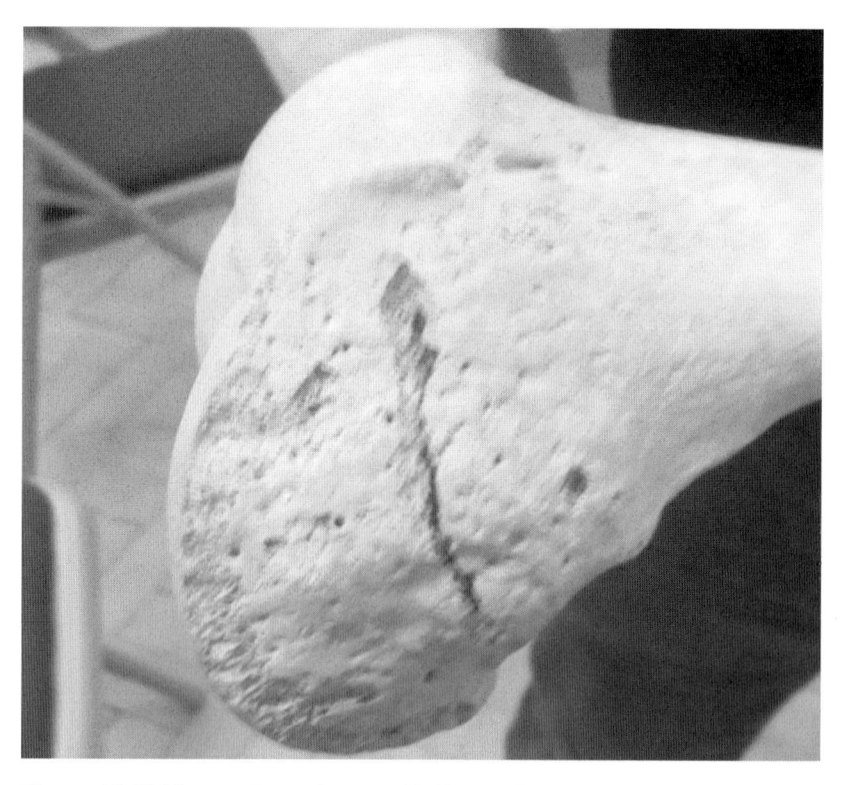

Picture 15. Evidence of sword cut to thighbone of a fifth-century warrior. From Highdown Hill. (Worthing Museum)

Weapons and Warfare of the Fifth and Sixth Centuries

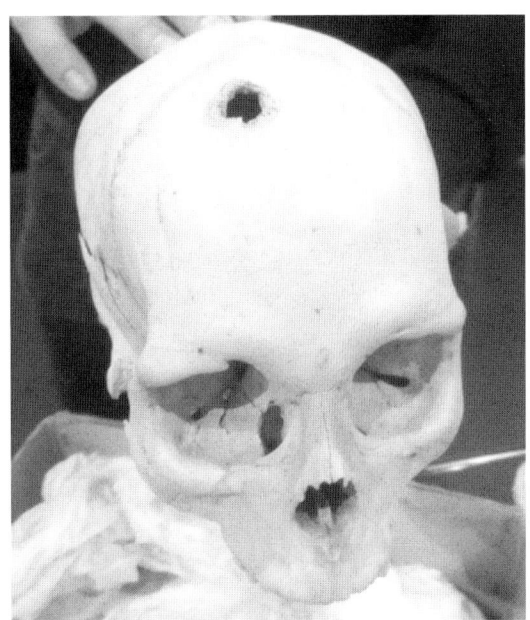

Above left: Picture 16. James Sainsbury, curator at Worthing Museum compares the thighbone of a fifth-century warrior. (Worthing Museum)

Above right: Picture 17. Skull from early Anglo-Saxon period showing likely fatal blow from axe. From Highdown Hill. (Worthing Museum)

Right: Picture 18. Replica of the c. seventh-century Benty Grange helmet. (Wikimedia Commons)

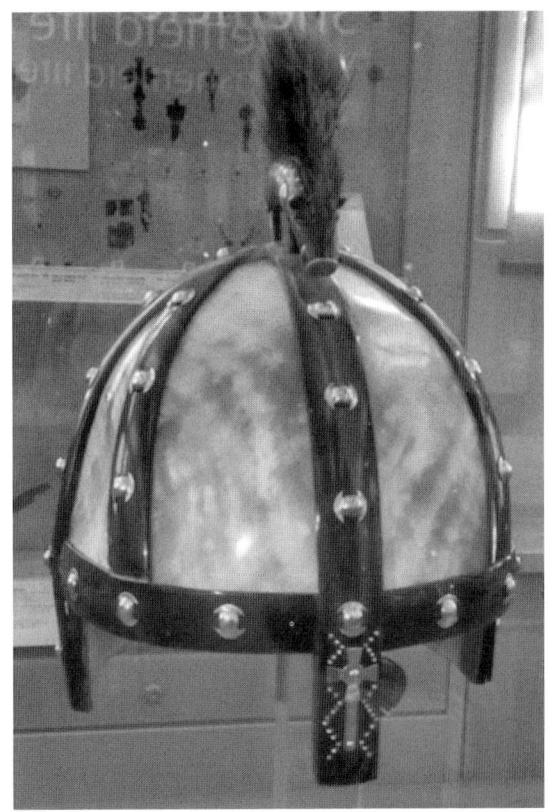

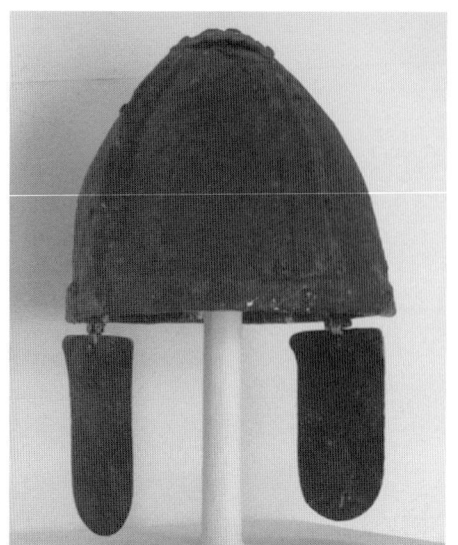

Above left: Picture 19. Spangenhelm (iron), helmet from the Migration Period. (Wikimedia Commons)

Above right: Picture 20. Late Romano-British warrior from fifth century. (Sean Poage, author of 'The Retreat to Avalon')

Left: Picture 21. Dark Age warrior. (Wikimedia Commons)

Weapons and Warfare of the Fifth and Sixth Centuries

Picture 22. Taeppa's Mound, Taplow, Buckinghamshire. (Wikimedia Commons)

Picture 23. Drinking horns, late sixty century from Taplow. (Wikimedia Commons)

Picture 24. Burial mound 2 at Sutton Hoo. (Wikimedia Commons)

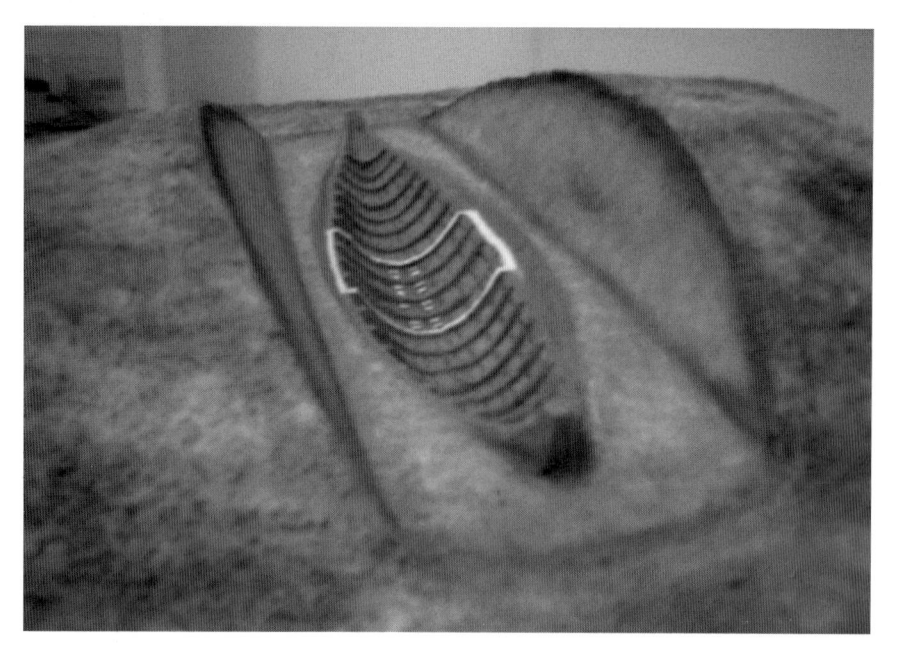

Picture 25. Model of Sutton Hoo ship-burial. (Image by Wikimedia Commons)

Weapons and Warfare of the Fifth and Sixth Centuries

Above: Picture 26. Burial chamber of the Sutton Hoo ship-burial. (Wikimedia Commons)

Right: Picture 27. Replica of Sutton Hoo helmet. (Wikimedia Commons)

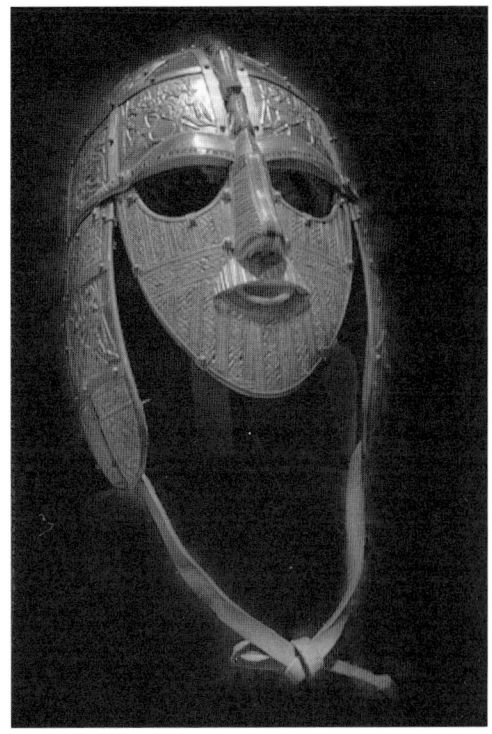

Picture 28. Shield from Sutton Hoo burial mound. (Wikimedia Commons)

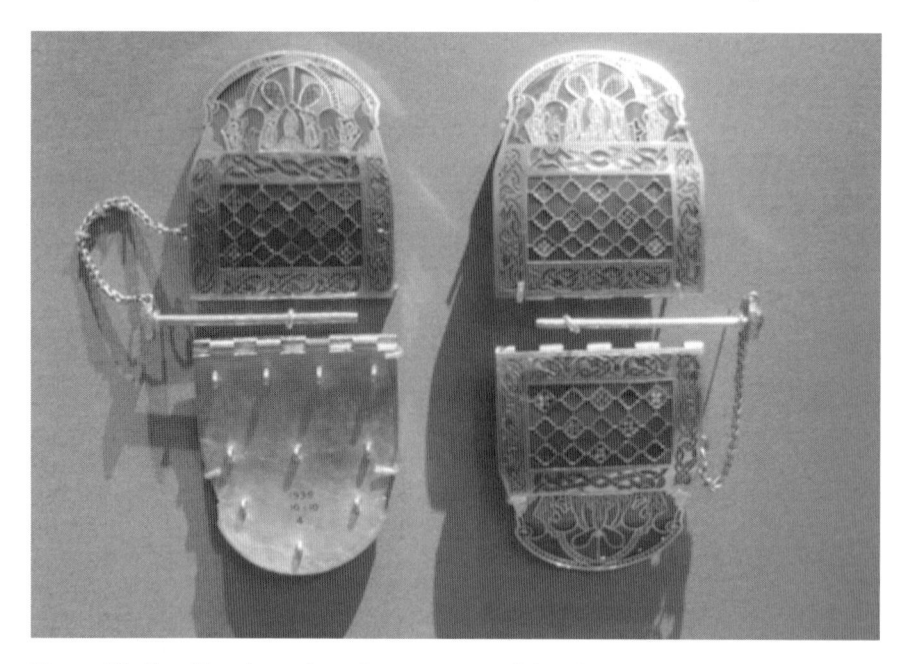

Picture 29. Shoulder clasps from Sutton Hoo. (Wikimedia Commons)

Weapons and Warfare of the Fifth and Sixth Centuries

Above left: Picture 30. Helmet from the seventh-century ship-burial at Vendel. (Wikimedia Commons)

Above right: Picture 31. Migration period sword from Saint-Dizier. (Wikimedia Commons)

Picture 32. Anglo-Saxon warriors from the migration period. (Yahushan Ram, Seaxia Dark Ages Re-enactment Group)

The Early Anglo-Saxon Kings

Above left: Picture 33. Anglo-Saxon warrior. (Yahushan Ram, Seaxia Dark Ages Re-enactment Group)

Above right: Picture 34. Anglo-Saxon warrior. (Yahushan Ram, Seaxia Dark Ages Re-enactment Group)

Picture 35. Two early period Anglo-Saxon warriors. (Yahushan Ram, Seaxia Dark Ages Re-enactment Group)

Chapter Five

The Empire Strikes Back

'Ambrosius Aurelianus … under him our people regained their strength, and challenged the victors to battle. The Lord assented and the battle went their way'.

Gildas, DEB, chapter 25, sixth century

'Then Arthur fought against them in those days, together with the kings of the British; but he was their dux erat bellorum [leader in battle].'

HB, chapter 56, ninth century.

We have read how post-Roman Britain experienced a significant economic shock alongside a period of de-urbanisation and increased cultural change and Germanic immigration. The GC seems to confirm the main thrust of the other sources. An event occurred that caused a significant part of the former diocese to 'fall to the power of the Saxons'. The HB describes the first fight back was by Vortimer, son of the infamous Vortigern. However, neither Gildas and Bede mention him. In contrast, the HB gives a slightly different narrative to the revolt of mercenaries in these earlier sources. Instead, there is a massacre at a peace conference after which various regions are ceded to Hengest. We have already covered Vortimer in chapter two but what of the man both Gildas and Bede credit for leading the fight back against the barbarians?

Gildas is our first source that names Ambrosius Aurelianus. The 'impious easterners' devastated town and country 'from sea to sea … licking the western ocean with its fierce red tongue'. All the major towns were 'laid low', and 'church leaders, priests and people alike' were left to rot in town squares. Some people emigrated, others were 'caught in the mountains and butchered wholesale', and some surrendered, 'fated to be slaves forever'. The 'cruel plunderers' returned home, presumably to the east of the island. We then read 'after a time', and are left to speculate what timeframe Gildas is referring to? The survivors gathered together and we get the first and only glimpse of our hero: their leader was Ambrosius Aurelianus, 'a modest man who, perhaps alone of the Romans had survived the shock of this storm'. His parents had been killed in these upheavals and we learn they had 'worn the purple'. Some have speculated his family were related to one of the emperors, Magnus Maximus or Constantine III for example. But this could refer to someone of senatorial class such as a consul or even a bishop.

Saint Ambrose (340–397) was the bishop of Milan and his father may have been Aurelius Ambrosius, a praetorian prefect of Gaul. There are examples of members of the gens Aurelii becoming consul in the fifth century, such as Quintus Aurelius Symmachus who was consul with Flavius Aetius in 446. His son, Quintus Aurelius Memmius Symmachus, was consul in 485. It is possible Ambrosius Aurelianus was a member of, or adopted by, someone of the Aurelii.

We recall Gildas describes one of his tyrant kings, Aurelius Conanus, as 'thou lion's whelp'. He also states the descendants of Ambrosius have 'become greatly inferior to their grandfather's excellence'. A comment that ties in well with the interpretation of forty-four years having passed. We have another example from the life of a sixth-century saint from South Wales who is recorded as one of the seven founding saints of Brittany and a bishop of the See of Léon. According to his ninth-century hagiography Paulinus Aurelianus, or Paul Aurelian, was the son of the ruler of Penychen in Glamorgan. Interestingly, his father's name, Porphyrius, means 'clad in purple'.

From Gildas we can discern three things. First, Ambrosius was considered to be 'Roman' by Gildas and it is worth noting the distinction he makes between those he describes as Roman and those as his 'countrymen'. He describes Britain in the time of Maximus as being 'Roman in name, but not by law or custom'. Maximus himself is a 'sprig of its own bitter planting'. The Romans offer help but eventually go back 'home'. He makes repeated distinctions between Britons and barbarians, but Ambrosius is neither. Whether he was actually Roman, or the last of the Romans is debatable. The second point is that Ambrosius is very likely Christian. It was the official religion of the empire but given Gildas's rhetoric and outlook, it is extremely unlikely he would praise someone who wasn't. Last, the Britons were willing and able to resource and fight a successful war and win battles against Germanic armies.

The next section of the text is perhaps the most hotly debated. Under Ambrosius 'our people regained their strength ... and the battle went their way'. A first victory, but then victory went back and forth, 'now to our countrymen now to their enemies'. This carried on: 'up to the siege of Badon Hill, pretty well the last defeat of the villains and certainly not the least. That was the year of my birth; ... one month of the forty-fourth year since then has already past.' The question arises, does this mean forty-four years has passed since Badon, or the first victory of Ambrosius?

If we take a literal translation without attempts by modern translators at punctuation, it would be even less clear:[1] '... now citizens now the enemies were victorious ... up to the year of the siege of Mount Badon almost the last defeat of the rascals and by no means the least one month of the forty-fourth year as I know having passed which was of my birth'.

We will discuss the dating and possible location of Badon a little later. Can we interpret this as meaning Ambrosius was the victor at Badon? This is indeed one possible explanation. However, it could equally mean Ambrosius won the first victory but the war went back and forth for some considerable time. Interestingly, Welsh tradition never associates the battle with Ambrosius. There, Gildas leaves us concerning Ambrosius. The only date we have in his narrative is the death of Magnus Maximus, who we know died in 388. We then get a presumably considerable timeframe that includes constant raids, an appeal (which *if* to Aetius in c. 446 gives us another date), the hiring of mercenaries and a subsequent revolt. If Gildas can be dated to the second quarter of the sixth century *and* we interpret the forty-four years as having passed since Badon, then we can place it c. 490s. This would allow us to estimate the floruit of Ambrosius Aurelianus to the last quarter of the fifth century. Given the GC gives our earliest estimate of a shift in power to the Saxons, then his earliest floruit would be after c. 450.

In terms of location Gildas tells us the first arrivals 'fixed their dreadful claws on the east side of the island'. A second larger group arrived and joined up with the first 'false units'. The revolt spread from sea to sea and then they returned to the east. One might expect a fight back to be 'in the east'. But this wouldn't prevent further attacks from 'sea to sea'. Gildas also states the war left his countrymen unable to visit the shrines of the martyrs, notably that of St Alban, in the modern town of the same name. There is some debate about the nature of this passage: 'the holy martyrs, whose tombs for their bodies and places of suffering now, if they had not been taken from the citizens through the grievous divorce from the barbarians [lugubri divortio barbarorum]'. Some have translated this as 'unhappy partition'. This would imply a border of some sort. However a more accurate translation of *divortio barbarorum* would be as above, a 'divorce', which implies the breaking of an agreement. If this is the case then no single border can be assumed. Yet Gildas is adamant he cannot access certain sites, St Albans and the graves of Aaron and Julius, 'citizens of Caerleon'. The interpretation leading to Caerleon is also disputed but this is rather academic as it is their graves and not their birthplace that are inaccessible. In addition, there is no clear indication the graves are inaccessible because of destruction or the presence of the 'barbarians'.

We also don't know where Gildas is writing from. Later, *Saints' Lives* links his family to the far north, yet his five tyrant kings all seem to be from the (perhaps) former province of Britannia Prima. It is also worth noting that the earliest evidence of Germanic material culture and settlement all come from south of the Humber. On the other hand, the north is a likely location in which to place mercenaries to defend from Picts and Irish raiders.

Bede, writing 200 years later, follows Gildas for much of his narrative. The first group of mercenaries are settled in 'the eastern part of the island'. But the larger group received a 'grant of land in their midst'. This of course could mean anywhere but towns such as Lincoln, Chester, York and forts along Hadrian's Wall would be likely locations. Once more the revolt covered 'almost the whole face of the doomed island' from 'the east to the western sea'. Ambrosius is a 'discreet man' and 'the sole member of the Roman race who had survived'. His parents perished in the storm and 'bore a royal and famous name'. Again we read of a victory won 'with God's help' and battles going back and forth. At this point Bede seems to interpret Gildas rather differently: 'the siege of Mount Badon, when the Britons slaughtered no small number of their foes about forty-four years after their arrival in Britain'. He may well have had access to other sources or an earlier version of Gildas's manuscript. If so, given Bede dates the *adventus saxonum* to c. 449, we can date Badon to c. 493. Unfortunately we cannot be sure he hasn't mis-interpreted Gildas. We do, however, get another clue concerning dating. In his earlier *Chronica Majora* Bede dates Ambrosius to 'the time of Zeno', the Eastern Roman Emperor, 474–91.

We learn nothing more about Ambrosius from Bede. Nor does he appear in the AC. The HB gives us a very different Ambrosius. After Hengest has received Kent in return for his daughter's hand, another forty ships arrive with Octha and Ebissa, fight the Picts, and are given land in the north. St Germanus then berates Vortigern for having a child with his own daughter. The king flees and later we read Vortimer is fighting his four battles. But at this point in the tale, Vortigern attempts to build a castle in Gwynedd, North Wales, which repeatedly collapsed. His 'wizards' tell him he must sacrifice a 'child without a father'. His men travel to Glywysing in South Wales, find a such a boy and take him to Vortigern. When learning of his potential fate the boy tells the king his wizards are wrong and he reveals the reason why the castle keeps collapsing. Two 'worms' lay underneath the castle, one red, one white, causing the collapse. These were discovered and the king asks the boy his name: 'I am called Ambrosius … My father is one of the consuls of the Roman people.' Ambrosius then makes various prophecies and from this, the legend of the two dragons is born. Geoffrey of Monmouth later fused the character with the sixth-century figure from Welsh tradition, Myrddin Wylit, to form part of his composite character Merlin. He introduced this figure in the twelfth century.

According to the HB Vortigern ceded the fortress and the western part of the island to 'Emrys the overlord' before heading north to the region called Gwynessi. This is clearly the same Ambrosius as in Gildas but there is no association with battles of Badon. Instead the HB later attributes twelve battles, including Badon, to Arthur. Here though is a very different Ambrosius from Gildas and Bede. He's associated with South Wales and with Vortigern. Vortigern in turn is connected to North Wales and allegedly descended from the founder of Gloucester. The Pillar of Eliseg, erected in the ninth century in Denbighshire, connects him with Powys.

The HB refers to Ambrosius in a later chapter: 'From the reign of Vortigern to the quarrel between Vitalinus and Ambrosius are twelve years, that is Guoloppum, the battle of Guoloppum.' This is thought to be Wallop in Hampshire, but the date is unknown. Is it twelve years from the start or end of his reign, and which of the many dates in the HB should we use? The text also gives us Vortigern's genealogy working backwards: 'Vortigern "the thin", Vitalis, Vitalinus, Gloiu who built … Gloucester'. So we see a Vitalinus was Vortigern's grandfather, yet in the tale above Ambrosius is a boy when Vortigern is king. Some have suggested an elder and younger Ambrosius, Vortigern or both. Others suggest Vortigern was a title and Vitalinus his name. After Vortigern's death we read that his son Pascent ruled in Builth and Gwertherynion 'by permission of Ambrosius who was the great king among all the kings of the British nation'.

These three sources appear to support a number of points. First, Ambrosius Aurelianus was considered Roman. This might reflect how the bulk of the population viewed the aristocratic elite. At the very least he came from a prominent family, one who had 'worn the purple'. He is associated with locations in the south and west, from Hampshire to Wales. The five tyrant kings of Gildas all appear to be from the same area, the former western province of Britannia Prima. One could speculate that is where he is writing from and this might point to the location of the fight back led by Ambrosius and the subsequent victory at Badon. In Wiltshire, Amesbury might be an echo of his name. A ninth-century record names it Ambresbyrig, possibly 'the burgh of Ambrosius'. It was later used as a 'royal villa' by the kings of Wessex. The Domesday Book names it Amblesberie. There are other sites in the south such as Ambrosden in Oxfordshire and Amberley in both Gloucestershire and Herefordshire. While all these are speculative, it does seem that Ambrsosius Aurelianus was active in the south of the island at least.

Geoffrey of Monmouth, writing c. 1136, gives us much more information, although it's hardly trustworthy. Confusingly, Geoffrey names him Aurelius Ambrosius, the son of a Breton prince. Constantine is the brother of King Aldoneous, the great-grandson of its alleged founder, Conanus Meriodocus, who Geoffrey claims was placed there by Magnus Maximus. (This is clearly not to be confused with Constantine III. The only similarity is that they both have a son called Constans.) He is invited over to take the throne of Britain. Geoffrey thus appears to date the father of Aurelius as being an adult in the mid-fifth century. This seems to fit with the only date he does give, which is the death of Arthur at the battle of Camlan. Working backwards one can estimate Arthur's birth to be after c. 500 according to Geoffrey. His father, Uther, lives a long life and dies when Arthur is 15. Uther took the throne when his brother Aurelius died. We can thus estimate their floruits.

Geoffrey seems to be taking Bede's date for the arrival of Hengest. After the death of Constantine his son Constans takes the throne. Constans is assassinated, Vortigern seizes power, and the twin boys Aurelius and Uther, 'still in their cradles', are whisked off to Armorica to keep them safe. It is after this point in the story that Hengest and Horsa arrive. What Geoffrey is implying is that Aurelius Ambrosius, the same Ambrosius Aurelianus of Gildas, was still a child c. 450. He returns to Britain when he reaches adulthood, which would tie in with 'the time of Zeno', 474–91. Aurelius and Uther besiege Vortigern in the castle of Genoreu in South Wales, burning it and its occupants. Aurelius is crowned king, fights two successful battles, Maisbeli and Kaerconan, and has Hengest executed. Interestingly, while he 'rules from York' he allows Hengest's son, Octa, to rule Bernicia in Northumberland.

Next we get the fantastical tale of Merlin magically transporting the giant's ring from Ireland to build Stonehenge as a suitable burial place for the 300 nobles slaughtered by the Saxons. Uther leads an army to Ireland to capture the stones. An enraged Irish king joins forces with a son of Vortigern, Pascent, and invades. The king had fallen ill and Uther leads the army to victory. However, the night before the battle Aurelius, now in Winchester, had been poisoned in his bed.

From Uther's camp in the west a two-headed dragon appeared in the sky with a fiery tail. Geoffrey uses this to explain Uther's title of 'Pendragon'. Interestingly, there is a comet recorded for 497 in a fourteenth-century text, *Flores Historiarum*.

The earliest Welsh legends provide us with a slightly different genealogy for Arthur, and thus Ambrosius. First we have a variety of different versions of Geoffrey's Constantine:[2] Custenin Gornev or Kustennin vendigeit, who are linked to Cornwall.[3] These all post-date Geoffrey, but experts such as Bartrum find there is 'no good reason to doubt the pedigree'. It is possible Geoffrey got his information from existing genealogies and mistook parts of Cornwall for similarly named regions in Brittany.[4]

This allows us to make the following statements about the pedigree of Ambrosius. Firstly Gildas, Bede and the HB all describe him as 'Roman' and his parents being members of the aristocratic elite, either a consul or even related to an imperial family. Geoffrey's tall tale links him to the royal house of Armorica. However, later genealogies persist in connecting him with the south west. Concerning timeframe, all the sources seem to point to the second half of the fifth century, with his military campaign towards the latter end of this period.

Gildas tells us they are now free from 'external wars', but not civil wars. The cities are left 'deserted, in ruins and unkempt'. He praises the generation who witnessed these terrible events as they 'kept to their stations'. But the generation of his day get the full force of his ire. They are ignorant of that 'storm' and only know of the 'calm of the present'. They are rushing 'headlong in to hell'. The first generation are gone and the grandchildren of Ambrosius are adults. This all supports a forty-four year period having passed. Whether this is from his first victory or the battle of Badon is a question to which we will turn next.

The Battle of Badon

It is worth comparing what Gildas and Bede say about the battle. Both describe a war going back and forth up to this point.

> Gildas: 'the siege of Badon Hill, pretty well the last defeat of the villains but certainly not the least'.
>
> Bede: 'the siege of Mount Badon when the Britons slaughtered no small number of their foes'.

The first thing to note is it is described as a siege. The location is a hill or mountain rather than a fort, town or castle. Finally, this is not the last defeat or the least. Gildas gives a date, either forty-four years before the time of writing, or a few years later, after the first victory of Ambrosius. Bede gives us a firm date, forty-four years after Hengest arrived in 449. This leads us to 493, which conveniently supports Gildas writing in c. 537. Neither name the victorious commander, although some might interpret it as being Ambrosius Aurelianus.

The less reliable HB gives us more information, including a new hero: 'The twelfth battle was on Monte Badonis and in it 960 men fell in one day, from a single charge of Arthur's, and no-one laid them low save him alone; and he was victorious in all his campaigns'. It dates the battle, along with eleven others, as sometime between Hengest and Ida. This would suggest a generation either side of c. 500. Arthur seems to be attacking, which might suggest the Britons were besieging the Saxons. The size of the enemy killed might be a literary device; it's certainly an exaggeration for Arthur's personal tally. However, we might very tentatively suggest 960 is roughly the size of a late Roman legion or thirty ships' crews. Could this indicate two cohorts of dis-loyal Germanic mercenaries were besieged and destroyed?

The AC dates it to 516 and describes it as follows: 'The battle of Badon, in which Arthur carried the Cross of our Lord Jesus Christ for three days and three nights on his shoulders and the Britons were the victors.' We can compare this to one of the battles in the HB: 'The eighth battle was in Guinnion fort, and in it Arthur carried the image of the Holy Mary, the everlasting virgin, on his shoulders and the heathen were put to flight on that day, and there was a great slaughter upon them'. It would appear there was a tradition of Arthur carrying an image of Mary into battle, though which battle may have been confused.

Geoffrey of Monmouth describes the Saxons as besieging Bath. Arthur arrives and after a day's fighting the Saxons retreat to a nearby hill and the battle rages on the next day. Unusually for Geoffrey, he doesn't outdo the HB in exaggeration; only 470 Saxons are killed by Arthur's sword Caliburn. His spear, called Rhongomyant, and circular shield, Pridwen, are often forgotten. We get the first mention of the names of the enemy generals: Colgrin and his brother Baldulf and Cheldric. This last possibly a reference to Cerdic, king of the West Saxons in the early sixth century. Given the chronology Geoffrey seems to be dating this slightly later than our previous sources, perhaps c. 520.

There are a number of points we can make. First, Badon is always placed in the same place in the narrative. The Romans leave, followed by continued raiding by Picts and Irish. This causes the Britons to make an appeal for help from the Romans which is rejected. Mercenaries are hired and there follows a subsequent revolt. The GC implies this occurred in c. 440, whereas Bede places it after 449. Some modern scholars, such as Dumville, place this revolt much later. We then learn of a fightback led by Ambrosius Aurelianus and a war that goes back and forth. Badon is 'nearly the last' battle of this war. This might imply a Badon from as early as c. 450 to c. 500. However, the sources that do date Badon place it in c. 493 (Bede) or 516 (AC). If we take HRB date of 542 for Camlan, then we could work back and estimate c. 520 for Badon. From Gildas we can estimate a time of after forty-four years before the date he was writing. I would suggest the most likely timeframe is c. 490–520 depending on which source we trust most. Leaving an exact date to one side, the next important question is where was Badon?

The five kings who receive a tongue-lashing from Gildas are thought to reside in the former province of Britannia Prima. Constantine, 'whelp of the filthy lioness of Damnoniae', could be Dumnonia, centred on modern Devon and Somerset, but might be Damnonia in modern Strathclyde. Aurelius Caninus, 'lion-whelp', could be a Cynan from the genealogies of the kings of Powys. Cuneglasus, 'Bear … Red butcher', might be Cynlas from Rhos, eastern Gwynedd. Maglocunnus is often identified as Maelgwn, king of Gwynedd c. 534–47. Only Vortipor, 'bad son of a good king … tyrant of Demetae', is located with certainty to Dyfed in South West Wales.

The modern historian Nick Higham places Gildas in the western province, in particular the *civitas* of the Durotriges, or around the modern Dorset.[5] Another scholar, Kenneth Jackson, agrees, placing Badon 'somewhere in Wessex'.[6] Chambers too says Badon is 'likely in Wessex'.[7] Two later Saints' Lives of Gildas are of little help. The first from the ninth century was written by a monk in Rhuys, modern Brittany. The second is from the twelfth century written by Caradoc of Llancarfan in Wales. Both place his birth in modern Scotland but place him in either Wales or Somerset as an adult. The first has him writing DEB in Brittany where he is buried. The second has him interceding between Arthur and a King Melwas, and being buried at Glastonbury. Neither can be trusted, but they also fail to mention Badon, Ambrosius, or a war between Britons and Saxons.

Bede is of no help in locating it, but the HB does contain some clues. After the famous battle list there is a section called 'The Wonders of Britain': 'The third wonder is the hot lake, where the baths of Badonis are in country of the Huich.' The Huich are almost certainly the Hwicce, a tribal group that evolved from the *civitas* of the Dobunni, on the east bank of the Severn. It continues: 'It is surrounded by a wall made of brick and stone, and men may go to bathe at any time, and every man can have the kind of bath he likes. If he wants it will be a cold bath and if he wants a hot bath it will be hot.' This would suggest that the author does indeed mean Bath. However, it is not that simple as we shall see although Geoffrey of Monmouth certainly accepted this in his HRB.

In Welsh tradition Bath is often referred to as Caer Faddon. One example is the poem '*Dream of Rhonabwy*' from the fourteenth-century *Red Book of Hergest*. Yet it describes Caer Faddon as half a days ride from Rhyd-y-Groes (the ford of the cross), near Welshpool. This is over 100 miles north of Bath, causing some to suggest Breidden Hill, an iron age hill fort, a few miles to the east. Some view this poem as a spoof of the HRB and it's worth noting that at the end of the dream Arthur rides for Cornwall and will arrive that very night, suggesting time and place belong in the realm of dreams rather than historical reality. The enemy here is 'Osla Big-Knife', listed as one of Arthur's men in the earlier poem *Culhwch and Olwen*. Perhaps this is a reference to Octha of Kent. Alternatively the Mercian king Offa was known as *Offa Kyllellvawr urenhin Lloegr*, Offa Great-Knife, king of England.

The name 'Badon'

All these later musings could be based on an assumption. The first recorded Anglo-Saxon name for Bath was *Hat Bathu* in a seventh-century charter. Later names include *Badum, Badan* and *Badon*. The Anglo-Saxon Chronicle names it *Badanceastre*. All this suggests both the Anglo-Saxons referred to Bath as Badon as early as the seventh century. Yet Gildas was writing in the sixth century, at least a generation before the ASC records the battle of Dyrham in 577 when Wessex expanded that far west. The HB author in the ninth century might well have accepted the obvious similarity between the sixth-century word Badonis and the ninth-century Anglo-Saxon place-name Badanceastre. But why would Gildas, a Briton writing in Latin, give a later Saxon name to what was then a British town?

The first point to make concerns the actual form of words Gildas uses, Gildas's *Badonici montis*. The 'd' should be a hard 'd' sound, as in 'bad'. This sound would be reflected in Anglo-Saxon 'bad-' type place names like Badbury, or *Baddanbyrig*. There are many similar examples in an arc from Dorset to Lincolnshire. A softer 'th' sound would result from 'dd' and hence 'Baddon'. Old English would have had its own letter to represent this Old Welsh 'dd' or soft 'th' sound: 'ð' as in Baðon, which would produce a soft 'th' sound.[8] Bennett and Burkitt, writing in 1985, found that Badan was the most commonly used medieval term for Bath and they see no objection to Gildas dropping a 'd' to Latinise it to Badonis. They also point out that in the seventeenth century, the hill to the north of the Roman City walls were known as Badonca.[9] However, let us assume Gildas did not 'drop a d' and knew exactly what he meant.

The consensus is that Badon was indeed Brittonic and that Gildas was Latinising a Brittonic place name. Badonicus would thus be a Latinised variation of 'Badon'. In Brittonic this may have derived from *boddi* or *baditi*, 'drown/flood/submerge'.[10] This would be similar to old Irish *baided* or badun, 'fortified enclosure'. It's possible that Badon – derived from 'the very wet place' or 'fortified enclosure'. What we don't have is any evidence Bath ever had a Brittonic name resembling that. The Roman name Aquae Sulis derives from 'the waters of Sulis', a local deity whose name may derive from eye or sun. The first Germanic speakers named the town Acemannesceaster. Later names, Baþan or Baþum, mean simply 'at the Baths'. So it might be that the Anglo-Saxons arrived at Baþanceaster independently of any Brittonic influence. If Gildas had Latinised an earlier 'Bath-' type sound, it would be more likely take a different form such as 'bathama'.

Interestingly, we have an example of this from the other Spa town of Roman Britain. Buxton in Derbyshire, *Aqua* Armemetiae, has the Batham Gate Road running north-east towards Doncaster. Surrounded by much larger hills than Bath, it is also closer to Lincolnshire and Chester, which may be relevant in the context the battles list in the HB. If, however, we assume a hard 'd' sound, then we start looking at the very many 'bad-' type names mostly across the South.

Additionally there is a distinction in Latin between a long vs short 'a' sound. This is indicated by a line above the 'a' called a macron, meaning the 'a' Bādon or Badon would sound like the 'a' in father or fatter respectively. If Gildas, or a later copyist, neglected the macron, as often happened, Badon could be Bardon, such as Bardon Hill in Leicestershire. In addition a hard 'd' sound could evolve over time to a 't' sound. This has caused innumerable suggestions from the many Bad – or Barton type names. Bierton in Buckinghamshire is recorded in the Domesday book as *Bortone* meaning 'farmstead near the stronghold'. Bardon or Braydon Forest in Wiltshire; Breedon-on-hill Leicestershire; Baumber in Lincolnshire (called *Badeburg* in the Domesday book); Badbury Rings hill fort in Dorset; Badbury Hill in Berkshire; Badbury (Baddeburi in Old English) and Bedwyn in Wiltshire; Mynydd Baedan near Bridgend in South Wales; Badden west of Loch Lomond in Scotland; and Dumbarton (fort of the Britons) in Scotland to name just a few.

There is one further point worth considering. While there is a lack of archaeological evidence of Germanic material culture and settlement that far west, we don't know what language dominated large parts of lowland England in the fifth century. It is possible, with the posting of Germanic soldiers, notably in the south along the Saxon Shore Command, that a form of early English was already widespread. The Belgae and Atrebates of southern England may have had Germanic roots.

It has been suggested, most recently by Susan Oosthuizen in *The Emergence of the English*, that the origins of the English and thus the language, should rather be sought among late Romano-British communities. It is thus possible an early Frisian or English was widespread across southern Britain over a hundred years before Gildas put pen to paper. If that is the case then there would be nothing to prevent fifth-century locals referring to Bath with a 'Bath' sounding name. It would just require Gildas or a later copyist to write one 'd' instead of two, a common error of the time.

Leaving an exact location to one side, we have seen there's a fairly broad consensus among scholars that it is in the south. Kenneth Jackson, writing in 1959, placed it somewhere on a border, perhaps near Salisbury Plain, and suggests: Badbury, Swindon; Badbury Hill, Farringdon; or Badbury Rings, Blandford.[11] There are in fact many other 'bad-' type names on or near a Gewissae/Brittonic border. We have one further clue that may allow us more confidence as to a general area.

The AC record for the year 665 states as follows: 'The first celebration of Easter among the Saxons. The second battle of Badon. Morgan dies.' Who Morgan is and what, if any, connection there might be, is unknown. Nor can we tell if this is at the same location or a reference to a similar defeat of the 'Saxons'. Someone today naming something a 'second Dunkirk' or 'second D-Day' could mean any number of things. Only one version, the A text, mentions the battle. Yet both the A and B texts refer to the first celebration of Easter among the Saxons and place it four years before the death of Oswy, king of Northumbria (died 670).

There is one ASC entry that may be synonymous. The year 661:

> This year, at Easter, Kenwal fought at Posentes Bryg [Posent's stronghold]; and Wulfere, the son of Penda, pursued him as far as Ashdown. Cuthred, the son of Cwichelm, and King Kenbert, died in one year. Into the Isle of Wight also Wulfere, the son of Penda, penetrated, and transferred the inhabitants to Ethelwald, king of the South-Saxons, because Wulfere adopted him in baptism. And Eoppa, a mass-priest, by command of Wilfrid and King Wulfere, was the first of men who brought baptism to the people of the Isle of Wight.

So the only 'first celebration of Easter among the Saxons' for this time was in the Isle of Wight and Sussex. The question arises was this raid by Wulfhere the same conflict in which the second battle of Badon occurred?

Posentes Bryg could be Posbury near Exeter in Devon, but this seems unlikely as it's too far west and nowhere near any likely battles involving Mercians. A better location might be Pontesbury a few miles south-west of Shrewsbury. This might suggest a raid by Kenwal into Mercian territory. No victor is declared, but the Wessex king seems to be on the back foot after the battle. Wulfhere pursues him deep into Wessex territory.

Wulfhere's father was Penda and a generation before Cadwallon of Gwynedd had joined forces with Penda to defeat Edwin of Northumbria at the Battle of Haethfelth (possibly Hatfield Chase, Yorkshire). In 655, at the Battle of Winwaed, Penda was accompanied by 'thirty royal ealdormen'. One of these was Cadfael of Gwynedd who escaped the defeat with his army, 'rising up in the night', earning him the title 'Cadfael the battle dodger.' Immortalised in the Welsh Triads 'The three faithless/disloyal war-bands of the island of Britain.' Thus we have a tradition of early Mercians and Britons being in alliance; an entry in the AC with elements synonymous with parts of an ASC entry; with one mentioning a second battle of Badon and the other a raid 'as far as Ashdown'. Here we have a possible source for the AC entry. Not Cadfael the battle dodger, but perhaps another British prince or king accompanying Penda's son against Wessex.

Where then is Ashdown? Unfortunately this is a fairly common name and there is an example in Sussex and Wiltshire to name but a few. An Anglo-Saxon charter from the mid-tenth century, the will of Ealdorman Æthelwold, included bequests of land to the bishop and episcopal community at Winchester. One example was Æscesdune in Berks. Given that the South Saxon king is persuaded to receive baptism by Wulfhere one might assume it is Ashdown Forest in Sussex. However, one further clue is also in the ASC for the year 648, just thirteen years before Wulfhere's raid and also involving Kenwal of Wessex: 'This year Kenwal gave his relation Cuthred three thousand hides of land by Ashdown. Cuthred was the son of Cwichelm, Cwichelm of Cynegils'. This would suggest this Ashdown is in Wessex and the Wiltshire example near Swindon is a strong candidate. Whatever the case, a raid 'as far as Ashdown' from Mercia could easily pass through several of the most likely locations for Badon.

At the very least, if the AC entry is synonymous with the ASC entry it places Badon in the south, specifically the Wessex area, which falls into line with where it is suspected Ambrosius Aurelianus was operating and Gildas was writing. Another possibility occurs in the ASC five years after Oswy's death rather than before as the AC states. 675: 'Here Wulfhere, Penda's offspring, and Escwine, fought at Bedan [or Biedan] Heafde.' Bedan or Biedanheafde is translated as Bieda's or Beda's Head but unfortunately hasn't been located as either. It would require a convoluted etymology to get from Badonicus to Biedanheafde and it isn't thought to be a candidate.

The Early Anglo-Saxon Kings

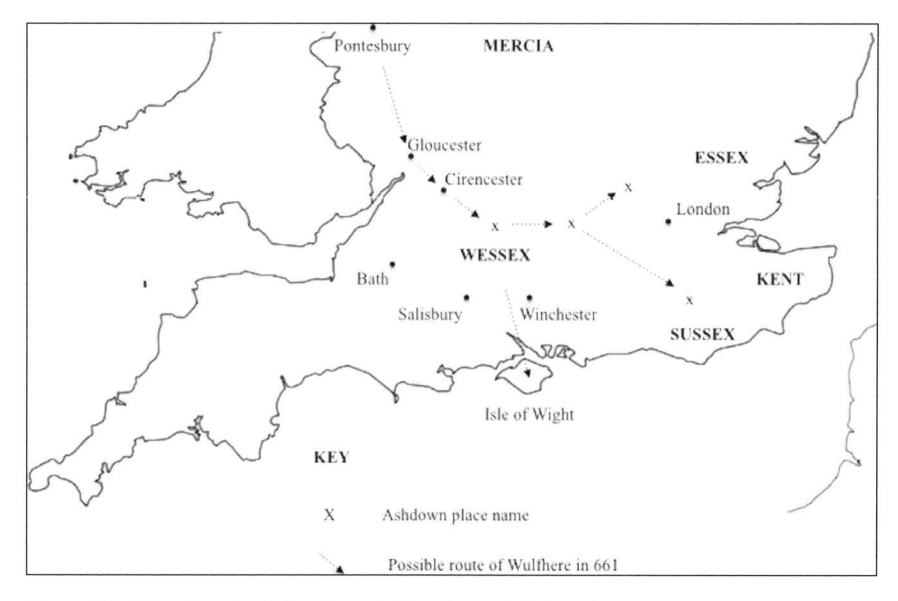

Figure 21. Map showing Mercian raid 'as far as Ashdown'.

In summary, the exact location of Badon has proven elusive. Bath may well have been a medieval assumption. This leads us to a large number of alternatives involving a, ar, ea, ae, ie, ee sounds followed by a hard 'd' or 't' with any number of endings. Yet through this mist we get some clues. It appears to be southern and most likely in the Wessex area. The consensus of academics, the likely zone of operations for Gildas and Ambrosius and the archaeology of the late fifth, and early sixth, centuries all point to this area. My best guess would be one of the hills around Bath, which may require earlier Germanic language presence than we currently have evidence for. Or Gildas, or a copyist, neglecting to write a double 'dd'. I am far more confident in pointing to the Wessex area as the site of any likely border that would prevent Gildas accessing shrines further east. This becomes interesting when placed in the context of the HB's battle list.

Arthur and the battle list

I have covered the evidence for and against a historical Arthur in my previous book, *King Arthur Man or Myth*. It is quite possible he was purely a mythical figure, invented by fifth-century Welsh bards. Indeed the earliest Welsh tradition does paint a more magical and darker figure than the chivalry hero of the medieval French Romances. If, however, he was a historical figure, it is worth repeating the three options for his likely floruit: an early Arthur, c. 450–480; and middle Arthur, c. 480–510; or a late Arthur c. 510–540. Which option we choose is important given the historical context. An early Arthur may be operating in the context of a surviving provincial and *civitas* structure alongside a political and military organisation. A later Arthur would be living in a world of emerging petty kingdoms and war-bands with little, if any, of the Roman political, social or military structures present.

Another interesting point is that the Welsh tradition rarely associates Arthur with his most famous battle, in fact he isn't portrayed as fighting Saxons at all. Rather he fights giants, witches and monsters, and raids Ireland and the underworld for magic cauldrons and other treasures. The HB, however, presents us with both a historical character, '*dux erat bellorum*' (leader in battle), and a more magical figure in the later 'Wonders of Britain' with magical stones and graves. Many do not accept the battle list as genuine, but it is useful exercise to consider the implications of taking it at face value.

In my second book, *The Battles of King Arthur*, I did just that. I do not claim to have identified all the battles. However, there is a consensus from scholars about some of them even if they disagree over whether it reflects a genuine Old Welsh battle poem. The battles are as follows:

1. At the mouth of the River *Glein*.
2–5. The River *Dubglas* or *Duglas* in *Regione Linnuis*.
6. River *Bassas*.
7. *Silua Celidonis* also called *Cat Coit Celidon*.
8. *Castellum Guinnion*.
9. *Urbe Legionis*.
10. River *Treuroit*, *Tribruit* or *Ribroit*.
11. *Monte Agned Cat Bregomion* or *Monte Breguoin*.
12. *Monte Badonis*

For some there are small clues. Glein is possibly the Northumberland Glein mentioned by Bede for 627, or the Lincolnshire river of the same name. Bassas might be Baschurch in Shropshire, or any number of the 'Bas-' type names from Lincolnshire to Hampshire. The battles at castle Guinnion, Tribuit and Breguoin have proved impossible, although northern sites are perhaps the most promising. For the latter, the Roman fort of Bremenium near High Rochester is the most favoured. However, four of the battles are almost certainly in Lincolnshire. The exact location of the River Dubglas is academic, as Linnuis is accepted as deriving from late British *Lindes*, through Old English *Lindissi*, to *Linnes* and then *Linnuis*. Four battles in Lincolnshire makes perfect sense given the distribution of early Germanic material culture and settlement as well as the literary sources referring to mercenaries settled 'in the east of the island'. Battle seven, in *Silua Celidonis*, is also widely accepted as being the forested area in southern Scotland and we have an early reference to the area just north of Hadrian's Wall being called just that. Battle nine is perhaps the easiest to locate. While Chester is usually referred to as *Caer Legionis*, the AC does use the word *urbe*, meaning city. The only other location similarly named is Caerleon in South Wales. This would require a copyist to neglect the 'on-Usk' suffix. No other town or city in Britain is ever referred to in this way. Both Chester and Caerleon have the same alleged problem as Celidonis: They are far away from early evidence of Germanic presence. The last battle, Badon, we have seen is very likely in the South.

I would therefore suggest we can actually locate seven out of the twelve battles. The fact that they are widely dispersed and away from areas of Germanic presence is no reason to dismiss them. First, an Arthur operating from Hadrian's Wall to Lincolnshire, Chester and as far South as the Thames Valley might suggest an earlier Arthur of our three options for his floruit. It might indicate some sort of provincial or military structure has survived. The fact the literary sources state Ambrosius Aurelianus fought an ultimately successful campaign and that the Western Britons held out for many centuries supports the possibility. Figures in the seventh century such as Penda, Cadwallon and the Northumbrian kings campaigned similar distances. There is no reason why someone a hundred years earlier could not.

The idea that lack of archaeological evidence for early Germanic presence is a barrier to these sites does not stand up to scrutiny. At the end of *The Battles of King Arthur* I presented several possibilities: first, a defensive war with Arthur reacting to Germanic incursions and raids either by sea or land. Chester and Caerleon are both accessible by sea and two days' march (or one day's hard ride) from areas with Saxon or Angle settlements. Second, a border war between two distinct polities, for example fragmenting provinces and *civitates* aligning themselves with eastern Germanic-Romano-Britons or western Romano-Britons. Perhaps religious schisms even between Christians, such as Pelagianism and Arianism. Third, he could be a roving war-band leader fighting in a range of campaigns from Irish or Pictish raiders to civil wars across different areas and the battle poem remembers the place-names but not the enemies. Last, a war of ethnic cleansing with Arthur clearing out Germanic settlers and/or *foederati* within Romano-British *civitates*.

This option would fit the literary sources and follow the narrative of the HB. Vortigern posts mercenaries to fight off Pitcish and Irish raiders. Hengest is given Kent, and Octha and Ebissa are given land 'in the north about the Wall...'. Chester, Caerleon, Lincolnshire, Saxon Shore forts and the Thames Valley are all likely places for mercenaries to be posted. According to the HB Octha comes from the north to Kent and then Arthur fights his battles. It is telling none of the likely locations are in the south-east where Octha now rules. No mention of London, seemingly abandoned in the mid-fifth century. Nothing to suggest any of the Saxon Shore forts or ports of the Kent coast. Nor the *civitas* capitals at Canterbury or Chichester.

Instead we have four battles in Lincolnshire, where we have strong evidence of a ring of Germanic settlements around the provincial capital at Lincoln. One battle near Hadrian's Wall, where some of Octha's men may still have resided. Another at Chester (or Caerleon), former legionary bases, ideal locations from which to defend the western coasts from Irish raids. Lastly, a battle somewhere in the Thames Valley

1. At the mouth of the River *Glein*: River Glen, Northumberland
2-5. The River *Dubglas* or *Duglas* in *Regione Linnuis*: A river in Lindsey.
6. River *Bassas*: Baschurch
7. *Silua Celidonis* also called *Cat Coit Celidon*: Forest near Clyde and Tweed
8. *Castellum Guinnion*: Vinovium Roman Fort at Binchester
9. *Urbe Legionis*: Chester
10. River *Treuroit, Tribruit* or *Ribroit*: In border region of Gododdin.
11. *Monte Agned Cat Bregomion* or *Monte Breguoin*: Bremenium Roman Fort.
12. *Monte Badonis*: Bath or Wessex area.

Figure 22. Map showing most likely locations of Arthur's battles. Camlan, numbered 13, has been added to the 12 battles of the HB.

close to areas of significant Germanic presence and the centre of Gewissae, and later West Saxon, power. This last one is very likely a hill-fort, since it is described as a siege and a hill. The map in figure 22 shows the most likely sites. I have highlighted the four locations and seven battles which we can be reasonably confident about.

We must consider the possibility that the situation was far more nuanced than once thought. This may not have been a simple Britons versus Saxons conflict. Instead we have emerging and diverging cultural identities. Gildas may well have seen the world in black and white with barbarian Saxons on one side and Christian Britons on the other. But the truth might be closer to a civil war type situation with ethnicity, religion, class and politics all influencing people and events in different ways. Gildas himself tells us that civil wars continue.

The Battle of Llongborth

A thirteenth-century Welsh poem, *Elegy to Geraint*, refers to a battle at Llongborth which not only mentions Arthur, or rather his men, but also Geraint, who features in Arthurian legends. There are numerous references to horses, 'swift chargers … under the thigh of Geraint' which suggests a cavalry engagement.

> In Llongborth I saw Arthur's
> Heroes who cut with steel.
> The Emperor, ruler of our labour.
>
> In Llongborth Geraint was slain,
> A brave man from the region of Dyvnaint,
> And before they were overpowered, they committed slaughter.

There may be a link in the *Irish life of Finnian of Clonard*. The Irish annals date his death to c. 549 although another Finnian (of Moville) is dated to c. 579. The *Betha Fhindein* survives in a collection of saints' lives known as *The Book of Lismore*, taken from a fifteenth-century manuscript.[12]

> Once upon a time Saxons came to ravage the Britons. They pitched a camp on the side of a lofty mountain. The Britons betook themselves to Findian to ask for a truce for them from the Saxons. Findian went on the service. The Saxons gave him a refusal. Findian gave a blow of his staff on the mountain, so that the mountain fell on the Saxons, and not a man of them escaped to tell the tale.

It is suggested that one interpretation is 'they [the Saxons] captured longphort near a tall mountain'. The argument is that we have an Irish source placing a battle on a mountain just after the Saxons capture Llongphort. Additionally, the ASC entry for 501 states: 'Here Port and his two sons, Bieda and Maegla, came with two ships to Britain at the place which is called Portsmouth, and immediately seized land and killed a certain young British man, very noble'. Some have argued that this reference is synonymous with the battle in the *Elegy to Geraint*. This would make Llongphort or Longborth possibly Portchester at the head of Portsmouth harbour. It has the longest and most continuous occupation of the Saxon Shore Forts.[13] Alternatively, and possibly more likely etymologically, it is Langport on the River Parrett in Somerset. Although this appears too far west. Bieda may be linked to Biedan or Bedan Heafde in the entry for 675. Interestingly, like Cerdic, Maegla is thought to be a British name.[14]

The theory is that we can interpret these sources as meaning the Saxons defeated an initial force led by Geraint at Llongphort. Subsequently they encamped on a mountain nearby, where they were destroyed. A neat theory which is undermined by the lack of mountains in Hampshire and the absence of any reference to Arthur in the *Life of Finnian*. Not to mention any reference to Finian in any sources referring to Badon.

From Camlan to Catraeth

Sandwiched between his long rant about the woefulness and wickedness of the Britons and the five tyrant kings, Gildas tells us about the fightback at Badon. But even here he can't confine himself to a positive comment about the great victory. A new generation are rushing 'headlong to hell', and while external wars have ended, civil ones have not. The implication is that such conflict was, and continues to be, endemic. If Gildas was writing in the second quarter of the sixth century as suspected, then he very likely was aware of one of our most famous battles. It may come as surprise to learn we can be almost as confident as Camlan as we can about Badon. Unlike this later battle Arthur is always associated with it and there are enough references to it to lead us to accept its historicity.

The AC entry for 537 reads: 'The battle of Camlann, in which Arthur and Medraut fell: and there was plague in Britain and Ireland.' Text A of the annals records it as *Gueith cam lann* with the last 'n' added. Text B gives us *Bellum camlam*. Geoffrey of Monmouth spells it *Camblan* and other Welsh sources give us *Gamlan*. It has proved as difficult to locate as many of the other battles, but the likely candidates are once again in the west or north. This is also discussed in *The Battles of King Arthur*, but as *Cam lann* is likely derived from 'crooked/twisting enclosure', it could be anywhere. Suggestions include Cambuslang south of Glasgow; Camelon near Falkirk; Camboglanna on Hadrian's Wall; the River Gamlan in Wales; and various Camlan type names surviving on maps on the Powys–Gwynedd border that can be traced back to the sixteenth-century lordship of Mawddwy.

The Welsh Triads mention the battle in various places:[15] Camlann is described as one of the three 'futile battles'. Mordred is one of the three men of shame and copies the narrative from the HRB. Interestingly, another triad states it was caused by the contention between Gwenhwyfar and her sister Gwenhwyfach rather than their husbands. The three violent ravagings describe how Mordred came to Arthur's court at Celliwig and dragged Gwenhwyfar from her chair and struck her. This is followed by Arthur coming to Mordred's court and 'leaving neither food nor drink in the court or the cantref'; The three faithless war-bands of Britain concerns one that left the night before; the three unfortunate counsels include Arthur's threefold division of the men with Mordred at Camlann. A fourteenth-century code of Welsh laws states when the queen wills it, 'let the bard sing a song respecting Camlann'.[16]

The HB fails to mention Camlan, but we have already covered the apparent civil war between Ambrosius and Vitalinus as well as Vortimer taking power from his father. The HRB has Ambrosius and Uther fighting a war against Vortigern before turning on the Saxons. Back in the HB there is a brief mention of another warrior who, like Vortimer and Arthur, 'fought bravely against the English…'. No further information about Outigern is given, but he seems to be a little later than Arthur as he is placed alongside the poets Aneirin and Taliesin, as well as Maelgwn of Gwynedd. In the next chapter we see a list of the kings of Bernicia starting from Ida. Taking the dates as accurate, one of his sons, Theodoric, reigned in the 570s. During his reign we read that four British kings fought against him with a familiar 'sometimes the enemy, sometimes our countrymen were victorious'. Urien, Rhydderch Hen, Gwallag and Morcant blockade the Angles on the island of Lindisfarne. The first three of these kings are recorded in the later genealogies of Rheged, Alt Clut and Elmet. It would seem the Angles were at risk of being pushed into the sea. Yet events conspired against the northern Britons. Morcant was jealous of Urien's military skill and generalship and arranged for his assassination.

If we accept this account, then the Angles of Bernicia were relatively weak and various British polities vied for control. We get another tale of civil strife in the AC entry for 573: 'The battle of Arfderydd between the sons of Eliffer and Gwenddolau son of Ceidio; in which Gwenddolau fell; Merlin went mad.' According to the genealogies, *Bonedd Gwŷr y Gogledd* (The Descent of the Men of the North), the sons of Eliffer and Gwenddolau were cousins and descendants of Coel Hen, a legendary figure from Welsh tradition in the fourth century. Welsh sources make Merlin, or Myrddin, an adversary of Rhydderch Hen.

Further evidence of civil wars might be seen when comparing the statement by Gildas with the ASC entries regarding Wessex. As we shall see in the next chapter, there is some debate over whether the entry for the arrival of Cerdic and Cynric in 495 are too early and should in fact be dated to c. 532. However, the fact remains that both these dates, and thus the subsequent battles, are before Gildas was likely writing. If that is the case, how can we account for the statement regarding the absence of external wars alongside the ASC list of battles? Perhaps Gildas is only referring to the province of Britannia Prima. However, another possibility is that Gildas did not regard Cerdic as a Saxon at all.

Another famous battle likely occurred after Gildas wrote DEB. Traditionally the battle of Catraeth has been dated to c. 600, but there is some evidence to suggest it was nearer to the mid-sixth century. There is also evidence that it may have been more of a civil war than one between Britons and Angles as is usually portrayed. It also gives us a vivid and entertaining insight into the nature of sixth-century warfare.

Y Gododdin

The *Y Gododdin* may be an authentic seventh-century account, but the earliest copy survives in a thirteenth-century manuscript of the *Book of Aneurin*. The poem is a series of elegies to the men of the Kingdom of Gododdin, centred around Din Eidyn – modern Edinburgh. The warriors are called from all over Britain and feasted for a year by the king, Mynyddog Mwynfawr, in preparation for an attack on the English to the south. In the earliest manuscript only Deira is mentioned, suggesting the battle may pre-date even the establishment of Ida as king of Bernicia c. 547. A force of 300 ride out in a valiant, but doomed, attack that reminds one of the charge of the light brigade in the Crimean War. The target is Catraeth, which is often declared to be Catterick although this is not certain. One rather excellent take on the battle can be seen in the 1988 book, *Men Went to Catraeth*, by John James, which is a first person account by the bard Aneirin.

Traditionally this has been viewed as conflict between Britons and Anglo-Saxons. However, recent analysis of the poem suggests a more nuanced and complex picture. The theory is that Urien of Rheged was the 'Lord of Catraeth' and the Deirians were his allies.[17] It is suggested that in the sixth century, 'warlord animosity' was the determining factor rather than ethnicity. Gildas may well view the world in a stark 'barbarians' versus Britons dichotomy, but perhaps not everyone shared his world view. Clearly not, given his polemic.

John Koch refers to other Welsh poems that may describe the same battle but from the defender's point of view:[18] in *The battle of Gwen Ystrad*, Urien leads the 'men of Cattaeth'; in the *Eulogy of* Cadwallon fierce Gwallawg is blamed for the 'mortality at Catraeth'; later Welsh Genealogies have Urien and Gwallawg as cousins; the HB describes their alliance against the Bernicians with no mention of Deira. An alliance destroyed by Urien's assassination by Morcant. If we take all these sources at face value an interesting sequence of events emerges. First, warriors from Gododdin lead an attack south against Urien, 'lord of Catraeth' and king of Rheged, and the Angles of Deira. Later, Urien leads an alliance with the kings of Elmet and Alt Clut (and Morcant) against the Bernicians at Lindisfarne, where he is murdered by a fellow Briton. A later version of *Y Gododdin* includes the Bernicians with the Deirians but an earlier version does not, leading us to wonder whose side the Bernicians were on and did Ida become the first Angle king of Bernicia before or after the battle?

Let us now turn to the text of *Y Gododdin*. A certain Cydywal leads a contingent of men from Gwynedd and during the battle slays Athrwys and Affrai, two very British sounding names. There is an Athrwys ap Mor in the thirteenth-century genealogy, *Bonedd Gwyr y Gogledd* (descent of the men of the north). He is the grandfather of our protagonists at the battle of Arfderydd in 573, which again might suggest a date closer to the mid-fifth century. We see here more evidence of a complex situation.

Mynyddog Mwynfawr attracts warriors to Din Eidyn from all over Britain: from Eidyn itself; Geraint and the men of Argoed from the south; Isag from 'the southern part'; 'Bubon ... beyond the sea of Iddew' (possibly north of the River Forth and thus a Pict); and Cydywal from Gwynedd. The king feasts them for a year as they gather and prepare. Then 300 set out, 'men went to Catraeth at dawn', but only one returns. Some of the lines mention three hounds and one numbers the warriors to 'three hundred three score and three'. Elsewhere the survivors number three, but we get the picture. A large force rides out to noble defeat with only one, or three, survivors.

The description of the enemy force is inconsistent: the Gododdin are outnumbered 'nine score to one', which equates to 54,000, or 100,000. The Gododdin slay 'seven times their number', (2,100 or 2,541). Or we read, 'Of the men of Deira and Bernicia there fell a hundred score into oblivion in one hour' (2,000). We get the idea. Around 300 warriors ride south (presumably without infantry or support troops) and attack Catraeth, but are met and defeated by a much larger force.

The warriors seem to be organised into various war-bands with 'three kings to the hosts' against the 'crafty Deirans'. Ywain is said to lead the Gododdin. Some warriors are given various animal epithets: Blaen is 'a bear in manner'; Merin, 'scatterer of the deirians … a fearful bear'; and Cibno is called a terrible bear. Boars and eagles also get referenced. We are reminded of Gildas's description of his five tyrants: 'lion-whelp'; 'leopard spotted with wickedness'; 'Bear… red butcher'; 'Dragon of the island'.

We can picture the scene as they left Din Eidyn: 'A host of horsemen in dark blue armour with shields spear shafts held aloft with sharp points' their mail armour is coloured 'blood' and dark blue over crimson under clothes. Spears are yellow, their shields white, 'light and broad' with spear points 'square pointed'. If the *Y Gododdin* is an authentic seventh-century account, then it is the closest contemporary account of a battle between Britons and Saxons.

The battle begins and 'spears were shattered' and we get one of the named warriors: 'Marchlew cast spears in battle from a bounding, wide tracked charger … he threw spears from his steaming slender bay horse.' Eithinyn casts spears between two armies 'before the cattle herds of the eastlands'. We read of the surging fury of the horsemen. Cynon 'with shattered shield … tore through armies his horses swift'. Morien 'set fire to the fleeing horsemen'. We get the impression of an initial cavalry engagement: 'from our successful assault on the day of the mighty charge … the host was broken'. Perhaps this is a synonymous with the three references to an attack on the borderland or at a ford. There appears to be more than one engagement with the first a success for the raiding Gododdin army.

Other parts of the poem point to a bloody infantry battle. They close ranks and form a 'wall of battle'; 'a stronghold of shields' sounding like thunder; Shields are shattered as spearpoints 'tore and cut'; Cadfannan is the 'defender … brandished javelins; the warrior Graid throws 'lances in the forefront of battle in the spear-fight and formed a battle pen against the spears'; the battlefield is a 'place of spears'. This reads very much like a shield wall type battle and we read spears are splintered and shattered, shields broken. Gwid's sword resounds 'above the rampart', which might be an earthwork or fortified position such as Catraeth. But it could also be a literary device to describe a shield wall. There is 'a charge of axe blows and sharpened swords', which must surely be an infantry charge. One sword is described as having a 'blue blade, fringes of worked gold'.

The warrior Gwawrddur 'fed black ravens on the rampart of a fortress' and 'charged before three hundred of the finest. He cut down both centre and wing.' Taking the poem as a whole it would appear the Gododdin won an initial cavalry engagement, possibly at a ford or border. They then attacked the old Roman fort at Catraeth. Perhaps they underestimated the defending force or reinforcements arrived to overpower them.

We get a glimpse into sixth-century warfare. The warriors wear dark blue coloured mail coats over crimson tunics. They carry white, round shields and are armed with yellow spears with square spearheads. They are organised into warbands led by kings, nobles, or the most able warriors. The Britons ride to battle and win an initial skirmish. But the real battle is one of the shield wall. The battle begins with javelins and other missiles. Axes are thrown, spear points clash, shields splintered. Blue bladed, pattern-welded swords flash over shields. Inevitably one side breaks and then the pursuit begins. The Gododdin and their allies are hacked down leaving a sole survivor. John James in his 1988 book has this man as the poet Aneirin, who immortalises the battle in *Y Gododdin*. Who was left the victor? The original author of *Y Gododdin*, and James 1,500 years later, would have us accept it was the Angles of Deira. But perhaps it was Urien of Rheged, 'lord of Catraeth', and his allies from the Brittonic kingdom of Elmet and the Angles of Deira.

One might speculate where these Angles came from. As it happens, we have some evidence to suggest they migrated north across the Humber from Lindsey. In fact the region of the Linnuis might be where the Bernician settlement at Lindisfarne derived its name. A reference to *Lynwyssawr* in the poem could be translated as the 'men of *Linnuis*'. A Brittonic polity, surviving into the sixth century, managed Germanic groups who appeared to have been placed in a defensive ring around the *civitas* capital at Lincoln. Later people from this area settled north in Deira and Lindisfarne. These settlers appear to have taken Germanic material culture and names with them. Yet Lindsey retained a 'Romano-British' identity until quite late.

Case study Lincolnshire

The Roman town of *Lindum*, or the Brittonic name *Lindocolonia*, lay in the former *Civitas Corieltavorum*. This formed the northern part of the province whose capital lay at modern Leicester, *Ratae Corieltavorum*. The name derives from a late British and tribal/district name, *Lindes*, roughly 'the people of the territory of the city of *Lindon*'.[19] Later Anglo-Saxon words, such as Lindisware or Lindisfaran, can be translated as the people who migrated, *faran*, to the territory of the *Lindes*. The Old English speakers thus borrowed the pre-existing Brittonic name. The *regione Linnuis* recorded in the HB is 'beyond reasonable doubt' derived from Late British *Lindes* to Old Welsh *Linnis* and then *Linnuis*.[20]

There is strong evidence that a church built in the centre of the forum at Roman Lindum in the fifth or sixth century was British.[21] An Anglo-Saxon origin is seen as 'not credible'. Instead, it is the likely location of an episcopal see. We know a Bishop Adelphius from Lincoln attended the Council of Arles in 314. The evidence strongly supports the existence of a British Christian community in Lincoln into the sixth century. There were likely British Bishops at other locations such as Gloucester, Lichfield and Exeter before Anglo-Saxon ones.[22]

Late fourth-century Lindum had a considerable population and thriving economy. Similar to other towns, there is evidence of deterioration in urban life toward the end of the fourth century. However, in Lindum we also see evidence of continuation into the fifth century: roads being resurfaced and nearby villas maintained to a high standard, possibly the residence of a the Roman provincial governor.[23] Evidence suggests the arrival of peoples in the early fifth century from North-West Europe in sufficient numbers for us to detect a change in burial customs. At the same time evidence shows a significant amount of population continuation. The distribution of material and burials suggest a defensive ring was formed around the provincial capital and episcopal see.[24]

Caitlin Green, in *Britons and the Anglo-Saxons, Lincolnshire 400–650 AD*, found that the 'boundary between the fourth-century provinces centred on Lincoln and London broadly corresponds with the archaeological observers boundary between 'Anglian' and 'Saxon' cultural areas in the fifth century'.[25] The implication appears to be that the provinces remained intact and in control. There is much archaeological evidence for post-Roman British continuation in specific areas.[26] We can thus make the following points:[27]

- There was little post-Roman reforestation in lowland Britain.
- We see a shift from arable to pastoral farming and away from intensive farming such as large scale grain crops.
- Continuation of Roman-era field systems and boundaries into the medieval period.
- Most areas remained almost as densely settled.

A ring of sites showing Germanic material presence and burials start to appear from the mid-fifth century. Their positioning, location and distance from Lincoln suggest they were placed there deliberately by a controlling authority based at Lincoln. Cemeteries only begin to appear close to the city in the mid-sixth century, but there is little evidence for Germanic presence within the city until the seventh century. The existence of British metalwork in the fifth and sixth centuries also point to a continuation of British authority.[28] Thus a British authority controlling the city and ringed by Germanic cremation cemeteries is 'the only plausible scenario'.[29]

A century later Bede records a mass baptism of the *Lindisfaran* in 627–8 with a *praefectus* called Blæcca. He also refers to the kingdom, or perhaps more accurately *provincia*, of *Lindissi* and the people, the *Lindisfari*, who lived there. The Tribal Hidage also refers to the region as having 7,000 hides. This is the same size as that recorded for the kingdoms of Essex and Sussex. It would appear to have been a significant area both economically and politically in the seventh century at least.

Overall, Green sees Lindsey as evolving out of the former Romano-British community centred on Lincoln.[30] The polity would have had British leaders from the former Romano-British aristocracy and church. The region experienced significant Anglo-Saxon immigration from the mid-fifth century. However, British influence continued perhaps to the mid-sixth century. In other words, for the entire period covering Ælle's supposed 'imperium' and the alleged activity of any historical King Arthur. We have seen that early Anglo-Saxon Kingdoms had their origins in the former Roman *civitates*: Kent, Wast Anglia, Essex and Sussex from the *Cantiaci, Iceni, Trinovantes* and *Regni*.

Green also states that the territory of the Middle Angles coincides with a 'coherent and archaeologically identifiable late fifth – to sixth-century cultural group'.[31] Many of the groups within the Tribal Hidage were found in this region. Far from being small independent tribal groups it may be that they were always part of a higher authority. If so, then what form might that authority take? One possibility is the surviving remnants of the former province. In fact, for Bede's description of Ælle and Ceawlin to be valid it is necessary for some political structure to exist. To get some idea of what that might be we only need to look across the English Channel. Clovis and his sons, as well as the Goths and Burgundians, were busy utilising the former Roman administrative structures. Here the church also played a major role.

Evidence also points to significant Anglo-Saxon immigration alongside large-scale British survival. The word 'significant' could mean as little as 5 per cent of the adult male population.[32] Place names in Lincolnshire point to widespread British survival: Walcot, Wlaton, Walesby, and Walshcroft. In addition Felix's *Life of St Guthlac* records 'Welsh' speakers in the Fens of South Lincolnshire. One of Lindsey's kings, Caedbaed, possibly mid-sixth century, has a likely British etymology. Some of the other names are quite rare (Cueldgils, Cretta, Bubba, and Winta) suggesting a genuine tradition. Although as with other Anglo-Saxon king lists, Lindsey traces back to Woden. The last king, Aldfrið, is thought to have ruled until c. 679 and is mentioned in a Mercian charter. It is thus very possible that the Britons of Lindsey developed a distinct cultural identity separate from those further west or north.

Lindisfarne, off the coast of modern Northumbria, is nearly fifty miles north of Hadrian's Wall and a 150 miles north of the Humber. The etymology is almost certainly from Old English, *Lindisfarnae*. No British or Irish etymology is likely and it can be read as 'the island of the *Lindisfaran*'. Given the likely British etymologies of both Deira and Bernicia, the question arises why there is an apparent early Old English name for the island. A plausible explanation is that Germanic people from Lindsey settled in the area. This seems to fit the literary and archaeological sources. First we have settlers in 'the east of the island'. The HB claims mercenaries were posted to the north, near the wall. We read in the HB Soemil was the first to separate Deira from Bernicia.

Both Bernicia and Deira have Brittonic etymologies and Soemil is five generations before the first attested king of Deira, Aelle, who ruled c. 560–588. If we accept this and assume each generation had their first born son at 20, then this places Soemil born c. 440. He would thus be of fighting age c. 460–500. By any measure he would pre-date Ida, first king of the Bernicians. Ida had a royal fort at Bamburgh opposite the island that carries the name of Germanic settlers from Lindsey. Green states that the 'simplest and most credible' explanation is that the origins of Anglo-Saxon Deira and Bernicia lay in the movement of groups from Lindsey.[33]

Summary

Two competing theories exist for the evolution of Dark Age Britain. First, Anglo-Saxon conquests destroyed the former political structures in the south and east and later smaller tribal units coalesced into the emerging kingdoms. Second, Anglo-Saxons took over former British territories in a patchy and opportunistic way. With a significant amount of assimilation, intermarriage of elites and in some cases violent take overs. The smaller units recorded in the tribal Hidage are merely examples of administrative sub-districts. The evidence points to the second of these two possibilities.[34] However, with increasing evidence of continuation of population and land use I would suggest a more nuanced picture. Perhaps some areas did indeed experience a take over by a Germanic elite. But others, such as Lindsey, may have evolved slowly over a century or more. Urban areas such as Wroxeter, Silchester and St Albans may have had similar pockets of surviving British authority.

The whispers of civil wars in the old Welsh poems and sagas alongside the statement by Gildas support this more complex political and cultural context. If a Brittonic authority placed Germanic mercenaries around a former provincial capital at Lincoln, what is Arthur doing fighting four battles in the 'regione of the Linnuis'? If that polity survived into the mid-sixth century, who was Soemil and who settled Lindisfarne? Were the battles of Catraeth, Arfderydd and Camlan examples of civil wars that Gildas complained about? If 'external wars' had indeed stopped, how do we explain the entries concerning Cerdic and Cynric fighting battles in what later became Wessex?

Gildas may be confined to Britannia Prima, but he doesn't seem to be complaining about the loss of most of lowland Britain. Instead his complaint is he cannot access specific locations. We can speculate this may include the whole of the former south-east province. Evidence from Lincoln suggests the Britons at this point still had the upper hand, although in a complex and fluid political context. In our next chapter we will see the emergence of Wessex. Taking the ASC at face value, the expansion in the second half of the sixth century was at the expense of the Britons. This strongly suggests the Britons were still in control of much of central England. Effectively, what later became Mercia. If our dating for Gildas is correct, then he is a contemporary of Cynric if not Cerdic himself. Yet he has nothing to say about the Gewisse or Saxons along the Thames Valley. It is to these we will now turn.

Chapter Six

The Rise of Wessex

> 'Here two *ealdormen* [chieftains] Cerdic and Cynric, his son, came to Britain with five ships at the place that is called *Cerdices ora* [Cerdic's Shore] and on the same day fought against the Welsh.'
> Anglo-Saxon Chronicle entry for 495

If we recall our timeline, Hengest and Horsa arrived c. 428 or 449 depending on which source one trusts. The subsequent revolt, in c. 440 or 450s was followed by a fight back by Ambrosius Aurelianus. This war went first to 'our countrymen, now to their enemies' until the battle of Badon Hill. The date is important, but unfortunately we are left to place it a decade or more either side of c. 500. At the same we have evidence for increased Germanic material culture and settlement, as well as significant continuation of population and land use. If we attempt to believe all the sources at the same time we are left with some contradictions. The ASC tells us that our two adventurers quoted above were the first kings of the West Saxons. As we shall see, the 495 date is highly debatable and might be as late as 532. Whatever the case they landed around the time or just after the famous battle at Badon. Either a generation before, or at the same time as, Gildas dips his quill into his ink. By either calculation, they are sandwiched between two of Bede's and the ASC's Bretwalda's: Ælle at the end of the fifth century and Ceawlin after the mid-sixth.

Wessex

The ASC includes the genealogy for the kings of Wessex. However, when added up, the regnal dates included in the text do not lead back to 495. Instead the academic consensus is that the more likely date for Cerdic's arrival is 532.[1] It is possible kings have been missed off the list, and indeed we do have a Creoda mentioned by Asser in his *Life of King Alfred* but not in the ASC. In some manuscripts Creoda is placed between Cerdic and Cynric, and thus he may have been an older son of Cerdic. Yet in others he is absent, leading some to dismiss his historicity. Leaving that to one side let us look at the entries in the ASC:

> 495 Cerdic and Cynric arrive with five ships at Cerdic's shore and fight the Welsh.

501 Port and two sons, Bieda and Maelga, arrive with two ships at Portsmouth and kill a 'noble British man'.

508 Cerdic and Cynric kill a British king, Natanleod, along with 5,000 men (near Charford and Netley in Hampshire).

514 West Saxons Stuf and Wihtgar arrive with three ships at Cerdic's shore and fight Britons, putting them to flight.

519 Cerdic and Cynric succeed to kingdom of West Saxons, fight the Britons at Cerdic's Ford.

527 Cerdic and Cynric fight Britons at Cerdic's Wood.

530 Cerdic and Cynric take the Isle of Wight.

534 Cerdic passed away and Cynric continued to rule for twenty-six years. They give the Isle of Wight to their nephews, Stuf and Wihtgar.

Whether they arrived in 495 or 532, the sources agree that six years later they 'conquered the West Saxon kingdom' and were the first kings. A number of interesting points arise. They conquer the West Saxon's kingdom before the West Saxons, Stuf and Wihtgar, arrive with three ships at the same spot as Cerdic. Cerdic and Cynric have Brittonic sounding names and are not described as Saxons. Yet they are said to be uncles to Stuf and Wihtgar by the ASC and Asser, Alfred's biographer, in the ninth century. If Cynric arrived at fighting age then he was nearly 80 when he died, assuming, as the ASC does, it is the same person. Asser includes Creoda in his genealogy and in fact the earliest records, the *Anglian Collection*, has Cerdic-Creoda-Cynric.[2]

There also appears to be duplicate entries with an arrival in 495 and 514 and then a battle thirteen years later in 508 and 527. These anomalies have added to the weight of academic opinion pushing the date to 532.[3] However, if we accept Creoda as historical then we could easily reinstate our original date. In this case it is Creoda who succeeds his father and Cynric, a much younger brother or even grandson, comes of age c. 534 and takes the throne.

Another interesting possibility is that Cerdic wasn't actually Saxon himself, or perhaps half British. Additionally the locations the ASC names for the landing and battles are all on the south coast. We are told by Bede that the New Forest area was considered Jutish and only recently conquered by the West Saxons in his lifetime by the Wessex king Cædwalla (reigned 685–8).[4]

Bede tells us the West Saxons were originally called the *Gewisse*, although he uses both terms.[5]

The name *Gewissae* means 'sure' or 'reliable', which might suggest they were considered loyal to at least one power at one time. The unreliable Geoffrey of Monmouth describes Vortigern as the leader of the *Gewissei*. What we do know is that Gewisse power was centred on the Thames Valley region, notably around Abingdon in Oxfordshire. So on one hand we have a series of battles that seem to be located in the New forest and Isle of Wight areas; on the other hand the Gewisse were located across the former *civitates* of the Atrebates and Belgae inland and further north. We can also see in Bede's writings that the name Gewisse was still being used. Agilbert is described as a Bishop of the Gewisse in the third quarter of the seventh century.

Contrary to the narrative in the ASC we are told by Bede the south coast was considered Jutish land up to the late seventh century. The centre of West Saxon power was actually the upper Thames Valley.[6] We see this from the later battles in the ASC and the archaeological evidence which points to the Abingdon area. In addition, the first West Saxon Episcopal see was Dorchester-on-Thames. The last battle recorded before the mid-sixth century is the 530 entry for the Isle of Wight. We can see the map in figure 23 shows the initial battles of the fifth end early sixth century were all confined to the coastal areas of southern Britain. The later expansion of the Gewisse was from the Thames Valley. The Towns of Winchester and Silchester showed some continuation of British occupation between the early battles and later expansion. This suggests a patchwork or local petty polities in the south, which is a contrast to the possible survival of larger polities to the west in Britannia Prima and the east with Kent.

Below we see the ASC record showing the expansion of the nascent West Saxon kingdom and the appearance of Ceawlin, our second Bretwalda:

> 552 Cynric fought against the Britons at Salisbury and 'put the Britons to flight'.
>
> 556 Cynric and Ceawlin fought the Britons at *Beran Bryg* (Bera's stronghold, possibly Barbury castle, a Wiltshire hill-fort south of Swindon).
>
> 560 Ceawlin succeeded to the kingdom in Wessex.
>
> 568 Ceawlin and Cutha fought against Æthelbert at Wibbandun (Wibba's Mount) and drove him into Kent.
>
> 571 Cuthwulf fought the Britons at Bedcanford and took four settlements: Limbury, Aylesbury, Benson and Eynsham. And died that same year.
>
> 577 Cuthwine and Ceawlin fought the Britons at Dyrham against three British kings (Coinmail, Condidan and Farinmail) and took three cities: Gloucester, Cirencester and Bath.
>
> 584 Ceawlin and Cutha fought the Britons at *Fethan leag* (Battle Wood, possibly Stoke Lyne, Oxfordshire). Cutha was killed and Ceawlin captured many towns and 'war-loot' and returned to his own territory in anger.
>
> 592 Great slaughter at Woden's Barrow (Adam's Grave, Alton priors, Wiltshire) and Ceawlin was driven out.
>
> 593 Ceawlin, Cwichelm and Crida perished.

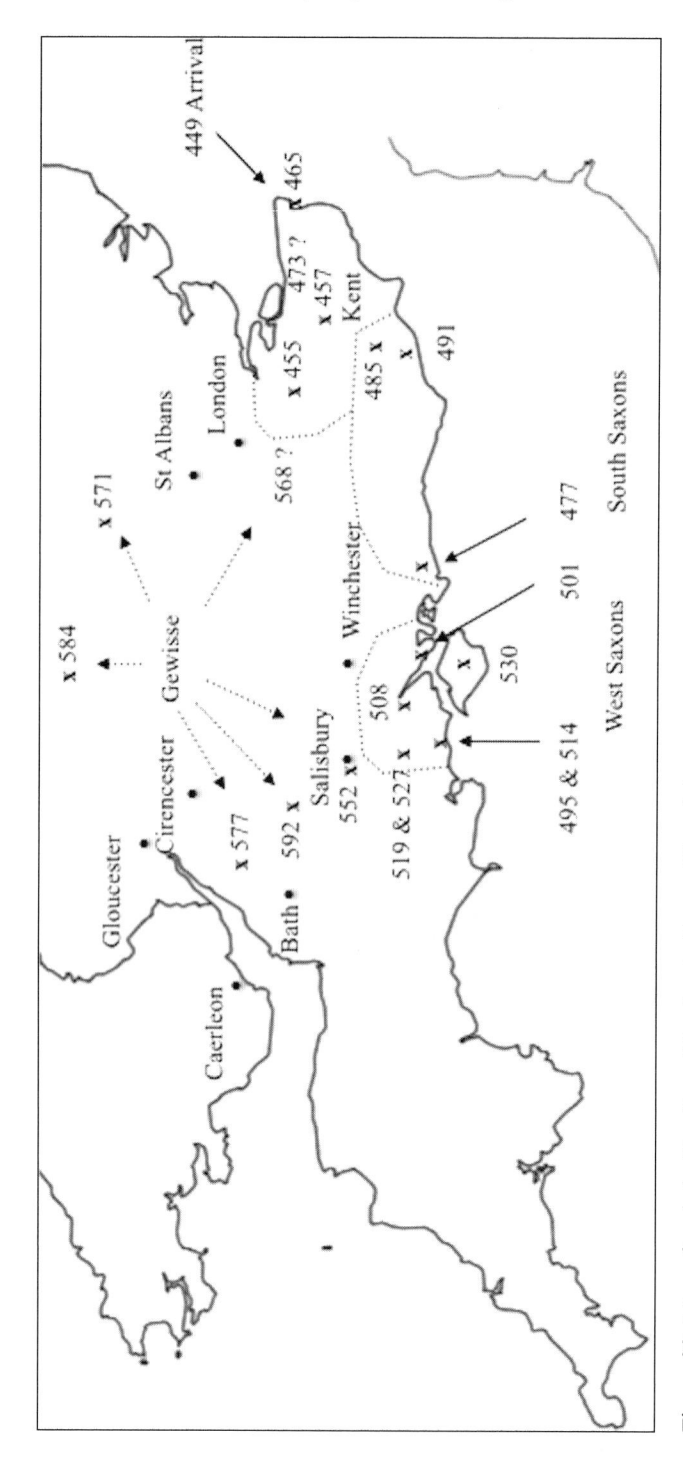

Figure 23. Map of early battle sites of the Anglo-Saxon Chronicles.

Ceawlin seems to have been a victim of a civil war as he was 'driven out' and died the following year. His successor was Ceol, who ruled for six years and was succeeded by his brother: in 597 'Ceolwulf began to rule in Wessex' and he fought against the Angles, Welsh, Picts and Scots. Up to this point, aside from 568, all the battles were against Britons, suggesting north and west of the Thames Valley around Abingdon were under British control well beyond the mid-sixth century. The first definite record of conflict between Wessex and Mercia is 628 when Cynegils and Cwichelm fought Penda at Cirencester. We can summarise the ASC as follows: first, a series of landings and battles c. 495–530 confined to the New Forest area and Isle of Wight on the south coast. If the later dates are more accurate we could move this timeframe to c. 530–65. Second, an expansion from the mid-sixth century that results in a nascent kingdom centred on the Thames Valley and Ceawlin (reigned c. 560–593) described as Bretwalda. Although his reign may have to be shortened if the later arrival date is accepted.

What does the archaeological evidence tell us? The record shows a marked contrast between west and east Wessex:[7]

- Extensive Saxon presence in the fifth century in east Wessex.
- Earliest settlements around the river Meon in east Hampshire.
- Artefacts dated prior to 475 are only found in eastern Wessex and the earliest is 425.[8]
- The finds are centred on the *civitas* of the *Atrebates* as well as eastern *Belgae* and western *Regnenses*.
- The towns of Abingdon and Winchester are especially notable for early settlement as well as Reading, Mildenhall, Andover, Pewsey and Maidenhead.
- Anglo-Saxon cemeteries as early as the second quarter of the fifth century are found at Abingdon and from around 475 at Wallingford, Reading, West Hendred, Harwell, East Shefford and Long Wittenham with a more isolated case at Market Lavington.[9]

Kate Mees, in *Burial, Landscape and Identity in Early Medieval Wessex*, finds the change between the fifth and sixth centuries was not a straightforward, linear process. Rather it was a 'series of interdependent paradigm shifts' which caused society to coalesce from around 600.[10] These changes were the 'cumulative result of both external and insular post-imperial transfigurations'. The distribution of new burial practices and material culture do appear at face value to correlate with the literary accounts from Bede and Gildas.[11] New burial practices and material culture appeared rapidly in eastern and central Wessex. However, a recent study found a number of caveats:[12] The burial practices were not uniformly 'Anglo-Saxon' (a debatable term); they often preserved Romano-British traditions; and there is little that unequivocally identifies them as culturally Anglo-Saxon.

We recall Bede's account seems to contradict the ASC as it implies that southern Hampshire and the Isle of Wight did not come under Wessex control until the area was conquered by Cædwalla in the late AD 680s. A number of names from the early kings of Wessex suggest a British connection: Cerdic, Cædwalla and Cenwalh. We thus get a complex picture from the one traditionally taught: Jutes in south Hampshire, a group calling themselves the Gewisse in the Thames Valley, a very British sounding 'ealdorman' but with West Saxon nephews, Stuf and Wihtgar. Not only that, but 'West Saxon' appears to have been a name that was applied retrospectively. One is left to speculate what happened to those who identified as belonging to the *civitates* of the Atrebates or Belgae?

Kate Mees states, 'it is now generally accepted, however, that the West Saxon kingdom emerged as an amalgam of what appear to have been twin clusters of population and power: one in the Hampshire area and the other in the upper Thames region'.[13] The *Geuissae* or *Gewisse* appear to have formed in the latter area and then branched out from the Thames Valley. The main drivers of social development were internal by the indigenous population.[14] Settlers, or even invaders, may have added to the mix rather than being the catalyst.

New burial rites and practices, and material culture appeared in southern and eastern England in the fifth century. In the past some assumed this could be explained by the appearance of large numbers of 'Anglo-Saxon' invaders and settlers killing or pushing out the indigenous Romano-Britons. However, recent evidence and studies show this is far too simplistic. By the late sixth century 'princely burials' appear in this region. Although it must be noted these high-status burials were the exception rather than the norm.[15] The pagan Saxons often reused existing barrows and other earthworks to bury their dead.[16] The area around the Salisbury Avon valley and the Marlborough Downs is particularly worthy of note.[17]

The situation could be said to resemble a kaleidoscope of ethnic, social and political groups all influencing, shifting, competing and evolving. Some growing in power, others diminishing. One could interpret Gildas as meaning a political or military border now exists, preventing his access to the east and specifically St Albans. Bruce Eagles in *From Roman Civitas to Anglo-Saxon Shire* has attempted to map this 'unhappy partition with the barbarians'.[18] A number of locations across Hampshire and Wiltshire have been identified that might represent a such a border: Teffont, Bokerley Dyke, Charlton, Kemble, Pewsey, West Ashton, Market Lavington. Archaeological evidence from as early as 475 suggests Germanic material culture and burial practices had spread only twenty miles, or a day's march, from Bath. This would make any arguments concerning Bath not being a suitable location for Badon null and void. Linguistic arguments remain, but a raiding force could easily reach any post-Roman towns or settlements of the Severn Valley.

Who was Ceawlin? Taking the ASC at face value he was likely born c. 530–540. Bartrum, in *A Welsh Classical Dictionary*, states the name Cerdic is recognised as the British name Ceredig.[19] Yorke, in *Kings and the Kingdoms of Early Anglo-Saxon England*, finds that Ceawlin likely reigned for either seven or seventeen years and dates him c. 581–8.[20] Cerdic's father's name, Elesa, is similar to the Welsh Elise. His son Cynric is also similar to the Welsh Cynwrig. A descendant, Cædwalla, also has a distinctly Welsh name. It is possible Cerdic's grandfather Gewis is linked to the city of Gloucester, deriving from a corruption of the Latin Gleuenses (inhabitants of Gloucester) to Gewisse. Bartrum suggests the possibility that the West Saxon kingdom derived from the Jutes of Hampshire and Isle of Wight, the West Saxons of the Thames Valley and the Gewisse from further west. To this we should perhaps add the significant percentage of indigenous Romano-Britons and perhaps a Brythonic elite intermarrying with Germanic settlers.

Ceawlin gets his first mention in the ASC in 556 fighting the Britons at *Beran byrg* (Bera's stronghold), identified as Barbury hill fort in Wiltshire. In 560 Ceawlin succeeded to the kingdom. Eight years later he and Cutha drive Æthelberht into Kent. Taking the family tree from Yorke, Ceawlin's son is called Cutha, or Cuthwine. Confusingly, his brother is Cuthwulf or Cutha. The ASC records Cutha defeating the Britons in 571, but another version gives the name as Cuthwulf.[21] This is important to note as a certain Ceol, Cuthwulf's son, and Ceawlin's nephew, features in the Bretwalda's downfall. Seven years after Ceawlin and Cuthwine's victory at Dyrham in 577 we read: 'Ceawlin and Cutha fought the Britons at *Fethan leag* [Battle Wood, possibly Stoke Lyne, Oxfordshire]. Cutha was killed and Ceawlin captured many towns and "war-loot" and returned to his own territory in anger.' Presumably it is Ceawlin's son who died and his brother still lived because Ceol, Cuthwulf's son, doesn't succeed to the kingdom until 591. At this point Ceawlin may still have been king indicating a possible dual kingship. Possibly it indicates a political change or coup.

Whatever the case things came to a head the following year as we read: 'Great slaughter at Woden's Barrow [Adam's Grave, Alton priors, Wiltshire] and Ceawlin was driven out.' Another year later and the ASC records Ceawlin's death along with Cwichelm and Crida. Ceol's line ruled Wessex for nearly a hundred years before a descendant of Ceawlin took the throne. The very British sounding Caedwalla was the great-great-grandson of the second Bretwalda and from him the kings of Wessex extended to Alfred the Great and beyond.

Summary

The traditional story of the emergence of Wessex may be far too simplistic. Instead we see a provincial structure in Britain fragmented by the end of the fifth century. From its ashes emerges several petty kingdoms. Those in the far west and east appear to be loosely based on the former Roman *civitates*. Kent, Essex and Sussex from the Cantii, Trinovantes and Regni in the east. Dyfed, Powys, and Dumnonia from the Dematae, Cornovii and Dumnonii and Durotriges. These areas, east and west, later evolved a distinctive cultural identity, Romano-British or Anglo-Saxon respectively. However, in the fifth and sixth centuries no one would have called themselves 'Anglo-Saxon'. Additionally, down the centre of the island the *civitates* themselves appear to have fractured. While the Dobunni may have contracted into the Hwicce on the banks of the Severn, the Atrebates and Belgae are invisible. What became of the people who identified as members of those civitates?

Firstly, we know they did not disappear or get wiped out. Their DNA lived on in a significant percentage of the population, mostly rural and poor. Urban centres also limped on at Winchester, Silchester and Salisbury. Into this area we get an increase in Germanic material culture and burials often identified as 'Saxon' in nature. Mainly in the east of the region from c. 425 but shifting westwards throughout the fifth century. The Thames Valley around Abingdon appears to be especially significant. Two main groups are worth noting. First, the Jutes of the New Forest area. Second, the Gewissae of the Thames Valley.

The literary sources give some clues, although they are confusing and untrustworthy. Two ealdormen with British-sounding names land on the south coast in 495 (or 532) followed by others including the West Saxons. They fight a series of battles confined to the New Forest area. Later, after the mid-sixth century, they expand rapidly but not from the south coast. Instead, from the Thames Valley area. Much later, a century or more, these Gewissae identify as West Saxons and conquer (or reconquer) the Jutish areas of the south coast.

Back in the sixth century Ceawlin is named as the ASC's second Bretwalda. Bede gives him *imperium* over those living south of the Humber. This might be an exaggeration. He did push Æthelberht back into Kent in 568 and won a number of battles against the Britons to the north and west, but there is no indication he controlled East Anglia or Lindsey. In the north Ida is the first king of the Bernicians from 547. Yet they are under severe pressure from strong British polities right up to the end of the sixth century. Twenty years after the Britons in the north tear themselves apart at Arfderydd, the Gewisse are involved in a bloody dynastic dispute of their own. After Ceawlin's reign we start to see the appearance of various dynasties and our first attested kings or the emerging Anglo-Saxon kingdoms.

Chapter Seven

Kings and Kingdoms

'To other unspeakable crimes... they [the Britons] never preached the faith to the Saxons and Angles who inhabited Britain with them'. Bede, book 1.22.

'Here Pope Gregory sent Augustine to Britain with many monks who preached God's word to the English nation'. Anglo-Saxon Chronicle entry for 595.

Æthelberht

We have seen that Eormenric is the first attested king of Kent and his son Æthelberht was likely born c. 565. His marriage to the Christian Frankish princess Bertha was c. 585. His reign began c. 589–593 and he died 616. We can say a couple of interesting things about him. First, he was born a pagan but later converted to Christianity. Second, his law code was the earliest written code in a Germanic language.

Bede takes the kings of Kent back to Woden as do the 'stock [of] royal families of many kingdoms'. (book 1.5). He described Æthelberht as a 'king of Kent' and a 'very powerful monarch'. (book 1.25) He exercised 'suzerainty' as far as the Humber. Augustine landed at Thanet, which at that time is described as an island 600 hides in area and separated from the mainland by the River Wantsum, three furlongs wide. He was accompanied by nearly forty companions, 'servants of Christ' and interpreters from the Franks, commanded by the Pope, St Gregory. Bede states that some knowledge about the Christian religion had already reached him through his wife, Bertha. She had been allowed to bring a bishop, Liudhard, and practise her faith. At this point one might think Christianity was not as widespread in Kent as it had been 200 years before at the end of Roman rule.

A few days later Æthelberht came to Thanet and met Augustine 'in the open air'. Bede claims there was a 'traditional superstition' that their 'magic art' would have more power if he entered a building. Æthelbert replied to Augustine's preaching: 'The words and the promises you bring are fair enough, but because they are new to us and doubtful, I cannot consent to accept them and forsake those beliefs which I and the English race have held so long.' This seems to contradict the evidence concerning his Christian wife. Taking it at face value however, we read that Christianity is new to Æthelberht, he has a clear, distinct ethnic identity and his peoples' beliefs are equally distinct and have been held for a long time. Æthelberht gave his visitors a dwelling place in his 'chief city', Canterbury, and allowed them to preach. In fact, he seems to have positively encouraged them: 'we will receive you hospitably and provide what is necessary for your support; nor do we forbid you to win all you can to your faith and religion by your preaching' (book 1.25).

Next we read that they use 'a church built in ancient times in honour of St Martin'. They began to preach and convert. Once Æthelberht himself had been baptised they 'received greater liberty to preach everywhere and to build or restore churches'. Does this suggest the restoration of churches already in use? Next we learn Augustine went to Arles and was consecrated 'archbishop of the English race'. A letter between the pope and Augustine refer to the Kentish or English church and do not at this point mention Britons at all. Bede then gives us the text of a letter sent by Gregory to Augustine along with the pallium, his symbol of office. He requests he ordains twelve bishops and specifically places London above York in precedence. One is left to wonder which other cities might receive a bishop. Lincoln and Wroxeter are very likely candidates.

Gregory also sends a letter to Æthelberht, adressing him as 'most worthy son, the glorious lord Æthelberht, king of the English' (book 1.32). He is commanded to 'extend the Christian faith among the people who are subject to you, increase your rights zeal for their conversions; suppress the worship of idols; overthrow their buildings and shrines...'. It is unclear how prevalent Christianity is, if at all. Bede had left us after the chapters concerning Germanus and the battle of Badon, stating one of the crimes of the Britons was not preaching the faith to the Saxons and Angles. We can be confident that most Germanic immigrants and their descendants had not converted.

Bede then, for the first time, tells of the the bishops of the Britons. With 'the help of King Æthelberht', Augustine summoned the bishops of the 'neighbouring British kingdom'. Interesting the use of the singular here. They meet at a place that is still called in Bede's time Augustine's Oak on the borders of the Hwicce and West Saxons. Does it follow the Hwicce were the British kingdom? And did Æthelberht have sovereignty over the West Saxons?

Bede gives a us a hint about the Hwicce a little later. In the mid-seventh century, Æthelweah king of the South Saxons was baptised in c. 661. His wife was Eafe of the Hwicce. Bede states she and her family were already Christian 'as were their people'.[1] There is strong evidence the Hwicce evolved from the territory of the Dobunni, whose *civitas* capital at Cirencester was also the provincial capital of Britannia Prima.[2] Worcester later became a seat of a bishopric and may have been one of the twelve Pope Gregory had in mind in his letter to Augustine. Bede lists the bishoprics in his own day and these might indicate administrative boundaries.[3] Kent and the West Saxons have two bishops; Essex, Lindsey and Wight, one. Interestingly, Merica and the Hwicce are separate bishoprics with a bishop each, along with a bishop of those who Bede states 'dwell west of the River Severn'.

In the country of the Hwicce the towns of Bath, Gloucester and Cirencester were captured by the West Saxons in 577. It would thus seem likely the area was a British polity until the later sixth century, and archaeological evidence supports this.[4] It appears to have continued as a sub-kingdom and as late as 680 had a king, Osric.[5] So here, Bede implies the West Saxons and the Hwicce were still separate kingdoms in the early seventh century, despite the previous victory, and Æthelberht was able to arrange a meeting on the border and get British bishops to attend.

Augustine requested the British bishops do three things: keep Easter at the proper time; perform baptism according to the Roman church; and 'preach the word of the Lord to the English people in fellowship with us'. The Britons refused and ignored Augustine's demands and warnings. Bede is in no doubt that they deserved their divine judgement. Some years later, Æthelfrith of Northumbria attacked Chester and 'made a great slaughter of that nation of heretics'. Accompanying the Britons were over 2,000 priests from the monastery of Bangor, although Bede later claims over 1,200 were killed and only fifty escaped.

In 604 Augustine, now called Archbishop of Britain, consecrated two bishops, Mellitus and Justus. Mellitus was sent to the East Saxons whose king was Sæberht, a nephew of Aethelberht, son of his sister Ricule. Their chief city was London and here Æthelberht built a church dedicated to St Paul. Interesting that Æthelberht has sovereignty over land south of the Humber, but his ability to encourage the adoption of Christianity is confirmed to Essex. Justus became bishop of Rochester.

Gregory refers to Æthelberht as an Angle and talks of the 'English people'. He seems unaware of other ethnic labels such as Saxon or Jute. Æthelberht most likely was descended from Jutes and had a significant population of Saxons and Frisians as well as of course descendants of the indigenous Romano-Britons. He also assumes London, the old Roman diocese capital, would be the seat of the bishops. The political reality was that London was in the territory of the East Saxons but Canterbury retained its primacy. The establishment of Rochester may reflect an original administrative difference between east and west Kent.

While Æthelberht is described by Bede as holding *imperium*, it is perhaps significant he can only encourage the adoption of Christianity in one other early kingdom, Essex. This appears to have evolved from the former Roman *civitas* of the *Trinovantes*. However, recent analysis shows a lack of early Germanic material culture around major urban sites such as London, St Albans, and Colchester.[6] Evidence is largely confined to coastal areas and waterways.[7] In a recent extensive study, Rippon finds an absence of evidence for early Anglo-Saxon settlement within 'all but the fringes' of *Catuvellauni* and *Trinovantes* areas.[8] They were confined to a small area, possibly a grant of land peripheral to existing Romano-British communities.[9] Thus sparsely populated areas, such as fens, woodland and rivers, perhaps near civitas boundaries.[10] This suggests 'immigration may have occurred within the context of Romano-British socio-political control'.[11]

The literary sources suggest that the mercenaries were initially settled 'in the east of the island' and after the revolt returned to their areas. The HB then has Vortigern ceding Essex, Middlesex and Sussex to Hengest. This then may be an echo of how far an early bretwalda held sovereignty, or imperium. The former Roman province of Maxima Caesariensis may have retained some integrity before it also fragmented. This might explain how first Ælle and then Æthelberht could be considered to rule a wide area even extending to the possibly weaker province to the north, Flavia Caesariensis.

I would suggest the evidence points to the provincial structure surviving in some form up to the war between Ambrosius Aurelianus and the Saxons. This war may have created new polities and new boundaries. Yet we also have support for the survival of *civitas* boundaries and these administrative areas evolving into early kingdoms. What we cannot determine is the process, the 'how' and 'why'. Recent genetic evidence shows that there was not a wholesale removal of the indigenous population. Although this may have occurred in specific local areas and times. This leaves us with two likely options. First, an 'elite takeover' of former provinces or civitates similar to Clovis in northern Gaul. We recall him being asked to administer Belgica Secunda. It is possible Ælle was asked to perform the same role across the channel just as Clovis was defeating Syagrius in Soissons. Second, a change in cultural identity where the Romano-Britons decided to reject their former Roman identity. We have seen a number of reasons why they might do so. The corruption and maladministration of the crumbling fifth-century regime is one. The inability to defend from repeated attacks from raiders is another. Heavy taxation may have caused resentment and we have seen evidence of widespread inequality and social unrest. Third, the imposition of an increasingly intolerant Christianity cannot be ignored. With the prevalence of Plagiarism and Arianism, siding with the more tolerant 'pagans' might be more attractive than defending an harsh, intolerant, elite who tax you heavily and are seen to be unfair and corrupt.

In Essex the first recorded king was Sledd c. 587. We have seen he was related to Æthelberht, and Kent exerted control. What is interesting is the extent of the original London diocese, after the founding of the bishopric, which included Middlesex, Surrey and south-eastern Hertfordshire.[12] It seems the original East Saxon Kingdom extended further west and south than the present county, surrounding London. There is no evidence of an earlier fifth – or sixth-century royal power. Perhaps some 'princely grave' equivalent to Sutton Hoo awaits discovery. But we have evidence for pockets of Brittonic power surviving into the late sixth century, such as at St Albans.[13] And we have a later 'princely burial' at Prittlewell.

We know even less about Surrey, which is called Sudergeona, or 'Southern District', by Bede. A certain *Frithuwold* is said to be of 'the province of the men of Surrey', and a 'sub-king of Wulfhere, king of the Mercians'.[14] Middlesex also gets few mentions although there is a land grant referring to the Middle Saxons in 704.[15] If there were small groups of Germanic settlers in Surrey and Middlesex and these areas reflected former Roman administrative boundaries, then they may have been subsumed by their larger neighbours very early.

We get a possible clue in the ASC entry for 825. The West Saxons conquer what is referred to as the 'East Kingdom', which included Kent, Sussex, Essex and Surrey.[16] This is two to three centuries after our period but it is curious this is same territory mentioned in the HB being ceded to Hengest and that it also resembles the south-eastern Roman province.

In summary, the HB tells us Hengest was given control of a former *civitas*, Kent, before forcing Vortigern to cede the entire south eastern province. By the end of the sixth century, Kent has emerged as an established kingdom yet Æthelberht still seems to be exercising authority over a wider area.

Northumbria

While Caewlin and then Æthelberht are fighting it out for control of the south, the literary sources tell us the Angles were exerting pressure north of the Humber. The Northumbrian kingdoms, Deira and Bernicia, both had British etymologies, coming from *Bernech* and *Deura* (the latter deriving from the river Derwent). Deira possibly evolved from the *civitas* of the *Parissi*, north of the Humber. It would seem Germanic material culture and burials spread across the Humber to Deira before reaching the more northern Bernicia.[17] The boundary between these nascent kingdoms is thought to have been River Tees,[18] Bernicia spreading north of Hadrian's wall to the borders of the Gododdin in modern Lothian.

The literary sources place Hengest's son Octha in the north 'near the wall'. However there is little archaeological evidence north of the Tees and west of the Vale of York until the seventh century. The largest concentration of cemeteries in Bernicia are in the extreme south and there is little evidence of any Anglo-Saxon materials in the fifth or sixth centuries aside from isolated burials.[19] We get some material culture appearing between York and Catterick in the second half of the fifth century.[20] These are associated with Romano-British military centres.[21] So we seem to have some evidence supporting the HB's assertion that Soemil was the first to separate Deira from Bernicia, with the genealogies pointing to the second half of the fifth century. We don't get evidence supporting the literary sources placing Octha in Bernicia in the fifth century. However, finding and identifying evidence from around 1,000 warriors (forty ships) might be difficult; especially if they were posted to just a couple of locations away from more common sites.

The first confirmed king of Deira is Ælle c. 568–598.[22] Soemil is listed as five generations before in both the HB and eighth-century Anglian Chronicles. Carver, writing in 2019, describes 'the creep of Anglo-Saxon burial grounds' north of the Humber after 475.[23] The interesting thing here is that the evidence suggests Deira and Lindisfarne were settled from Lindsey, where we have seen evidence of a British polity surviving into the sixth century. We also recall four of Arthur's battles were in the *regione linnuis*. This could be interpreted as a Romano-British-Germanic polity pushing north and west. The example in the battle list may be more indicative of a civil war with Arthur leading forces of the north and west against a nascent kingdom of Lindsey emerging out of the fragmenting former province of Flavia Caesariensis. The later battle of Catraeth may well have pitted the Gododdin and their allies against Urien of Rheged, the 'Lord of Catraeth', and his allies from Deira and Elmet.

If so, this isn't the last time we see an alliance between Britons and pagans. Several decades later Cadwallon and the Mercians join forces to fight the Northumbrians. The royal palace site at Yeavering, in Bernicia, confirms the existence of a great hall similar to Hrodgar's Hall in *Beowulf*.[24] At this site we see evidence of both Brittonic and Germanic influences. Other example of the fusion of Brittonic and Germanic influences.

The first king of Bernicia is said to be Ida c. 547. The HB claims he joined Din Guaire, the British name for Bamburgh, to Bernicia. Interestingly, Bede tells us Bamburgh was named after a certain Bebba, which appears Brittonic. There are no records of battles in the ASC although some of Arthur's battles may be northern, such as the Roman forts at Bremenium and Bincheseter. We have seen linguistic, political and economic links north and south of the Humber. If this region developed a distinct political identity then perhaps this was at odds with their neighbours to the north and west.

A surviving French document from c. 850 gives us Oesa and Eosa as the first Bernician royal dynasty to arrive, two generations before Ida.[25] This would place Oesa around 500 or possibly a generation before.[26] The HB names Ida's father as Eobba. We recall the HB and Hengest's son Octha and his cousin Ebissa being given land 'near the wall'. Octha eventually becomes the first king of Kent but there is no mention of Ebissa. However, a corruption of *Ebissa* to *Eoppa* and then to *Eobba* is considered very possible.[27]

> Anglian Collection, eighth century: Oesa, Eoppa, Ida.
> Historia Brittonum, early ninth century: Ossa, Eobba, Ida.
> Anglo-Saxon Chronicle, late ninth century: Esa, Eoppa, Ida.

If Hengest's kin, Octha and Ebissa, are synonymous with Oesa and Eosa, then we have a link between the Kentish and Bernician royal families. It is one of Ida's sons who we read was besieged for three days and nights on Lindisfarne by Urien and his allies c. 572–9. Clearly at this point the Bernicians were still not the powerful force they would prove to be a century later. The kingdoms of Alt Clud, Gododdin and Rheged likely emerged from the mid-fifth century after the Picts were driven back.[28] We can speculate that the Brittonic polities still had the upper-hand north of the Humber as Caewlin exerted his influence further south. It may be that disastrous civil wars such as Arfderydd in 573 and Catraeth (which I would date earlier rather than the conventional c. 600) weakened them. The emergence of strong Bernician rulers from Æthelfrith, c. 593–616, continued this trend. Yet Bede does not label him as holding *imperium*. Instead he applies this description to four southern rulers Ælle, Caewlin, Æthelberht and then Rædwald of East Anglia. All of whom were born pagan.

East Anglia

Our earliest evidence of significant Germanic immigration appears in East Anglia in the early fifth century.[29] The first attested king is our fourth Bretwalda, Raedwald c. 599–627. His father and grandfather were named as Tytil and Wuffa respectively. It is from the latter we get the name of the royal house, the *Wuffingas*. The HB claims one further generation, Webha, as the first to rule. Later medieval sources such as Roger of Wendover in the thirteenth century, date Wuffa's reign from c. 571. In other words, the line of kings only go back as far as the late sixth century and one is left to speculate as to the situation between the *adventus saxonum* and the emergence of these first kings. We do see a continuation of farming practices such as at West Stow in Suffolk covering this gap.[30]

The region had a separate socio-economic identity as early as the first half of the fifth century.[31] This doesn't necessarily mean separation or independence, but it may show a distinctive social and political area. Different material cultures existed between East Anglia and further South such as the area occupied by the *Trinovantes*.[32] Importantly, early immigrants are spread out across the landscape rather than be confined to specific areas.[33] This is unique to East Anglia when compared to areas such as Wessex.

Once again we see a similarity between the civitas of the Iceni and the later kingdom although the county names of Norfolk and Suffolk (literally North and South folk) imply two separate early polities. Archaeological evidence demonstrates Scandinavian influences especially from Sweden. Some links have been drawn with the earliest written Anglo-Saxon epic poem *Beowulf*. There are signs it originated in East Anglia as early as the seventh century.[34] In the poem, Queen Wealhpeow married to King Hrodgar, was a *Wuffinga* princess from southern Sweden and the storyline has been placed in the early sixth century.[35] The *Wuffingas*, are linked to south-west Sweden and south-east Norway, and the name is 'etymologically identical' to the *Wylfingas* in Beowulf and *Wulfingas* in another tenth-century Anglo-Saxon poem, *Widsith*.[36] There are also interesting parallels in *Beowulf* with stories of Anglian Saints' lives, folklore tales of Fenland monsters and place name evidence.[37] Archeological evidence, not least the royal ship funeral and Sutton Hoo, demonstrates that East Anglia had the strongest links to Scandinavia than any other Anglo-Saxon kingdom.[38]

We see an interesting pattern emerge from the poetry of the time. An audience sitting in a great hall somewhere in the East Anglia of the seventh century, listening to a poet present Beowulf, still seemed to regard their ancestral homeland as overseas. By the tenth century, poems such as the *Battle of Brunanburh* and *Battle of Maldon* suggest the 'ancestral lands are no longer overseas'.[39] They now considered themselves English and their homeland England. This process took 300 years. It is possible a Romano-British audience, disenchanted with Roman rule, heavy taxes and corruption, may have changed their outlook much quicker. We see dykes appear in South Cambridgeshire which show a fluctuating boundary between what became East Anglia and Mercia.[40] However, their construction and positioning (facing inland) indicate locals were defending attacks from the west, suggesting they may have been defending against Britons.

Mercia

Mercia was the last kingdom to coalesce into a single unit many decades after Wessex.[41] The ASC records the expansion of the West Saxons but Caewlin, aside from the entry for 568 concerning Aethelberht, is always recorded as fighting Britons. It is not until 597 that a West Saxon king, Ceowulf, is recorded as fighting against 'the Angle race'. Is this an indication of Angles now north of the West Saxons? The first historically attested figure is Penda c. 626–655. The genealogies name Pybba as his father. Bede tells us Cearl was king before Penda and that Edwin of Northumbria married his daughter while in exile during the reign of Æthelfrith, 593–616. The founder of the dynasty is said to be Icel, five generations before Penda, which might place him at the start of the sixth century. On the other hand, if this records the reigns of kings, rather than successive generations, we might reduce this estimate to the mid-sixth century.

Later medieval writers such as Roger of Wendover, Matthew Paris and Henry of Huntingdon state the first king of Mercia was Creoda or Cridda in 585, succeeded by Pybba in 593.[42]

Roger of Wendover and Matthew Paris, both writing in the thirteenth century, state the expansion of the Mercians derived from East Anglia. Bede gives the origins of the Mercians as from Angulus along with the 'East Angles, the Middle Angles, and all the Northumbrian race'.[43] If we take this and the battles of the ASC at face value then we can postulate that the Britons were still in control of much of what became Mercia as late as the beginning of the last quarter of the sixth century. Around the same time Urien is besieging the Bernicians at Lindisfarne, the Britons are fighting a bloody civil war at Arfderydd and the Gododdin are charging the Deirans at Catraeth.

A cemetery of the period has been found which may shed light on how the region evolved a new cultural identity. Wasperton in Warwickshire presents Romano-British burials along side later Anglo-Saxon graves. Twenty-two were cremations dated to around 480, which is early when considering the dates of the first Mercian kings. It suggests continuity of use, possible adoption of material and cultural behaviours and later assimilation of Anglo-Saxon settlers. It is about seventy miles south-east of the Roman city of Viroconium at Wroxeter near Shrewsbury, where we have seen evidence of a Brythonic polity into the sixth century. Similarly, in the East Midlands and the Trent valley there was significant evidence of Germanic settlers yet also evidence of Brythonic polity at Lincoln and further south at St Albans.

We have seen that it is likely the Hwicce was under British authority prior to the battle of Dyrham in 577 and archaeological evidence supports this.[44] The fact that Bede tells us Augustine had a meeting with British bishops on the border of Hwicce and Wessex might suggest it was still considered a British kingdom despite that defeat. Bede lists the bishoprics in his own day which might indicate administrative boundaries.[45] Interestingly, Merica and the Hwicce have separate bishoprics. We get a sense that some former Roman civitates were able to maintain some sort of integrity and evolve into early kingdoms such as the Hwicce and Kent. Some provinces may have lingered on in some reduced form, such as Britannia Prima and Maxima Caesariensis. Other areas fragmented completely and new polities emerged. Mercia seems to be an example of this. The possibly seventh-century Tribal Hidage lists various 'peoples', many across what later became Mercia.

If we lay this alongside surviving Brythonic polities and urban centres we see an interesting picture. The Hwicce contracted around the towns of Cirencester, Gloucester and Worcester and the Cornovii around Viroconium, Wroxeter. A similar process seems to have occurred around Lincoln and St Albans. In the middle of these potentially surviving Brythonic powers we see many of the peoples from the later Tribal Hidage. We also have the cemetery at Wasperton showing early presence of Germanic culture, along with similar evidence down the Trent Valley and Lincolnshire. The ASC battle entries appear to match with our genealogical evidence. The West Saxons are fighting Britons to their north until 597. The first Mercian kings are said to rule from 585.

The first kings

All the historically attested kings appear in the late sixth or seventh centuries. What is interesting to note is the potential dates of the first alleged kings. The literary sources, though potentially unreliable, give us two distinct periods. The first is the late fifth century concerning Kent, Sussex and potentially Wessex (taking the ASC date over modern historians). To this we should add Deira, allegedly separated from Bernicia by Soemil. The second timeframe is the second half of the sixth century where first Bernicia and then East Anglia and Mercia establish dynasties. The reader will note this doesn't fall in line with the archaeological record. East Anglia experienced the earliest settlement in the fifth century yet it takes 150 years for Wuffa to establish his power. It is possible earlier dynasties existed and were destroyed or forgotten. But it is equally possible these dynasties emerged out of a Romano-British-Germanic hybrid polity.

It is worth recalling table four, the earliest Anglo-Saxon kings. This indicated broadly two timeframes. The first in the second half of the fifth century, perhaps a generation after a marked increase in Germanic material culture appears. Hengest arrives in Thanet and thirty years later Ælle lands in Sussex. If the HB is to be believed, Soemil is separating a Brittonic-sounding Deira from presumably a nascent Brittonic polity, Bernicia. To confuse matters this might indicate the expanding influence of Lindsey, which appears to have been still a Brittonic polity in the sixth century despite being surrounded by Germanic settlements. Lastly, towards the end of the fifth century (or early sixth if Dumville is correct) Cerdic lands in Hampshire and takes over a nascent West Saxon kingdom in the Thames Valley, although his early battles are in the New Forest area.

Our second timeframe is hundred years later in the second half of the sixth century. The Gewisse begin their expansion in the south, largely at the expense of Britons with the exception of a campaign against Æthelberht. At the same time, Ida becomes the first king of Bernicia. In the last quarter of the sixth century the first dynasties of East Anglia, Essex and Mercia appear. It is in this period the first 'princely burials' appear. This would suggest a change in social practices or cultural identity was taking place.

Princely burials

Recent studies show 'over-kingship' probably existed by the 560s, importantly before 'princely burials' enter the archaeological record.[46] These burials are defined as follows:[47] 'graves so rich and elaborate that they can only be those of the very highest ranking members of a hierarchical society'. The grave goods are 'exceptional in their number, diversity and high quality' and marked by 'substantial burial structures'.

The practice emerged in Britain after the war-band had established itself as a dominant social unit. We have seen that, not only were military forces often made up of several warlords, but the emerging kingdoms themselves were often ruled by two kings with several sub-kings. Burial mounds had been a 'long-standing practice in barbarian Europe', although not specifically associated with Angles or Saxons.[48] It was adopted by high status people in Britain in the late sixth century. It is also worth noting that it was not forbidden by Christianity, although it fell out of favour in the seventh century. It is thought 'highly likely' that some occupants had converted to Christianity at some point.[49] In contrast, on the Continent we see moves to ban the practice, such as an eighth-century ruling by Charlemagne and a tenth-century text that punishes burials in mounds.[50]

Pollington, in *Anglo-Saxon Burial Mounds, Princely Burials in the Sixth and Seventh Centuries*, describes 'princely burials' that appeared in Britain as distinguished by a large mound of up to eighteen metres across and taller than a man.[51] The chamber found within the mound, or ship as at Sutton Hoo, could be viewed as a substitute for the meadhall. It often contained drinking vessels, gaming pieces, harps and cauldrons. The largest chamber type burial is at Prittlewell in Essex which is four metres by four metres. The practice was not confined to warriors and included high status females too.

The Franks appear to have adopted mound burials from the mid-fifth century. The most famous is of the Frankish king, Childeric, father of Clovis, at Tourney in modern Belgium dated to c. 481–2. At the same time it appeared in Scandinavia and 'English and Swedish traditions evolved side by side'.[52] This might be true of East Anglia, but the south east corner of Britain was more influenced by events in Frankia. Kent's wealth appears to have been heavily influenced by the Merovingian court.[53] It is perhaps noteworthy that mound burials in Gaul appear to have died out by the sixth century and this may indicate the practice was abandoned in Kent well before Aethelberht's reign.

However, it is interesting to consider if earlier kings of Kent did use burial mounds. One site associated with Horsa's grave is *Hawsborrow* or *Horseborough* overlooking Folkestone Harbour. Pollington cites a tradition that claims the mound was destroyed and a quantity of treasure found within.[54] There is also a White Horse Stone in Westfield Wood in Kent. Another location seems unlikely as it's too far from the alleged battles, *Horsan hlaw*, Orslow in Staffordshire. Bede states Horsa was killed in battle by the Britons and a monument or tomb bearing his name 'in the eastern part of Kent' is still visible in Bede's day in the early eighth century.[55]

The HB, a century later, repeats the tradition of Horsa's death but adds the battle name, *Episford*, in Saxon or *Rithergabail* in British. It also adds that Categern died and his brother Vortimer was leading the Briton. The later ASC records that Horsa dies in battle at *Aegelesthrep*. It is possible Bede's 'monument' was a mound still visible in his day. The suffix '-low' comes from the Old English *hlaw*, meaning burial mound.

Thus a grave mound at Taplow is likely the burial mound, *hlaw*, of Taeppa, dated to the sixth century. A mound attributed to Horsa in East Kent might have a similar name, Hors or Ors -low. An investigation into the history of the traditions regarding Horsa's grave revealed a number of interesting points.[56] The theory that a Roman inscription HORS was misinterpreted is undermined by the absence of any similar examples. Kits Coty House was associated with the grave of Catigern as early as the sixteenth century. A tradition of Horsa's tomb at nearby Horsted was recorded in the seventeenth century but reported as having been destroyed. A nineteenth-century investigation revealed a quantity of flints rather than remains of any large stones. Excavation of a nearby 'tumulus' (only about a foot in height) revealed evidence of a cremation but nothing else. Horsham, Horsmonden, Horsley, Horsenden, Horsley and Horsted all likely derive from a horse-related etymology, although not necessarily directly from Horsa's name. One possibility is simply a steading for horses. In fact, Horsted may well derive from *herst*, wood, and *stede*, a place.

It would be reasonable to suggest that if Catigern and Horsa perished in a battle near Aylesford, then a burial at nearby Kit Coty House and Horsted would make sense. However, we must be wary of legends that appear many centuries after the events. It is common to assume that the Medway forms the boundary between east and west Kent. However the original boundary may have been further east at Rainham. If the grave site was near the battle then it was very close to the border of east and west Kent. Bede could still be correct in placing this in East Kent.

In the HB (chapter 43–4) Vortimer requested to be buried in a specific location. The twelfth-century HRB tells us he was poisoned by his new mother-in-law, Renwein, daughter of Hengest. We can imagine him laying in bed asking his friends to bury him in a tomb by the coast at the port from which the invaders had fled, presumably in the battle 'in open country by the inscribed stone on the shore of the Gallic sea. This might be Richborough Roman Fort in east Kent near to the Isle of Thanet: 'I entrust it to you. Wherever else they may hold a British port or may have settled, they will never again live in this land.' But they went against his wishes and buried him at Lincoln.

Regarding Kit Coty House, the earliest reference, *Citscotehouse*, is in 1570. 'Cat' is Old Welsh for 'battle', and Catigern, could derive from 'War-Lord'. Coty may derive from the word for 'wood' and some have attempted to link the name to one of Arthur's twelve battles, Cat Coit Celidon. Alternatively, Coty could simply refer to coits or stones. A last suggestion is the Saxon word *cota* or hut. This would leave us with battle or the wood/stones/hut depending on one's preference. This all seems very speculative. The stones at Kit Copy House are part of a chambered

The Early Anglo-Saxon Kings

long barrow dated to the early Neolithic, c. 4,000 BC. This wouldn't prevent a fifth-century burial, but without evidence we must put it to one side. It is possible that Horsa's remains were transferred, either before or after cremation, back to Thanet or the coast and interred in a mound likely overlooking the coast or a major river similar to the site at Sutton Hoo.

Pollington lists a number of mounds in southern and central England and it is possible our second Bretwalda, Ceawlin may also have been interred in a mound. We recall Saxons tended to inhumation rather than cremation and so we are more likely to have skeletal remains. Two sites known as *Cwichelmes low* are found at Ardley in Oxfordshire and Scutchamer Knob, also in Oxfordshire.[57] Alternatively, Challow may derive from 'Ceawa-' which could come from Ceawlin.[58] Should his grave ever be discovered it would likely rival that at Sutton Hoo.

There are over 400 known ship burials in northern Europe.[59] The earliest is from the fifth century at Wremen in Germany and the latest in c. 950 at Lady in Denmark. In c. 922 Ibn Fadlan witnessed the Scandinavian Rus on the Volga placing the dead leader's corpse in a 'ship chamber' for ten days. The body was laid on a couch within a tent placed on the deck. Food, beer and musical instruments were placed about him. After various rites the man and ship were burnt on a large pyre after which a mound was erected. On top was erected a birch post with the man's name written on it. Pollington lists a sequence of funeral rites:[60] after the grave is cut it is lined with timber and a roof structure erected. The grave is furnished with various grave goods and various rites and sacrifices carried out. A mound is then erected over the chamber and a large timber post inserted into the top of the mound.

In the Scandinavian Scyldingas sagas, written in the middle ages, we read of the funeral of Sigurd Hring. He placed himself in a ship with the body of Alfsola, who had been poisoned to prevent her marriage to Sigurd. The ship was 'fired with pitch, bitumen and sulphur and with the raised sails pushed by the offshore winds he steered the prow while he harmed himself with his own hand'.[61] At the end of *Beowulf* the nobles of the Geats made a 'balefire on earth'. They placed helms, mail shirts and battle-shields then 'laid in the middle the famed leader'. When the fire had done its work they built a 'barrow on a spur of land, it was high and broad, widely seen by seafarers'. We are told it was built in ten days, building a wall about the 'battle-bold man's' remains. Into the grave they placed 'ring and circlet', gold and 'wealth of the heroes'. Twelve sons of nobles then rode round the mound mourning their king and singing his praises.

Perhaps the most famous 'princely burial' is the ship burial at Sutton Hoo dated to 550–650.[62] Martin Carver's excellent *The Sutton Hoo Story* gives a vivid account of the discovery, dig and finds of the famous ship burial under mound one. The man buried inside the ship chamber had been laid to rest in 'parade dress', with his accoutrements carefully placed around him: sword, spears, shield, helmet, purse, baldric and gold garnet connectors.[63] A silver dish bears the name of Anastasius I, Byzantium Emperor 491–518. Analysis of the thirty-seven gold coins in the burial have dated the grave to nearer 625, making Rædwald the prime candidate.[64] The first burial mounds at the site appear to be cremations followed by a horse burial and then two ship burials.[65] Mound two had a small ship placed over a chamber which measured 1.2m x 3.6m and 1.8m deep. Unfortunately this grave was later robbed, but some evidence of grave goods survived: shield, spears, sword, buckles, drinking horns, buckets and bronze bowls.

The more famous mound one has the chamber inside the ship. A trench 28m x 6m and up to 3.5m deep had been dug east to west on a promontory overlooking the river. The 27m long ship itself is the largest pre-Viking era ship known.[66] It contained 3,000 rivets and twenty-six ribs pegged to the hull. In the chamber was placed a large cauldron (100 litres), hanging bowls, a lyre, axe-hammer, five spears, three angons and a 'coptic' bowl from North Africa. Drinking vessels and gaming pieces were also present. Shoulder clasps were similar to Roman military officers and the sword pommel, connectors, bosses, buckles and pyramids were all made in gold inlaid with cut garnets. The sword was 85cm and pattern welded with a wool-lined wooden scabbard. The body was laid in a coffin and the famous helmet likely placed on top of the coffin lid, wrapped in cloth. The remains of a ring-mail coat is the only one found in Britain. A similar example in Vimose, Denmark, extends to the hip and elbows and contains 20,000 8mm iron rings.

Silver bowls with crosses might have been finger-bowls and may indicate the presence of Christianity, although it's possible they were simply booty, tribute or trade goods. The presence of a sceptre with a stag figure on top may indicate high office. We are reminded of Bede's comment about Edwin not only having banners carried before him in battle, but also being preceded by a standard bearer in times of peace. Edwin was a contemporary of Rædwald and owed his throne to the East Anglian king when he first protected him from, and then helped defeat, Æthelfrith in 616.

About ten miles to the north-east another ship burial (also dated to seventh century) was discovered at Snape in a cluster of nine or ten mounds. The ship itself was 14m in length, 3m wide and positioned on an east-west axis. The graves were an equal mixture of inhumations and cremations and the ship burial is thought to have contained the body of a ranking male. Unfortunately the grave had been robbed, but some items were found: two iron spear heads, the gold Snape Ring and a glass claw beaker.

One last example matches mound one at Sutton Hoo for its contents. Prittlewell in Essex is a chamber burial that measures 4.35m by 4m and 1.5m deep.[67] The mound constructed over this chamber is thought to have been 12m across and 2.5m high, although time has eroded it completely. As at Sutton Hoo there a variety of bowls, glass vessels, drinking horns, a harp and gaming pieces. A shield and two iron spear-heads were also found. Evidence from coins and buckles has enabled academics to narrow the date from 570–630 to c. 590–610.[68] The gold foil crosses and other finds are indicative of Christianity. Hirst and Scull, in *The Anglo-Saxon Princely Burial at Prittlewell Southend-on-Sea*, tentatively suggest that due to the presence of grave goods, some with Christian symbology, the burial is a young man who had converted to Christianity. He may have been related to Sledd (c. 587–604) or Sæberht (c. 604–616). The latter figure married Ricula, the sister of Æthelberht of Kent. Hirst and Scull suggest Sæberht's brother, Seaxa, although they admit this is 'highly speculative'.[69]

The 'golden age' of princely burials was between 550–650. Some princely burials were cremations: Asthall, Oxfordshire; Coombe, Kent, and Sutton Hoo mound three. Others were inhumations: Taplow, Buckinghamshire; Caenby, Lincolnshire; Sutton Hoo, Suffolk, mounds one and two; Snape, Suffolk; Broomfield and Prittlewell, Essex.[70] However, evidence from Gaul shows pagan Frankish kings were being buried in mounds in the late fifth century. It is possible some of the figures we have discussed are lying undiscovered, their mounds flattened long ago by time and centuries of farming. One can only imagine what treasures a grave of Ælle or Ceawlin might contain.

Christianity

It has been suggested some burial mounds were raised in defiance of the advance of Christianity.[71] In the case of Sutton Hoo we see some ambiguity which might reflect the situation at the time. Bede tells us that Rædwald kept a foot in both camps so to speak:

> Long before, his father Redwald had been instructed in the sacraments of Christ's faith in Kent, but to no purpose; for on returning home he was seduced by his wife and unrighteous teachers, and left the first purity of Christ's faith… he was seen to serve Christ as well as idols; and in the same sanctuary he had an altar for Christ's sacrifice and another for sacrifice to devils.[72]

The table below shows how the new faith took several decades to spread across the Anglo-Saxon kingdoms. Whether it was still present among the descendants of the Romano-British is unknown.

Table 6: The conversion of the Anglo-Saxon kingdoms.

Kingdom	Date of converseon	Source
Kent	Before 601	Pope Gregory wrote to Æthelberht, four years after Augustine's arrival calling him a 'Christian King'.
East Saxons	604	ASC: 'Here the East Saxons received the faith and baptismal bath under King Sæberht'.
Northumbria	627	ASC: King Edwin 'with his nation was baptised at Easter'. Bishop Paulinus also preached baptism in Lindsey.

Kings and Kingdoms

Kingdom	Date of converseon	Source
East Anglia	After 627 636	Bede (book 2.15) states Edwin of Northumbria persuaded Eorpwald son of Rædwald to be baptised. ASC: Here Bishop Felix preached the faith of Christ to the East Anglians'.
Wessex	634 635	ASC: 'Here Bishop Birinus preached baptism to the West Saxons'. ASC: King Cynegils baptised.
Mercia	653	Bede (book 3.21) Penda's son Peada was baptised with all his 'gesiths and thegns' and servants. ASC: 'The Middle Angles under Ealdorman Peada received the true faith'.
South Saxons	661	ASC: Æthelwald, king of the South Saxons, baptised and given Isle of Wight which received baptism for the first time.

Seeing this steady march of Christianity in the early seventh century, one might think it was inevitable. However, there were a number of setbacks. Æthelberht was succeeded by his pagan son Eadbald, who also took a Frankish bride. A similar situation occurred in the kingdom of the East Saxons when Sæberht died. His three sons had remained heathen and drove out Bishop Mellitus from London. Bede tells us that Rædwald had 'long been initiated in to the mysteries of the Christian faith in Kent'.[73] Returning to his kingdom he was seduced by his wife and certain 'evil teachers'. His son Eorpwald's reign was short and he was succeeded by a pagan, Ricberht. He in turn was succeeded by Sigeberht, a devout Christian who had been in exile in Gaul. Four years later Christianity returned to Kent. Eorcenberht succeeded his pagan father Eadbald and Bede gives us a number of interesting facts.[74] He was the first king to order idols banned and destroyed throughout the kingdom. He ordered forty days of Lent to be observed by Royal authority. He also imposed suitably heavy punishments for offenders who neglected these commands.

One could argue it took six decades to convert the major Anglo-Saxon kingdoms. Did a similar process happen in reverse from the mid-fifth century in lowland Britain? Did several decades of Anglo-Saxon control result in the rejection of the Roman religion?

Our last pagan king of Mercia was Penda, but it's worth noting he allowed his son to convert and for the faith to be preached in his kingdom. He was also not adverse to allying himself with Christian British kings. One of those kings,

Cadwallon, was himself not adverse to attacking a slaughtering fellow Christians in his campaign against the Angles of Northumbria. The dynastic disputes and wars of the early sixth century are reminiscent of the popular *Game of Thrones* series, or the Wars of the Roses in the fifteenth century on which it is based.

Conflict between Mercia and Northumbria in the sixth century

We have seen that Deira was likely established as an Anglo-Saxon kingdom before Ida ruled in Bernicia. These early kingdoms had their enemies. First the Gododdin at Catraeth then Urien of Rheged besieging Lindisfarne. It wasn't until the reign of Æthelfrith 592–616 that we get the impression the Angles were now the dominant force in northern Britain. Bede tells us Æthelfrith 'ravaged the Britons more than all the great men of the English'. He won a decisive victory over Áedán mac Gabráin of Dál Riata at Degsastan in c. 603. The Irish were never again to campaign against the English, even up to Bede's own time. A year later he gained control of Deira.

The first attested king of Deira, Ælle, had died c. 590, and was apparently succeeded by his brother Ælfric. Perhaps his death prompted Æthelfrith to make his move. He married Ælle's daughter Acha, giving him legitimacy which caused Ælle's son Edwin to flee. This sets in motion the bloody events of the next half century. It is during Æthelfrith's reign that the Northumbrians attack the kingdom of Powys and win a battle at Chester. Meanwhile, Edwin seems to have spent his exile in various kingdoms. First possibly Gwynedd, then Mercia where he married Cwenburg, a daughter of Cearl. Æthelfrith may have applied pressure on Mercia because we next hear of Edwin at the court of Rædwald, king of the East Angles. Æthelfrith tries to persuade Rædwald to hand Edwin over or have him killed, but Rædwald's wife reminds him of his obligation to his guest and instead he helps Edwin, riding out to defeat and kill Æthelfrith at the River Idle in Nottinghamshire. The same year, 616, sees the death of Æthelberht of Kent, leaving Rædwald as the most powerful king and the fourth to be described as Bretwalda. Edwin now takes the Northumbrian throne.

On Æthelfrith's death his sons, including the two future Bretwaldas, Oswald and Oswiu, were in their turn forced into exile to the Scottish kingdom of Dál Riata. We see the shifting allegiances and political alliances at work as this was the very kingdom their father had defeated at Degsastan in c. 603. Áedán mac Gabráin had died c. 609 and been succeeded by his son, Eochaid Buide, and it is to his protection the sons of Æthelfrith fled. Edwin soon expanded his kingdom and expelled the British king Ceretic from Elmet. Bede puts Edwin's victory down to divine providence. Not only does the new king marry a Christian Kentish princess, Æthelburg daughter of Æthelberht, but he later converts to the new faith.

In 633 Edwin was killed at the battle of Hatfield Chase by Penda of Mercia and Cadwallon of Gwynedd, both of whom likely knew Edwin during his exile. He had married a Mercian princess after all. Bernicia passed back to a son of Æthelfrith,

Eanfrith and Deira to Edwin's cousin Osric. Bede castigates these two for their paganism, they 'reverted to the filth of their former idolatry'.[75]

Because of this they were later expelled from the list of kings. The previous dynasties now back in place, Deira was once more independent. This wasn't to last long; within a year both were killed. Bede's description of events is significant. Cadwallon, with 'bestial cruelty' killed and tortured as he 'raged through all the land meaning to wipe out the whole English nation from the land of Britain'.[76] Clearly by the sixth century Cadwallon at least had developed a deep animosity towards the Angles of Northumbria. He paid no respect to those of the Christian faith either and it was here we read that it is 'the habit of the Britons to despise the faith and religion of the English and not to cooperate with them in anything any more than with the heathen'. Yet he was content to ally himself with Penda.

After Edwin's death, the following summer Osric, the new king of Deira, tried to besiege Cadwallon in 'a fortified town'. The king of Gwynedd sallied out surprising and destroying Osric's forces and killing the Deirian king. Cadwallon occupied Northumbria for a whole year behaving like a 'savage tyrant, tearing them to pieces with fearful bloodshed'.[77] Eanfrith of Bernicia unwisely came to Cadwallon accompanied by just twelve thegns. Cadwallon killed them all leaving him seemingly in control. One is left to speculate how history would have unfolded if Cadwallon had succeeded in conquering the north for good.

Oswald was another son of Æthelfrith, but his mother was Acha, sister to Edwin, and so he was able to gain support from both kingdoms. The following year he rode out to meet Cadwallon despite being outnumbered. In 634, at the battle of Heavenfield near Hexham, Cadwallon was defeated and killed. Bede praises Oswald for his piety but it's clear others perceived a potentially different side to the new king of Northumbria. Edwin's widow took her infant sons and grandson into exile to France. Oswald ruled until 642 when he was killed in a 'great battle' by Penda at Maserfield on 5 August, which is thought to be Oswestry near the modern Welsh border. If so, then Oswald was on the offensive and paid with his life at the age of 38.

It is likely Cadwallon was the senior party in the alliance and with his death the Northumbrians were once again able to exert pressure on the Mercians just as Æthelfrith had done. This dominance may have been the reason of Penda's alliance with Cadwallon in the first place. With Cadwallon dead Oswald went on the offensive but events went against him and Penda was victorious. Penda now was in the ascendency and thirteen years later it was his turn to invade.

On Oswald's death the Bernician throne passed to Oswiu, Bede's last king to hold *imperium*. Oswine took power in Deira. He was the son of Osric, one of the two pagan kings killed by Cadwallon. Oswiu attempted to reunite the kingdoms, first by legitimate means, then by murder. But on Oswine's death the Deiran throne went to Oswald's son, Æthelwald. It's possible Oswiu held authority over his nephew but it is noteworthy that Æthelwald fought on the side of Penda when he invaded in 655. It was during this campaign that the last great pagan king of the Anglo-Saxons was killed at the battle of Winwaed in 655.

Penda launched what Bede describes as a 'savage attack' on the Northumbria kingdom. Oswiu was forced to promise him an 'incalculable and incredible' amount of treasure and gifts, but Penda would not accept. According to Bede, Oswiu was outnumbered thirty to one. Penda had 'thirty legions' led by thirty *duces regnii*, royal commanders. The HB perhaps tells the story from the British side.[78] Penda was accompanied by the kings of the Britons and they had actually already received the treasure at a city called Iudeu, the location is of which is unknown. Oswy, or Oswiu, had actually handed over all the treasure of the city and Penda distributed it among the kings. It is unclear if Cadfael 'the battle dodger' received his share as he 'rose up in the night' before the battle. He was the only one to escape the battle, implying the bulk of the army remained. Whatever the case, Penda's army was defeated by a much smaller force just as the outnumbered Oswald had defeated Cadwallon. Nearly all the thirty 'royal ealdormen' were killed, including Æthelhere, son of Anna, king of the East Angles who Bede says was the cause of the battle.

How he caused it is not explained, but with Æthelwald fighting for Penda against his uncle the political and dynastic context must have been complex. Oswiu ruled Mercia directly for three years, allowing Penda's son, Peada to rule as a sub-king. Peada had converted to Christianity and married a daughter of Oswiu. A son of Oswiu, Alhfrith had also married Penda's daughter. These and other inter-marriages didn't stop more bloodshed. Peada was murdered and his brother Wulfhere took the Mercian throne. To make these dynastic struggles clearer there is a list of the battles in table 7, and figure 24 gives a simplified family tree of the kings of Deira and Bernicia.

These conflicts over a fifty-year period show examples of British rulers allied with a pagan Mercian king fighting against Christian Anglo-Saxons. We also see

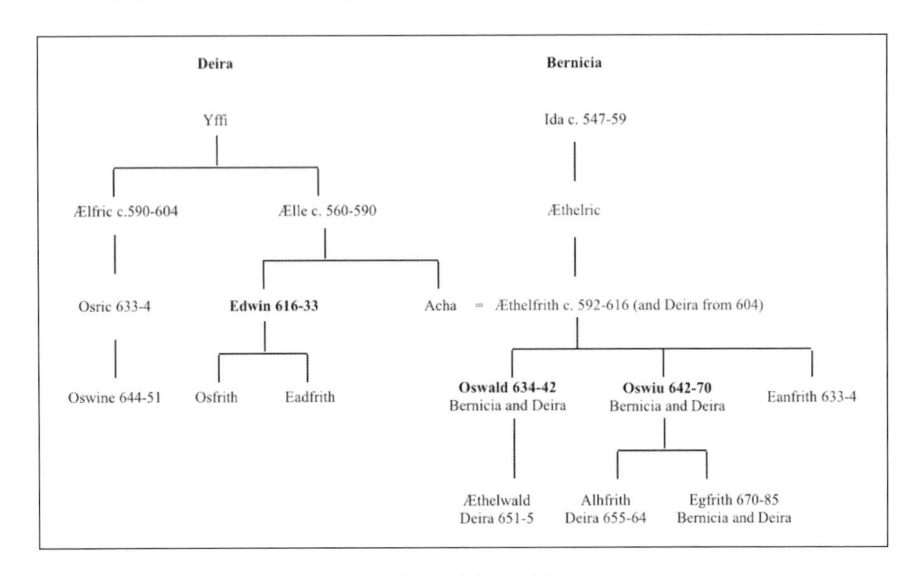

Figure 24. Family tree of the kings of Bernicia and Deira.

dynastic struggles, shifting allegiances and civil wars. We recall the Gewisse fighting first against Britons, but later against Kent and Mercia. Cultural differences between the Britons and Anglo-Saxons were not the only factors in conflict in the late sixth and early seventh centuries. It is likely similar conflicts were taking place in the late fifth or early sixth century. It is possible a fifth-century British ruler of Lincoln led sub-kings of the Angles, such as Soemil. Just as Cadwallon appeared to be the senior party in the alliance with Penda. But instead of fighting against the Angles of Northumbria they fought with Arthur in the *regione Linnuis*, or at one of the Roman forts of the north. Or perhaps Ambrosius and his allied Gewisse fought against Ælle and the men of the former south-eastern province.

Table 7: Battles of the early sixth century

Date	Location	Result	Comment
616	River Idle	Edwin and Rædwald defeat Æthelfrith	Edwin becomes king of Northumbria
633	Hatfield Chase	Cadwallon and Penda defeat Edwin	Osric king of Deira. Eanfrith king of Bernicia. Cadwallon ravages Northumbria
634	unknown	Osric defeated and killed by Cadwallon. Eanfrith killed	Cadwallon rules like a 'tyrant' for a year
634	Heavenfield	Oswald defeats and kills Cadwallon	Oswald becomes king of Northumbria
642	Maserfield (Oswestry)	Penda defeats and kills Oswald	Oswiu becomes king of Northumbria
655	Winwaed	Oswiu defeats and kills Penda possibly near Leeds	Oswiu rules in Mercia for three years with Peada as sub-king

Summary

We have a number of seemingly contradictory pieces of evidence concerning the nature of the Germanic settlement and take over of lowland Britain. On one hand we have the apparent replacement of the Brittonic language with Old English. The literary sources from Gildas and Bede suggest a conquest by fire and sword from sea to sea, dipping its 'red and savage tongue in the western ocean'. On the other hand we have evidence for significant continuation of population and land use. Initial settlements appear to have been directed by a Romano-British authority and mercenaries likely placed on marginal lands, borders, coastal strips and rivers. Additionally, the DNA evidence does not support the replacement of the indigenous population. Estimates are of tens of thousands into a population of about 2 million over many decades. There is no suggestion of a movement of people as large as the Goths or Vandals. While Bede mentions the three main tribes, Angles, Saxons and Jutes, he also lists many others including Danes, Huns and Friesians.

We recall that sixth-century Angles visiting Constantinople don't mention Saxons at all, but see Friesians as distinct with no mention of Jutes. However, Gildas, writing c. 530s, is quite certain of a cultural difference. The Romano-Britons are his fellow citizens, whereas the Saxons are barbarians. A hundred years later Cadwallon is slaughtering Northumbrians regardless of whether they are Christian or not.

Later Welsh poems *Marwnad Cynddylan* and *Canu Heledd* refer to Cynddylan, a prince of Pengwern, a sub-kingdom of Powys in the seventh century. Taking these at face value, Cynddylan fought alongside Penda at Maserfield but survived Winwaed, only to be killed and his kingdom conquered by the Mercians. The tenth-century *Armes Prydein* urges the Welsh to join the other Brythonic people to drive out the English: 'there will be reconciliation between the Welsh and the men of Dublin, the Irish of Ireland and the Isle of Man and Scotland, the men of Cornwall and of Strathclyde will be made welcome among us, the Britons will rise again when they prevail'. Conan, Cadwaladr and St David will return to lead the Welsh, who will defeat the English and 'possess the entire land from Stirling to Brittany, from Dyfed to Thanet, it will be theirs'. Conan refers to Conan Meriodoc, the legendary founder of Brittany. Perhaps surprisingly, rather than Cadwallon, it is his son, Cadwaladr, who is invoked. There is no mention of Arthur, indicating he wasn't considered as highly by the Welsh in the tenth century as by later writers. The HB, written in ninth-century Gwynedd, also shows a distinct cultural identity had formed in opposition to the Anglo-Saxon kingdoms of the east.

However, we should not assume the apparent loathing Bede attaches to the Britons for the English was always there or that it was held by everyone. Gildas may well have seen the world in black and white, but if we are to believe the HB Vortigern was happy to hire Germanic mercenaries and marry the leader's daughter. Penda and Cadwallon were in alliance and perhaps so was Urien of Rheged and the Deirians. We saw how these complex social changes played out in Gaul in the fifth century.

It is interesting to consider all the things we don't know: the discrepancy in dating between the GC and Bede for the *adventus saxonum*; the nature and timeframe of the fragmentation of the provincial structure; the nature, timeframe and process of the Germanic settlement and 'take-over'; the extent, duration, timeframe and location of the fightback by Ambrosius Aurelianus which culminated in the Battle of Badon; the relationship between the indigenous Britons and Germanic incomers in the south and east; whether Christianity survived in those areas; the nature and process of cultural change between 400–600; why is there an apparent contradiction between the near total language replacement and the evidence of continuation form DNA and land use sturdies; and how and when kingdoms emerged from the provincial and *civitas* structure.

I would suggest the following narrative as a possibility. Economic decline, corruption, high taxation, social unrest and pressure from barbarian raids were already present by the beginning of the fifth century. Despite this a sense of 'Roman identity' was common, even if faith and trust in the centralised bureaucracy was not. The break from Roman authority may not have been universally welcomed, but nor should we assume the ruling elite were regarded any better by the population. Yet the former diocese appears, for a generation at least, to have maintained a sense of citizenship, Christianity and a functioning civic and military apparatus. Enough to fight off one Saxon and Pictish raid if St Germanus is to be believed, and defeat Irish and Pictish raiders according to Gildas. The sources suggest a council of sorts was able to post mercenaries to the east and possibly the north to fight off northern and western raiders. It is likely the diocese structure survived to the mid-fifth century. At the same time Britain had been experiencing significant Germanic immigration, notably in East Anglia and the Thames Valley. This was accompanied by an increase in Germanic material culture.

Now to the difference between the GC and Bede and the ambiguity of Gildas. The GC is generally reliable, but Bede is also usually a conscientious writer and had access to other sources. The HB, though untrustworthy, offers a reasonable solution. Nor is there any reason to doubt the historicity of some of the figures mentioned. A council, led by Vortigern, hired mercenaries in the time-honoured Roman fashion. Whether he married Hengest's daughter is open to question, but the appointment of a Germanic magister militum in c. 440 and the command of a *civitas* such as Kent or the Saxon Shore Forts might appear, to a Gallic observer looking back in 452, as Britain ceding control to the Saxons. Further arrivals, a subsequent revolt and according to the HB, Hengest's return after the war with Vortimer, might be the source of Bede's later date.

The result of this upheaval between 440–450s was the ceding of specific areas to a new Germanic elite. I would suggest much of the south-eastern province of Maxima Caesariensis was 'lost' by 460. This is no reason to assume the other provinces collapsed overnight. Roger White in *Britannia Prima, Britain's Last Roman Province*, suggests the western province at least may have survived to the end of the fifth century.[79] The fragmentation of the provinces and *civitates* may have taken several decades with shifting alliances and emerging power blocks. We should see the Saxon war with Ambrosius Aurelianus in that context. Most likely occurring in the south, with Badon somewhere in Wessex. We should not assume what side the Gewisse, the 'reliable', were on. Nor should we assume that the conflict neatly bisected ethnic lines. Yet power was becoming more localised and we see the emergence of petty local rulers, just as a 'war-band culture' was evolving across Britain. Hill forts were being reoccupied and dykes built as people sought to protect valuable resources.

In fifth-century Gaul we saw that many people had turned their backs on the centralised Roman state and were attempting independence as the *bacaudae* in northern Gaul or fleeing to the barbarians. A major change in cultural identity was taking place. There is no reason to believe similar events weren't playing out in Britain. Religion may have played a significant part with conflict between the Roman Church and other doctrines, such as Pelagianism, and the introduction of a new Germanic pagan tradition. What we know did not happen is a large one off invasion by a homogenous Germanic people which wiped out the indigenous population. Instead, we get a variety of different groups arriving over several decades. It may be that some local take-overs did involve violence and that Bede's Angles, Saxons and Jutes were more prevalent in specific areas, but evidence also shows a large degree of assimilation and continuation.

Gildas, however, sees the world in very simple terms. On one side are Christians and citizens, and on the other barbarians, hated by God and man. The culmination of the events he described are that he is unable to visit certain shrines, St Albans in particular. It is possible this is simply because the shrines had been destroyed, or it may be that the south-east is now under new management. This raises one of the most intriguing and frustrating questions. Is there a political and military border separating what's left of the western and northern provinces and the areas controlled by the Anglo-Saxons? Or are there pockets of Anglo-Saxon settlements within a fragmenting political, social and military context?

I would suggest Gildas is writing in a contracted Britannia Prima. The northern province may have already fractured into competing petty kingdoms of Rheged, Alt Clud, Gododdin, Deira and Bernicia. What's left of the south eastern province was controlled by Hengest then Ælle. Badon may have prevented any expansion, but the early Kentish dynasty seems to have had influence over Essex and Surrey. Lindsey is an interesting case study. It's possible to view it as the emergence of a distinct hybrid Romano British-Germanic cultural identity. The four battles of Arthur in the *regione linnuis* might be more significant than realised. The possible spread of Arthur's battles from Southern Scotland, Chester, Lincolnshire and Wessex also suggest the survival of some political or military structures.

It is important to note Gildas appears to be preaching over the heads of his five tyrant kings to one people or even one polity. If so, this may indicate the survival of provincial authority in to the sixth century. We get no hint from Gildas that most of lowland Britain is lost. The barbarians returned to the east and we hear of no further expansion after Badon, 'not the last or least slaughter'. Britain still has governors and judges, kings and priests. External wars have stopped but civil wars continue. His polemic is a warning of disaster to come rather than a lament of one passed. What then happened after Gildas? The expansion of the West Saxons, establishment of Bernica and emergence of new dynasties don't occur until the second half of the sixth century.

Firstly, not only does Gildas tell us civil wars are continuing, but we have various sources describing such conflict at Camlann, Arfderydd and possibly Catraeth. But there are two other events that may have influenced matters. The first is the extreme climatic event c. 535 recorded in literary sources and evidenced in tree ring and ice core studies.[80] The second is the plague of Justinian c. 541–9, which swept across the former Empire. It may have killed over a quarter of the population and affected urban areas more than rural. However, Procopius writes that the plague wiped out the farming communities.[81] Gaul suffered severely, so it is quite likely that Britain was also affected.[82] Maelgwn, the 'dragon' of Gildas, was recorded in the AC as dying from the 'great death' or 'yellow plague' in 547. The Byzantium Empire was affected more than the Goths with whom they were in conflict. It is therefore possible that the plague affected the Britons more than the Anglo-Saxons.

Whatever the case, it is towards the second half of the sixth century that we see a continued expansion after a time 'free of external wars' since the battle of Badon c. 500. We have seen that some Germanic tribes discouraged intermarriage and Æthelberht stated they had kept to their old beliefs for generations. The church also tried to prohibit such marriages, although sometimes they supported such matches to encourage conversion, such as between Edwin and Æthelberht's daughter Æthelburg. We have seen how Germanic law codes often made a distinction between Romans and their own people, just as Roman law codes distinguished between citizens and barbarians. Yet at the same time people did intermarry. From the marriage between Placidia, daughter of Valentinian III, and the Gothic king, Atlas, in 414, to that of the Rheged princess, Rhiainfellt, a great-granddaughter of Urien, to Oswiu of Northumbria. Her grandfather, Rhun, is said in the HB to have baptised Edwin in 627.

Gildas no doubt would have been dead against such unions, and we have seen from Bede that some Britons at least loathed the Anglo-Saxons even if they had converted to Christianity. Despite the literary references to ethnic division we also get just as many civil wars and alliances between Britons and Anglo-Saxons. We should not be surprised about this apparent contradiction. People have layers of cultural identities that change over time or context. Additionally, different forces could be prominent at the same time. While one warlord may be engaging in ethnic warfare another might be encouraging assimilation and inter-marriage.

As we peel away the veil that obscures the 'Dark Ages' we may well be presented with a more complex and dynamic political, cultural and military situation than we imagined. A fragmenting Roman administrative structure coupled with the emergence of local power blocks. Alongside increased immigration from a variety of Germanic peoples and a rapidly changing cultural identity in the indigenous population. Additionally, we see the beginnings of a war-band culture and a social order based around the warlord and mead hall. We see echoes of this in Old Welsh and Anglo-Saxon poems such as *Y Gododdin* and *Beowulf*.

The exciting thing to think about are all the discoveries yet to be made. The graves of Hengest, Horsa, Vortimer and our Bretwaldas, Ælle and Ceawlin, lie undiscovered waiting to reveal their secrets. Treasures likely to rival those at Sutton Hoo and Prittlewell. The locations of battle sites also need to be determined. Perhaps the Cray or Darent Valleys will reveal the remains of a mass grave of hundreds of warriors. Or building work near Paulinus Church on Mount Nod will uncover the bones and weapons that have been lying silent of over 1,500 years. A document hidden for centuries, or long forgotten in the Vatican archives, may reveal a marriage proposal, charter or appointment which will reveal something about the political situation in fifth-century Britain. Or an inscribed stone, its face hidden in the wall or foundations of an early church. The inscription will show a fifth-century ruler of a province, *civitas* or early kingdom. The name might be Vortigern, Ambrosius Aurelianus or even Arthur. Perhaps Ælle or Ceawlin. What we can be sure about is new discoveries and finds will be made. Archaeologists will keep digging, metal detectorists will keep detecting and historians will continue researching. With each new find, however small, we get closer to unravelling some of the mysteries and secrets that have so far eluded us.

Sources for Maps

Figure 3. Map of major Roman roads of Britain. Image from Wikimedia Commons. By Andrei Nacu at English Wikipedia – Transferred from en.wikipedia to Commons by Gpedro. Mason (2001. Public Domain, https://commons.wikimedia.org/w/index.php?curid=3575904

Figure 4. Map of infrastructure and Romanisation of the fourth century. Image from Wikimedia Commons. Based on Jones & Mattingly's Atlas of Roman Britain (ISBN 978-1-84217-06700, 1990, reprinted 2007). CC BY-SA 3.0, https://commons.wikimedia.org/w/index.php?curid=11638867

Figure 7. Map of Anglo-Saxon cemeteries in post-Roman Britain. Image from Wikimedia Commons. Based on Jones & Mattingly's *Atlas of Roman Britain*, CC BY-SA 3.0, https://commons.wikimedia.org/w/index.php?curid=11596162

Figure 9. Map of early Anglo-Saxon cemeteries in Kent. Image from Wikimedia Commons. Amended from Jones & Mattingly's *Atlas of Roman Britain*, CC BY-SA 3.0, https://commons.wikimedia.org/w/index.php?curid=11596162

Figure 14. Map of Ælle and the South Saxons. Author: Green, John Richard, 1837-1883. Image from Wikimedia Commons. https://commons.wikimedia.org/w/index.php?curid=44101450

Figure 16. Map showing Saxon, Angle and Jute homelands. Image from Wikimedia Commons. Author: mbartelsm – Own work, CC BY-SA 3.0, https://commons.wikimedia.org/w/index.php?curid=86531831

All other maps and figures by author

Sources and details of photographs

Picture 1: Outer ditch and wall at Richborough Roman Fort, East Kent. Major port for entry in Britain in Roman times and close to Isle of Thanet. Photograph by author.

Picture 2: Exterior wall at Pevensey Roman Fort, East Sussex. Taken by Ælle in 491. Photograph by author.
Picture 3: Interior of Pevensey Roman Fort, East Sussex. Photograph by author.

Picture 4: Highdown Hill, Sussex. Fifth-century Anglo-Saxon cemetery. Photograph by author.

Picture 5: Outer ditch at Cissbury Hillfort, Sussex. Photograph by author.

Picture 6: Cadbury Castle Hill Fort. Image from Wikimedia Commons. Author: Tim Heaton, CC BY-SA 2.0, https://commons.wikimedia.org/w/index.php?curid=41356913

Picture 7: Dark Age warriors guarding a reconstruction of a King's Hall from c. 700 in Lejre near Roskilde, Denmark. Photograph by permission of Ivanowich of Kobbeaa.

Picture 8: A Dark Age lord in reconstruction of hall c. 700 in Lejre near Roskilde, Denmark. Photograph by permission of Ivanowich of Kobbeaa.

Picture 9: Shield bosses, bowls and brooches found at Highdown Hill fifth-century Anglo-Saxon cemetery. Photograph by permission of Worthing Museum, Sussex.

Picture 10: Glassware found at Highdown Hill fifth-century Anglo-Saxon cemetery. Possibly from Rhineland and northern Gaul. Photograph by permission of Worthing Museum, Sussex.

Picture 11: Glassware found at Highdown Hill fifth-century Anglo-Saxon cemetery. Possibly c. 400 from Egypt. Photograph by permission of Worthing Museum, Sussex.

Picture 12: Two swords and spear found at Highdown Hill fifth-century Anglo-Saxon cemetery. Photograph by permission of Worthing Museum, Sussex.

Picture 13: Quoit military style brooches found at Highdown Hill fifth-century. Anglo-Saxon cemetery. Photograph by permission of Worthing Museum, Sussex.

Picture 14: Replica of Vendel helmet at Worthing Museum. Photograph by permission of Worthing Museum, Sussex.

Picture 15: Evidence of sword cut to thighbone of a fifth-century warrior. From Highdown Hill fifth-century Anglo-Saxon cemetery. Photograph by permission of Worthing Museum, Sussex.

Sources for Maps

Picture 16: James Sainsbury Curator at Worthing Museum compares the thighbone of a fifth-century warrior, who must have exceeded 6ft. From Highdown Hill fifth century Anglo-Saxon cemetery. Photograph by permission of Worthing Museum, Sussex.

Picture 17: Skull from early Anglo-Saxon period showing likely fatal blow from axe. From Highdown Hill fifth-century Anglo-Saxon cemetery. Photograph by permission of Worthing Museum, Sussex.

Picture 18: Photograph of the 1986 replica of the c. seventh-century Benty Grange helmet, on view at Weston Park Museum in Sheffield. Image from Wikimedia Commons, author: Museums Sheffield – Museums Sheffield CC BY-SA 4.0, https://commons.wikimedia.org/w/index.php?curid=66284652

Picture 19: Spangenhelm (iron), helmet from the Migration Period. Museum of the Cetinska Krajina Region – Sinj, Croatia. Image from Wikimedia Commons. Author: Völkerwanderer – Own work, CC0, https://commons.wikimedia.org/w/index.php?curid=21654634

Picture 20: Late Romano-British warrior from fifth century. A depiction of Arthur c. 500 by Sean Poage, author of 'The Retreat to Avalon'.

Picture 21: Dark Age axe-man re-enactor in period authentic costume. Sutton Hoo replica helmet. Image from Wikimedia Commons. Author: Chaosdruid – Own work, CC BY 3.0, https://commons.wikimedia.org/w/index.php?curid=15366880

Picture 22: Taeppa's Mound in the old churchyard, Taplow, Buckinghamshire. Image from Wikimedia Commons. Author: Stefan Czapski, CC BY-SA 2.0, https://commons.wikimedia.org/w/index.php?curid=40494701

Picture 23: British Museum description: 'Pair of drinking horns, Anglo-Saxon, late sixty-century AD. From the princely burial at Taplow, Buckinghamshire.' Image from Wikimedia Commons. Author: unforth – http://www.flickr.com/photos/unforth/2686728373/, CC BY-SA 2.0, https://commons.wikimedia.org/w/index.php?curid=11188549

Picture 24: Burial mound 2 at Sutton Hoo, Suffolk. Reconstructed to original height. Image from Wikimedia Commons. Author: Kim Roper – https://www.flickr.com/photos/mrandmrsbunny/, CC BY-SA 2.5, https://commons.wikimedia.org/w/index.php?curid=1633217

Picture 25: Model of Sutton Hoo ship-burial mound one, with burial chamber marked white. Image by Wikimedia Commons. Author: Eebahgum CC BY-SA 3.0, https://commons.wikimedia.org/w/index.php?curid=4515737

Picture 26: Burial chamber of the Sutton Hoo ship-burial 1, England. Reconstruction shown in the Sutton Hoo Exhibition Hall. Image from Wikimedia Commons. Author: Iestyn Hughes – https://www.flickr.com/people/traedmawr/, CC BY-SA 2.5, https://commons.wikimedia.org/w/index.php?curid=1609778

Picture 27: Replica of Sutton Hoo Helmet. Image from Wikimedia Commons. Author: Gernot Keller (Own work), Public Domain, https://commons.wikimedia.org/w/index.php?curid=4077937

Picture 28: Shield from Sutton Hoo burial mound. Image from Wikimedia Commons. Author: Gary Todd. CC0, https://commons.wikimedia.org/w/index.php?curid=108814351

Picture 29: Identical shoulder clasps from mound one at Sutton Hoo in British Museum. Image from Wikimedia Commons. Author: Jononmac46 – Own work, CC BY-SA 3.0, https://commons.wikimedia.org/w/index.php?curid=31938534

Picture 30: Helmet from the seventh-century ship-burial at Vendel, Sweden. Image from Wiki Commons. Swedish History Museum – Swedish History Museum: http://mis.historiska.se/mis/sok/fid.asp?fid=109204, CC BY 2.5, https://commons.wikimedia.org/w/index.php?curid=58203423

Picture 31: Migration period sword from Saint-Dizier (Haute-Marne) grave 11. Germanic Futhark or Anglo-Saxon Futhorc runic inscription alu on Bifrons-Gilton type ring sword pommel carved then effaced and replaced with niello ornaments. Image from Wikimedia Commons. Author: G.Garitan – Own work, CC BY-SA 3.0, https://commons.wikimedia.org/w/index.php?curid=19511211

Picture 32: Anglo-Saxon warriors from the migration period. Photograph by kind permission
of Yahushan Ram from the Seaxia Dark Ages Re-enactment Group.

Picture 33: Anglo-Saxon warrior. Photograph by kind permission
of Yahushan Ram from the Seaxia Dark Ages Re-enactment Group.

Picture 34: Anglo-Saxon warrior. Photograph by kind permission
of Yahushan Ram from the Seaxia Dark Ages Re-enactment Group.

Picture 35: Two early period Anglo-Saxon warriors. Photograph by kind permission
of Yahushan Ram from the Seaxia Dark Ages Re-enactment Group.

References

Adoman of Iona. *Life of St Columba.* (Penguin, London, 1995).
Arnold, C.J, *An Archaeology of the Early Anglo-Saxon Kingdoms,* (Routledge, London, 2000).
Alexander, Caroline, *Lost Gold of the Dark Ages, War Treasure and the Mystery of the Saxons*, (National Geographic, Washington, 2011).
Baring-Gould, Sabine, *The Lives of British Saints Volumes 1–4*, (Forgotten Books, London, 2012).
Barr-Hamilton, Alec, *In Saxon Sussex*, (The Arundel Press, Bognor Regis, 1953).
Bartrum, Peter, *A Welsh Classical Dictionary,* (National Library of Wales, 1993).
Bassett, Stephen, *The Origins of the Anglo-Saxon Kingdoms*, (Leicester University Press, London, 1989).
Bede, *The Ecclesiastical History of the English People,* (Oxford University Press, Oxford, 1994).
Birley, Anthony, *The Roman Government of Britain*, (Oxford University Press, Oxford, 2005). Bishop, M.C., *The Secret History of the Roman Roads of Britain*, (Pen and Sword, Barnsley, 2020).
Breeze, David, J. and Dobson, Brian, *Hadrian's Wall*, (Penguin Books, London, 2000).
Brookes, S and Harrington, S, *The Kingdom and People of Kent AD 400–1066 Their History and Archaeology*, (The history Press Port Stroud, 2010).
Brown, Peter, *Through the Eye of a Needle, Wealth, the fall of Rome, and the Making of Christianity in the West 350–550 AD*, (Princeton University Press, Princeton, 2012).
Brugman, B, *Migration and Endogenuous Change,* in Hamerow, H, Hinton, D, and Crawford, S, *The Oxford Handbook of Anglo-Saxon Archaeology,* (Oxford University Press, Oxford, 2011).
Bury, John, *The Life of St Patrick and His Place in History,* (Dover Publications, London, 1998).
Bury, J.B., *The origin of Pelagius*, (Hermathena, Volume 13, Number 30 (1904): 26-35, Trinity College Dublin).
Carver, Martin, *Formative Britain, An Archaeology of Britain Fifth to Eleventh Century AD,* (Routledge, Abingdon, 2019).
Carver, M., Sanmark, A., and Semple, S., *Signals of Belief in Early England, Anglo-Saxon Paganism Revisited*, (Oxbow Books, Oxford, 2010).
Carver, M, *The Sutton Hoo Story*, (The Boydell Press, Woodbridge, 2017).

Chadwick et al, *Studies in Early British History,* (Cambridge University Press, Cambridge 1959).

Chambers, E, K, *Arthur of Britain,* (Sidgwick and Jackson, London, 1966).

Charles-Edwards, T.M, *Wales and the Britons 350–1064,* (Oxford University Press, Oxford, 2014).

Clarkson, Tim, *The Men of the North,* (Berlinn Ltd, Edinburgh, 2016).

Clarkson, Tim, *The Picts: A History,* (Berlinn Ltd, Edinburgh, 2019).

Clearly, S, *The Ending(s) of Roman Britain* in Hamerow, H, Hinton, D, and Crawford, S, *The Oxford Handbook of Anglo-Saxon Archaeology,* (Oxford University Press, Oxford, 2011).

Clemoes, Peter, *Anglo-Saxon England Volume 5,* (Cambridge University Press, Cambridge 1976).

Collins, Rob, *Hadrian's Wall and the End of Empire,* (Routledge, New York, 2012).

Crabtree, Pam, *Early Medieval Britain, The Rebirth of Towns in the Post-Roman West,* (Cambridge University Press, Cambridge, 2018).

Cusack, Mary Francis, *History of Ireland from AD 400 to 1800,* (Senate, London 1995).

Cunliffe, Barry, *Britain Begins,* (Oxford University Press, Oxford, 2013).

Dark, K, R, *Civitas to Kingdom; British Political Continuity 300–800,* (Leicester University Press, London, 1994).

Dark, Ken, *Britain and the End of the Roman Empire,* (Tempus Publishing Ltd, Stroud, 2000).

Davidson, Hilda, Ellis, *The Sword in Anglo-Saxon England,* (Boydell Press, Woodbridge, 1998).

Davies, Hugh, *Roman Roads in Britain,* (Shire Archaeology, Oxford, 2008).

Davenport, Peter, *Roman Bath, A New History and Archaeology of Aquae Sulis,* (The History Press, Stroud, 2021).

De La Bedoyere, Guy, *Eagles over Britannia,* (Tempus Publishing, Stroud, 2001).

De La Bedoyere, Guy, *Gladius, Living Fighting and Dying in the Roman Army,* (Little Brown, London, 2020).

De La Bedoyere, Guy, *Roman Britain, A New History,* (Thames and Hudson, London, 2006).

Drinkwater, John, and Elton, Hugh, *Fifth Century Gaul: A Crisis of Identity,* (Cambridge Universety Press, Cambridge, 2002).

Dumville, David, *Britons and Anglo-Saxons in the Early Middle Ages,* (Variorum, Aldershot, 1993).

Dumville, David, *Saint Patrick,* (Boydell Press, Woodbridge, 1999).

Dyer, James, *Hillforts of England and Wales,* (Shire Archaeology, Risborough, 1992).

Eagles, Bruce, *From Roman Civitas to Anglo-Saxon Shire: Topographical Studies on the Formation of Wessex ,* (Oxbow Books, Oxford, 2018).

Elliott, Simon, *Romans at War,* (Casemate, Oxford, 2020).

Esposito, Gabriele, *Armies of the Late Roman Empire AD 284–476, History Organisation and Equipment,* (Pen and Sword Books, Barnsley, 2018).

References

Evans, Bryan, *The Life and Times of Hengest*, (Anglo-Saxon Books, Ely, 2014).

Evans, John, *The Tomb of Horsa*, (Archaeologia Catiana Volume 65, pages 101-113, 1952).

Evans, Stephen, *Lords of Battle,* (Boydell Press, Woodbridge, 2000).

Fitzpatrick-Matthews, Keith, J, *The textual history of the Historia Brittonum*, (http://www.historiabrittonum.net/wp-content/uploads/2018/09/The-textual-history-of-the-Historia-Brittonum.pdf, 2017).

Fitzpatrick-Matthews, Keith, J, The Arthurian Battle list of the Historia Brittonum, (http://www.historiabrittonum.net/wp-content/uploads/2018/09/The-Arthurian-battle-list-of-the-Historia-Brittonum.pdf)

Fleming, Robin, *The Material Fall of Roman Britain 300–525 CE*, (University of Pennsylvania, Philadelphia, 2021).

Flierman, Robert, *Saxon Identities AD 150–900*, (Bloomsbury Publishing, London, 2017).

Foster, Sally, *Picts, Gaels and Scots: Early historic Scotland,* (Berlinn Ltd, Edinburgh, 2014).

Gerrard, James, *The Ruin of Roman Britain an Archaeological Perspective*, (Cambridge University Press, Cambridge, 2016).

Goldsworthy, Adrian, *Pax Romana*, (Weidenfeld and Nicolson, London, 2016).

Goldsworthy, Adrian, *The Fall of the West,* (Phoenix, London, 2010).

Goldsworthy, Adrian, *The Complete Roman Army,* (Thames and Hudson, London, 2003).

Goldsworthy, Adrian, *Roman Warfare* (Phoenix, London, 2000).

Green, D.H., *Language and History in the Early Germanic World*, (Cambridge University Press, Cambridge, 2000).

Green, Caitlin, *Britons and the Anglo-Saxons, Lincolnshire 400–650 AD,* (History of Lincolnshire Committee, Lincoln, 2020)

Griffen, T, *Names from the Dawn of British Legend,* (Llanerch, Dyfed, 1994).

Grigg, Eric, *Warfare and Raiding and Defence in Early Medieval Britain*, (Robert Hale, Marlborough 2018).

Halsall, Guy, *Barbarian Migrations and the Roman West 376–568*, (Cambridge University Press, Cambridge, 2014).

Halsall, Guy, *Warfare and Society in the Barbarian West 450–900,* (Routledge, London, 2003).

Halsall, Guy, *Worlds of Arthur,* (Oxford University Press, Oxford, 2014).

Hamer, Richard, *A Choice of Anglo-Saxon Verse*, (Faber and Faber, London, 1970).

Hamerow, H, Hinton, D, and Crawford, S, *The Oxford Handbook of Anglo-Saxon Archaeology,* (Oxford University Press, Oxford, 2011).

Hamilton, Walter, *Ammianus Marcellinus, The Later Roman Empire AD 354-378* (Penguin Books, London, 1986).

Harding, Dennis, *Iron Age Hillforts in Britain and Beyond*, (Oxford University Press, Oxford, 2012).

Harrington, Sue and Welch, Martin, *Early Anglo-Saxon Kingdoms of Southern Briton AD 450–650: Beyond the Tribal Hidage,* (Oxbow Books, Oxford, 2018).

Hatfield, Edward, Pritanica, *A Dictionary of the Ancient British Language,* (Whiskey and Beards Publishing, 2016).

Higham, N.J, *The English Conquest, Gildas and Britain in the fifth century*, (Manchester University Press, Manchester, 1994).

Higham, N.J., *The Kingdom of Northumbria AD 350–1100*, (Alan Sutton, Stroud, 1993).

Higham, N and Ryan, R, *The Anglo-Saxon World,* (Yale University Press, New Haven, 2015).

Hills, C., *Anglo Saxon Identity* in Hamerow, H, Hinton, D, and Crawford, S, *The Oxford Handbook of Anglo-Saxon Archaeology,* (Oxford University Press, Oxford, 2011).

Hill, Paul, *The Anglo-Saxons at War 800–1066*, (Pen and Sword, Barnsley, 2014).

Hirst, Sue, and Scull, Christopher, *The Anglo-Saxon Princely Burial at Prittlewell, Southend-on-sea*, (Museum of London Archaeology, London, 2019).

Hobbs, R & Jackson, R., *Roman Britain,* (The British Museum Press, London, 2015).

Hooke, Della, *The Anglo-Saxon Landscape, The Kingdom of the Hwicce*, (Manchester University Press, Manchester, 1985).

Hughes, Ian, *Aetius, Attila's Nemesis*, (Pen and Sword Books, Barnsley, 2020).

Jarman, A., *Aneirin, Y Gododdin,* (Gomer Press, Ceredigion, 1990).

Joyce, Stephen, *A new source for Mons Badonicus? Returning to the Irish life of Finnian of Clonard,* (Journal of the Australian Early Medieval Association, p31–46, 2019). Koch, John, *Waiting for Gododdin: Thoughts on Taliesin and Iudic-Hael, Catraeth, and Unripe Time in Celtic Studies* in *Beyond the Gododdin : Dark Age Scotland in Medieval Wales : the proceedings of a day conference held on 19 February 2005 [St. John's House papers, no. 13.],* (The Committee for Dark Age Studies, University of St. Andrews,St. Andrews, Fife, 2013)

Lapidge, Michael and Dumville, David: *Gildas, New Approaches,* (Boydell Press, Woodbridge, 1984).

Laycock, Stuart, *Britannia The Failed State,* (The History Press, Stroud, 2011).

Leahy, Kevin, and Bland, Roger, *The Staffordshire Hoard*, (The British Museum, London, 2014).

Loveluck, C. and Laing, L., *Britons and Anglo-Saxons* in Hamerow, H, Hinton, D, and Crawford, S, *The Oxford Handbook of Anglo-Saxon Archaeology,* (Oxford University Press, Oxford, 2011).

Low, D.M, *Gibbon's The Decline and Fall of the Roman Empire,* (Chatto and Windus, London, 1981).

Lucy, Sam, *The Anglo-Saxon Way of Death*, (Sutton Publishing, Stroud, 2000).

Manco, Jean, *The Origins of the Anglo-Saxons,* (Thames and Hudson, New York, 2018),

Mathisen, Ralph, *Roman Aristocrats in Barbarian Gaul, Strategies for Survival in the Age of Transition*, (University of Texas Press, Texas, 1989).

Matthews, John, *Taliesin, The Last Celtic Shaman,* (Inner Traditions, Vermont, 2002).

References

Matthews, Robert, *Ceawlin, The Man Who Created England*, (Pen and Sword, Barnsley, 2012).

Marren, Peter, *Battles of the Dark Ages,* (Pen and Sword, Barnsley 2006).

Marsden, John, *Northanhymbre Saga: History of the Anglo-Saxon Kings of Northumbria,* (Kyle Cathie Ltd, London, 1992).

Mees, Kate, *Burial, Landscape and Identity in Early Medieval Wessex*, (The Boydell Press, Woodbridge, 2019).

Mierow, Charles, *Jordanes The Origin and Deeds of the Goths,* (Dodo Press, Princetown 1908).

Mills, A.D., *A Dictionary or British Place Names,* (Oxford University Press, oxford, 2011).

Milner, N.P., *Vegetius: Epitome of Military Science 2nd Ed* (Liverpool Universety Press, Liverpool, 2011).

Mitchell, Stephen, and Greatrex, Geoffrey, *Ethnicity and Culture in Late Antiquity,* (Duckworth and The Classical Press of Wales, London, 2000).

Moffat, Alistair, *The British: A Genetic Journey,* (Birlinn, Edinburgh, 2013).

Morris, J., *Arthurian Period Sources Volume 3 Persons: Ecclesiastics and Laypeople,* (Phillimore, Chichester, 1995).

Morris, J., *Arthurian Period Sources Volume 7 Gildas,* (Phillimore, Chichester, 1978).

Morris, J., *Arthurian Period Sources Volume 8 Nennius,* (Phillimore, Chichester, 1980).

Morris, Marc, *The Anglo-Saxons, A History of the Beginnings of England*, (Hutchinson, London, 2021).

Mortimer, Paul and Bunker, Matt, *The Sword in Anglo-Saxon England from the 5th to 7th Century*, (Anglo-Saxon Books, Ely, 2019).

Mortimer, Paul, *Woden's Warriors, Warriors and Warfare in 6th–7th Century Northern Europe*, (Anglo-Saxon Books, Ely, 2011).

Naismith, Rory, *Citadel of the Saxons,* (I.B. Tauris and Co. London, 2019).

Naismith, Rory, *Early Medieval Britain, c. 500–1000,* (Cambridge University Press, Cambridge, 2021).

Napper, H.F., *The Sussex Archaeological Society*, (Volume 39, 1904).

Newton, Sam, *The Origins of Beowulf and the Pre-Viking Kingdom of East Anglia,* (D.S Brewer, Cambridge, 1994).

O Croinin, Daibhi, *Early Medieval Ireland 400–1200 2nd Edition,* (Routledge, London, 2017).

Oousthuizen, Susan, *The Anglo-Saxon Fenland,* (Oxbow Books, Oxford, 2017).

Oousthuizen, Susan, *The Emergence of the English,* (Arc Humanities Press, Leeds, 2019).

Oppenheimer, Stephen, *The Origins of the British,* (Robinson, London, 2007).

Painter, K.S., *Villas and Christianity in Roman Britain*, (The British Museum Quarterly, vol. 35, no. 1/4, British Museum, 1971, pp. 156–75, https://doi.org/10.2307/4423079).

Pearson, Andrew, *The Roman Shore Forts,* (The History Press, Stroud, 2010).

Pollington, Stephen, *The Elder Gods, The Otherworld of Early England*, (Anglo-Saxon Books, Ely, 2011).

Reynolds, Andrew, *Anglo-Saxon Deviant Burial Customs*, (Oxford, University Press, Oxford, 2014).

Rippon, Stephen, *Kingdom, Civitas, and County: The Evolution of Territorial Identity in the English Landscape*, (Oxord University Press, Oxford, 2018).

Rivet, A.L.F. and Smith, Colin, *The Place-Names of Roman Britain*, (Batsford, London, 1982).

Salway, Peter, *A History of Roman Britain*, (Oxford University Press, Oxford, 2001).

Sayer, Duncan, *Anglo-Saxon Cemeteries, Kinship, Community and Identity*, (Manchester University Press, Manchester, 2020.

Sisam, Kenneth, *Anglo-Saxon Royal Genealogies,* The British Academy, London, 1953.

Snyder, Christopher, *An Age of Tyrants, Britain and the Britons A.D. 400–600*, (Sutton Publishing, Stroud, 1998).

Stenton, Frank, *Anglo Saxon England,* Oxford University Press, Oxford, 1989.

Swanton, Michael, *The Anglo-Saxon Chronicles,* (Phoenix Press, London, 2000).

Sykes, Brian, *Blood of the Isles,* (Corgi Books, London, 2006).

Syvanne, Ilkka, *Military History of Late Rome 425–457*, (Pen and Sword, Yorkshire, 2020).

Thomas, Charles, *Christianity in Roman Britain to AD 500,* (Batsford, London 1981).

Thompson, E.A., Procopius on Brittia and Britannia, (Cambridge University Press, The Classical Quarterly Vol. 30, No. 2, 1980: 498–507).

Thompson, E. A., *Saint Germanus of Auxerre and the end of Roman Britain*, (Boydell Press, Woodbridge, 1988).

Thornton, D., Kings, *Chronicles and Genealogies: Studies in the Political History of Early Medieval Ireland and Wales,* (Linacre College, Oxford, 2003).

Thorpe Lewis (translator), *Gerald of Wales,* (Penguin Books, London, 1988).

Thorpe Lewis (translator), *Gregory of Tours The History of the Franks,* (Penguin Books, London 1977).

Thorpe Lewis (translator), *Geoffrey of Monmouth, The History of the Kings of Britain,* (Penguin Books, London, 1966).

Todd, Malcolm, *A Companion to Roman Britain*, (Blackwell Publishing, Malden, USA, 2007)

Todd, Malcolm, *The Early Germans*, 2nd Edition, (Blackwell Publishing, Malden, USA, 2004).

Tolkien, J.R.R., *Beowulf, A Translation and Commentary,* (Harper Collins, London, 2016).

Tolkien, J.R.R., *Finn and Hengest, The Fragment and the Episode*, (Harper Collins, London, 1998).

Tomlin, R.S.O., *Britannia Romana, Roman Inscriptions and Roman Britain*, (Oxbow Books, Oxford, 2018).

References

Underwood, Richard, *Anglo-Saxon Weapons and Warfare,* (Tempus Publishing Ltd, Stroud, 1999).
Vermaat, Robert, Nennius, *The Historia Brittonum*, (http://www.vortigernstudies.org.uk/artsou/historia.htm).
Wacher, John, *The Towns of Roman Britain,* (BCA, London, 1995).
Wade-Evans, A.W., *The Lives and Genealogies of the Welsh Saints*, (Ashley Drake Publishers, Cardiff, 1988).
Wallace-Hadrill, J.M., *The Barbarian West 400–1000,* (Blackwell, Oxford, 1999).
Wallace-Hadrill, J.M., *The Long-Haired Kings,* (Methuen & Co, London, 1962).
Webster, L & Brown, M., *The Transformation of the Roman World AD 400–900,* (British Museum Press, London, 1997).
Webb, Simon, *Life in Roman London,* (The History Press, Stroud, 2011).
Welch, Martin, *Highdown and its Saxon Cemetery*, (Worthung Museum and Art Gallery Publications number 11, Worthing, 1978).
White, Roger, *Britannia Prima, Britain's Last Roman Province*, (Tempus, Stroud, 2007)
White, Roger, and Barker, Philip, *Wroxeter, Life and Death of a Roman City*, (Tempus, Stroud, 2002)
Williams, Ann, *Kingship and Government in Pre-Conquest England, c. 500–1066*, (MacMillan Press, New York, 1999).
Wilson, Roger J.A., *A Guide to the Roman Remains in Britain,* (Constable & Company, London, 1980).
Wolfram, Herwig, *The Roman Empire and it's Germanic Peoples*, (University of California Press, Berkeley, 1997).
Wood, Michael, *Domesday, A Search for the Roots of England*, (Book Club Associates, London 1987).
Woods, David, *Gildas and the Mystery Cloud of 536–537*, (The Journal of Theological Studies, NS, 2010, University of Southern California, April 5, 2014).
Yorke, Barbara, *Kings and the Kingdoms of Early Anglo-Saxon England,* (Routledge, London, 2013).
Zaluckyj, Sarah, Mercia: *The Anglo-Saxon Kingdom of Central England,* (Logaston Press, Logaston, 2013)

Endnotes

Introduction

1. Stenton, 1989:35
2. Gregory of Tours, History of the Franks, Book 4.4
3. Brooks in Bassett, 1989: 55
4. Painter, 1971: 161

Chapter 1: Fifth-century Britain

1. Rippon, 2018: 352
2. Halsall, 2014: 480
3. Gerrard, 2016: 215
4. Rippon, 2018: 327
5. Crabtree, 2018: 5–6
6. Crabtree, 2018: 18
7. Charles-Edwards 2014: 31
8. Dark, 1994: 10
9. Gerrard, 2016: 55
10. Dark, 1994: 15
11. Goldsworthy, 2010: 344
12. Dark, 2000: 17
13. Fleming, 2021: 18
14. Salway, 2001: 277
15. Salway, 2001: 280–281
16. http://www.vortigernstudies.org.uk/artsou/orosius.htm
17. Oosthuizen, 2019: 27
18. http://www.vortigernstudies.org.uk/artsou/zosim.htm
19. http://www.vortigernstudies.org.uk/artsou/procop.htm
20. Goldsworthy, 2010: 337
21. Bishop, 2020: 70–71
22. Bishop, 2020: 104
23. Fleming, 2021: 6
24. Wallace-Hadrill, 1961:2
25. Charles-Edwards, 2014: 43

Endnotes

26. Gerrard, 2016: 163
27. Halsall, 2014: 358
28. Fleming, 2021: 5
29. Higham and Ryan, 2015: 42
30. Hills, 2011: 9
31. Fleming, 2021, 10
32. Fleming, 2021: 177
33. Clearly, 2011: 13
34. Gerrard, 2016: 73–78
35. Gerrard, 2016: 114-117
36. Crabtree, 2018: 22-23
37. Wacher, 1995: 150
38. Snyder, 1998: 228
39. Davenport 2021: 219
40. Davenport, 2021: 215
41. Dark, 2000: 33
42. Bedoyere, 2006: 263
43. Salway, 2001: 347
44. Salway, 2001: 348
45. Carver, 2019: 37
46. Wacher, 1995: 188
47. Collins, 2012: 1
48. Collins, 2012: 110
49. Collins, 2012: 103
50. Salway, 2001: 341
51. Carver, 2019: 189
52. Carver, 2019: 192
53. Carver, 2019: 176
54. Carver, 2019: 145
55. Carver, 2019: 144
56. Crabtree, 2018: 84
57. Crabtree, 2018: 42
58. Cunliffe, 2013: 411
59. Charles-Edwards, 2014: 370
60. Todd, 2004: 208
61. Eagles, 2018: xxxiv
62. Arnold, 2000: 60
63. Manco, 2018: 129
64. Manco, 2018: 127
65. Hills 2011: 10
66. Zaluckyj, 2018: 2
67. Bede volume 5 chapter 9
68. Todd, 2004: 207
69. Green, 2012: 93 & 94

70. Carver in Bassett, 1989: 156
71. Rippon, 2018: 318
72. Fleming, 2021: 181
73. Todd, 2004: 210
74. Manco, 2018: 119
75. Oppenheimer 2007:382
76. Arnold, 2000: 23
77. Charles-Edwards, 2014: 48
78. Zaluckyj, 2018: 6
79. Arnold, 2000: 23
80. Arnold, 2000: 104-107, 116-118
81. Oppenheimer 2007: 380
82. Hills, 2011: 6
83. Eagles, 2018: 185
84. Eagles, 2018: 43
85. Eagles, 2018: 22
86. Rippon, 2018: 241
87. Higham and Ryan, 2015: 91
88. Eagles, 2018: xxx
89. Moffatt, 2013: 182
90. Cunliffe, 2013: 242
91. Cunliffe, 2013: 424
92. Arnold, 2000: 20 & 21
93. Oousthuizen, 2019: 59
94. Fleming, 2021: 5
95. Fleming, 2021: 187
96. http://www.vortigernstudies.org.uk/artsou/constex.htm
97. Bury, 1904: 26-35
98. Brown, 2012: 310
99. Wood in Dumville and Lapwood, 1984: 8
100. http://www.vortigernstudies.org.uk/artsou/prosp.htm
101. Wolfram, 1997: 241
102. Thompson, 1968: 39-46
103. Eagles, 2018: 14
104. Hughes, 2020: 93
105. Oosthuizen, 2019: 29
106. Charles-Edwards, 2014: 227
107. O Croinin, 2017: 46
108. O Croinin, 2017: 47
109. Dumville, 1999
110. Lapidge and Dumville, 1984: 52
111. Lapidge and Dumville, 1984: 47
112. Lapidge and Dumville, 1984: 50
113. Hughes, 2020: 130

Endnotes

114. Keys, 2000
115. Woods, 2014
116. Morris, 1978: 19
117. Chadwick in Chadwick et al, 1959: 21
118. Bede, book 1.15
119. http://www.vortigernstudies.org.uk/artsou/bede.htm
120. http://www.vortigernstudies.org.uk/artsou/chron452.htm
121. Wood in Lapidge and Dumville, 1984: 19
122. Wood, in Lapidge and Dumville, 1984: 16-20
123. Thomas, 1981: 198
124. Goldsworthy, 2010: 338, 345
125. Croinin, 2017: 37
126. Dark, 1994: 30 & 32
127. Brown, 2012: 359
128. Brown, 2012: 349
129. Brown, 2012: 352
130. Brown, 2012: 400–1
131. Charles-Edwards, 2014: 227
132. O Croinin, 2017: 46
133. Mathisen, 1993: 93
134. Bede, Book 1 Chapter 22
135. Mathisen, 1993: 33
136. Mathisen, 1993: 90–91
137. Bede book 1.25
138. Fleming, 2021: 11-2
139. Fleming, 2021, 11
140. Fleming, 2021: 11-2
141. Fleming, 2021: 7

Chapter 2: The First Kingdom

1. Tolkien, 1998: 167
2. Tolkien, 1998: 33
3. Charles-Edwards, 2014: 438
4. Higham, 2009: 120
5. Green, 2009: 9
6. Charles-Edwards in Bromwich et al, 1995: 21
7. Chadwick in Chadwick et al, 1959: 31
8. Morris, 1980
9. Baring-Gould, 1911: 60
10. Hills 2011: 10
11. Zaluckyj, 2018: 2

12. http://croniclau.bangor.ac.uk/documents/AC per cent20B per cent20first per cent20edition.pdf
13. Swanton, 2000
14. Morris, 1978: 28
15. Bede, Book 1.15
16. http://www.vortigernstudies.org.uk/arthist/vortigernquoteshb.htm
17. Brooks and Harrington, 2010: 24
18. Pollington, 2008: 49
19. Brooks in Bassett, 1989: 55
20. Yorke, 2013: 26
21. Manco, 2018: 131
22. Brooks and Harrington, 2010: 42
23. Crabtree, 2018: 46
24. Brooks and Harrington, 2010: 36
25. Yorke, 2013: 27
26. Yorke, 2013: 27
27. Brooks in Bassett, 1989: 64–67
28. Crabtree, 2018: 31
29. Webb, 2011: 132
30. Naismith, 2019: 43
31. Webb, 2011: 132
32. Gerrard, 2016: 48
33. Bailey in Bassett, 1989: 110
34. Pollington, 2011: 245
35. Carver et al, 2010: 150–1
36. http://www.vortigernstudies.org.uk/artwho/name.htm
37. http://www.vortigernstudies.org.uk/artwho/vitalinus.htm
38. Chadwick, 1959: 31
39. Snyder, 1998: 107
40. Snyder, 1998: 230
41. Snyder, 1998: 107
42. Morris, 1980: 33
43. Sullivan, 2020: 165
44. http://www.vortigernstudies.org.uk/artfam/faustus.htm
45. Wood, 1987: 75
46. Higham and Ryan, 2015: 75
47. Manco, 2018: 131
48. Evans, 2014: 10
49. Tolkien, 1998: 167

Chapter 3: Ælle, the First Bretwalda

1. Bede, Book 2.5
2. Swanton, 2000: 61

Endnotes

3. Barr-Hamilton, 1953: 12
4. Barr-Hamilton, 1953: 17
5. Barr-Hamilton, 1953: 18
6. Napper, H.F., *The Sussex Archaeological Society*, (Volume 39, 1904).
7. Pearson, 2010: 34
8. Welch in Bassett, 1989: 75–81
9. Welch in Bassett, 1989: 83
10. Barr-Hamilton, 1953: 21
11. Welch, 1978: 6
12. Welch, 1978: 4–8
13. Welch, 1978: 14-5
14. Welch, 1978: 18–9
15. Yorke, 2013: 46
16. Rippon, 2018: 269
17. Rippon, 2018: 284
18. Rippon, 2018: 352
19. Rippon, 2018: 285
20. Rippon, 2018: 103
21. Rippon, 2018: 240
22. Barr-Hamilton, 1953: 23
23. Halsall, 2014: 71
24. Charles-Edwards, 2014: 444
25. Drinkwater in Drinkwater and Elton, 2002: 217
26. Drinkwater in Drinkwater and Elton, 2002: 210–211
27. Drinkwater in Drinkwater and Elton, 2002: 208-217
28. Brown, 2012: 389
29. Brown, 2012: 404
30. Brown, 2012: 392
31. Brown, 2012: 393
32. Mathisen, 1993: 64
33. Wallace-Hadrill, 1961: 29
34 Stenton, 1989: 12
35. Dumville, 1993: II.83
36. Charles-Edwards, 2014: 70–71
37. Charles-Edwards, 2014: 71
38. Mathisen, 1993: 129
39. Halsall, 2014: 34
40. Halsall, 2014: 66
41. Elton in Drinkwater and Elton, 2002: 176
42. Brown, 2012: 394-5
43. Brown, 2012: 397
44. Brown, 2012: 399
45. Yorke, 1990: 158–9
46. Mathisen, 1993: 81
47. Mathisen, 1993: 82

48. Mathisen, 1993: 93
49. Mathisen, 1993: 121
50. Wiiliams, 1999: 51-2
51. Laycock, 2008
52. Eagles, 2018: 2
53. Lewis in Mitchell and Greatrex, 2000: 77
54. Brown, 2012: 503
55. Brown, 2012: 505
56. Rippon, 2018: 167
57. Oousthuizen, 2019: 59
58. Matthews in Mitchell and Greatrex, 2000: 31
59. Mathisen, 1993: 2
60. Mathisen, 1993: 42-43
61. Mathisen, 1993: 41
62. Mathisen, 1993: 106-107
63. Mathisen, 1993: 111
64. Mathisen, 1993: 13-14
65. Mathisen, 1993: 11
66. Mathisen, 1993: 20
67. Mathisen, 1993: 32
68. Mathisen, 1993: 59
69. Mathisen, 1993: 60
70. Mathisen, 1993: 25
71. Mathisen, 1993: 50
72. Mathisen, 1993: 68–69
73. Brown, 2012: 403
74. Brown, 2012: 446
75. Brown, 2012: 448
76. Brown, 2012: 449
77. Mathisen, 1993: 70
78. Mathisen, 1993: 78
79. Mathisen, 1993: 51
80. Fleming, 2021: 16
81. Brown, 2012: 434
82. Brown, 2012: 316
83. Matthews in Mitchell and Greatrex, 2000: 32
84. Oousthuizen, 2019: 76
85. Mathisen, 1993: 132-139
86. Mathisen, 1993: 72
87. Mathisen, 1993: 134-135
88. Matthews in Mitchell and Greatrex, 2000: 34
89. Harries in Mitchell and Greatrex, 2000: 48
90. Mathisen, 1993: 136
91. Mathisen, 1993: 34

Endnotes

92. Mathisen, 1993: 142-143
93. Mathisen, 1993: 6
94. Mathisen, 1993: 119
95. Halsall, 2014: 42
96. Greatrex in Mitchell and Greatrex, 2000: 278
97. Crabtree, 2018: 47
98. Gerrard, 2016: 262
99. Halsall, 2014: 472
100. Snyder, 1998: 79
101. Snyder, 1998: 70–2
102. Snyder, 1998: 70
103. Snyder, 1998: 71-2
104. Brown, 2012: 405
105. Brown, 2012: 337–8
106. Brown, 2012: 336–7
107. Todd, 2004: 1-2
108. Manco, 2018: 93
109. Wolfram, 1997: 4-5
110. Manco, 2018: 7 & 111
111. Tacitus, Germania, Chapter 2
112. Wolfram, 1997: 6–7
113. Todd, 2004: 9
114. Manco, 2018: 112
115. Manco, 2018: 115
116. Flierman, 2017: 28
117. Flierman, 2017: 37
118. Flierman, 2017: 29
119. Pearson, 2010: 168
120. Goldsworthy, 2010: 341
121. Flierman, 2017: 44
122. Flierman, 2017: 45
123. Flierman, 2017: 39
124. Flierman, 2017: 69
125. Flierman, 2017: 58
126. Flierman, 2017: 61
127. Todd, 2004: 204
128. Todd, 2004: 204
129. Flierman, 2017: 83
130. Flierman, 2017: 77
131. Flierman, 2017: 2
132. Green, 2000: 341
133. Flierman, 2017: 7–8
134. Green, 2000: 134
135. Green, 2000: 121

136. Yorke, 2013: 32
137. Pollington, 2011: 184
138. Mathisen, 1993: 121
139. Thorpe, Lewis, 1977:153
140. Thorpe, Lewis, 1977:154
141. Gregory of Tours: BkII.27
142. Williams, 1999: 4
143. Williams, 1999: 5
144. Wiiliams, 1999: 10
145. Pollington, 2011: 19
146. Tacitus, Germania, Chapter 2
147. Pollington, 2011: 68
148. Pollington, 2011: 452
149. Pollington, 2011: 448
150. Pollington, 2011: 450
151. Pollington, 2011: 41
152. Carver et al, 2010: xiiv
153. Carver et al, 2010: xiiv
154. Pollington, 2011: 450
155. Pollington, 2011: 457
156. Pollington, 2011: 167
157. Pollington, 2011: 171
158. Pollington, 2011: 174
159. Pollington, 2011: 177
160. Pollington, 2011:173
161. Pollington, 2011: 188–9
162. Pollington, 2011: 183
163. Pollington, 2011: 199
164. Pollington, 2011: 205

Chapter 4: Weapons and Warfare of the Fifth and Sixth Centuries

1. Goldsworthy, 2003: 205
2. Goldsworthy, 2003: 206
3. Goldsworthy, 2000: 168
4. Goldsworthy, 2000: 175
5. Goldsworthy, 2003: 169
6. Goldsworthy, 2003: 206
7. Esposito, 2018: 56-57
8. Esposito, 2018: 71
9. Brown, 2012: 447

Endnotes

10. Hughes, 2020: 19
11. Goldsworthy, 2010: 337
12. Green, 2000: 75
13. Green, 2000: 69
14. Green, 2000: 78
15. Green, 2000: 83
16. Marren, 2006: 3
17. Wolfram, 1997: 7
18. Wolfram, 1997: 74
19. Goldsworthy, 2000: 178
20. Goldsworthy, 2000: 197
21. Halsall, 2003: 130–132
22. Marren, 2006: 153
23. Swanton, 2001: 199
24. Mortimer, 2011: 189
25. Higham, 1992:8
26. Higham, 1992:79–80
27. Green, 2012: 109
28. Marren, 2006: 153
29. White, 2007: 203
30. Underwood, 1999: 41 & 47
31. Underwood, 1999: 24
32. Underwood, 1999: 25
33. Esposito, 2018: 73–74
34. Underwood, 1999: 32-34
35. Esposito, 2018: 111
36. Underwood, 1999: 73
37. Underwood, 1999: 70
38. Davidson, 1998: 9
39. Marren, 2006: 9
40. Davidson, 1998: 38
41. Davidson, 1998: 59
42. Underwood, 1999: 56-57
43. Davidson, 1998: 95
44. Underwood, 1999: 50
45. Marren, 2006: 10
46. Davidson, 1998: 197
47. Davidson, 1998: 197
48. Davidson, 1998: 108
49. Davidson, 1998: 165
50. Davidson, 1998: 109
51. Marren, 2006: 9
52. Underwood, 1999: 119
53. Underwood, 1999: 119

54. Davidson, 1998: 28
55. Davidson, 1998: 118
56. Davidson, 1998: 103
57. Davidson, 1998: 138
58. Davidson, 1998: 80
59. Hughes, 2020: 53
60. Underwood, 1999: 77
61. Underwood, 1999: 63
62. Esposito, 2018: 93
63. Underwood, 1999: 94
64. Marren, 2006: 10
65. Mortimer, 2011: 169
66. Esposito, 2018: 93
67. Evans, 2000: 136
68. Newton, 1994: 33
69. Underwood, 1999: 127
70. Halsall, 2003: 185
71. Halsall, 2003: 196
72. Halsall, 2003: 207
73. Davidson, 1998: 189
74. Davidson, 1998: 189
75. Davidson, 1998: 192
76. Davidson, 1998: 189
77. Hughes, 2020: 50–51
78. Evans, 2000: 1
79. Evans, 2000: 28
80. Evans, 2000: 26
81. Evans, 2000: 42
82. Bede Bk III.14
83. Charles – Edwards in Bassett, 1989: 30
84. Evans, 2000: 131
85. Gerrard, 2016: 242
86. Evans, 2000: 119
87. Evans, 2000: 135
88. Evans, 2000: 105
89. Evans, 2000: 91
90. Evans, 2000: 74
91. Evans, 2000: 84
92. Hill, 2014: 15
93. Bishop, 2020: 104
94. Bishop, 2020: 20
95. Bishop, 2020: 20–21
96. Bishop, 2020: 17
97. Bishop, 2020: 80

Endnotes

98. Mathisen, 1993: 82
99. Bishop, 2020: 99
100. Bishop, 2020: 70–71
101. Bishop, 2020: 66
102. Bishop, 2020: 85
103. Bishop, 2020: 76
104. Grigg, 2018: 55
105. Grigg, 2018: 28-29
106. Grigg, 2018: 31
107. Grigg, 2018: 20
108. Grigg, 2018: 135
109. Grigg, 2018: 77–78
110. Grigg, 2018: 122
111. Grigg, 2018: 46
112. Grigg, 2018: 81
113. Grigg, 2018: 60
114. Grigg, 2018: 86
115. Grigg, 2018: 33
116. Grigg, 2018: 67
117. Grigg, 2018: 53
118. Grigg, 2018: 48-49
119. Carver, 2019: 189-193
120. Alcock, 1989: 221
121. Harding, 2012: 164
122. Grigg, 2018: 72
123. Dyer, 1992: 24
124. Tacitus, Germania chapter 6
125. Hamilton, 1986: 435
126. Mierow, 1908, 66
127. Davidson, 1998: 150
128. Swanton, 2001: 106
129. Marren, 2006: 135
130. Thorpe, Lewis, 1977:153
131. Thorpe, Lewis, 1977:154
132. Marren, 2006: 156
133. Davidson, 1998: 149
134. Morris, 2013: 164
135. Swanton, 2001:198
136. Morris, 2013: 180
137. Morris, 2013: 183
138. Thorpe, 1966: 223-225
139. Milner, 2011: 103
140. Underwood, 1999: 133
141. Morris, 1978: 22

142. Milner, 2011: 2-3
143. Milner, 2011: 24 & 80–81
144. Milner, 2011: 13
145. Milner, 2011: 50
146. Milner, 2011: 95–6
147. Milner, 2011: 97
148. Milner, 2011: 26
149. Milner, 2011: 98
150. Milner, 2011: 104
151. Esposito, 2018: 71
152. Hill, 2014: 41
153. Hill, 2014: 40
154. Hill, 2014: 45
155. Hill, 2014: 46
156. Hill, 2014: 46
157. Gerrard, 2016: 59
158. Gerrard, 2016: 68–69

Chapter 5: The Empire Strikes Back

1. Halsall, 2014: 55
2. http://christophergwinn.com/wp-content/uploads/2016/09/achArthur.png
3. Bartrum, 1993: 158
4. Bartrum, 1993: 157
5. Higham, 1994: 112-3
6. Jackson, 1959: 4
7. Chambers, 1966: 199-201
8. Alcock, 1989: 69–70
9. Bennett & Burkitt, 1985: 5–8
10. Hatfield, 2016
11. Jackson, 1959: 2-3
12. Joyce, 2019: 31-46
13. Pearson, 2010: 36
14. Swanton, 2000: 15
15. Bromwich, 2014: 150, 153, 166, 217
16. Bartrum, 1993: 98
17. Carver, 2019: 609
18. Koch, 2013: 187–8
19. Green, 2020: 58–9
20. Green, 2020: 60
21. Green, 2020: xxv
22. Green, 2020: 67
23. Green, 2020: 27

Endnotes

24. Green, 2020: xxxv
25. Green, 2020: 93
26. Green, 2020: 15
27. Green, 2020: 44
28. Green, 2020: 87
29. Green, 2020: 62-4
30. Green, 2020: 113-5
31. Green, 2020: 166
32. Green, 2020: 109
33. Green, 2020: 248
34. Green, 2020: 267

Chapter 6: The Rise of Wessex

1. Yorke, 2013: 131
2. Yorke, 1990: 131
3. Yorke, 2013: 131
4. Yorke in Bassett, 1989: 89
5. Bede, book III chapter 7
6. Yorke, 2013: 132
7. Eagles, 2018: 185
8. Eagles, 2018: 43
9. Eagles, 2018: 22
10. Mees, 2019: 1
11. Mees, 2019: 1
12. Mees, 2019: 142
13. Mees, 2019: 9
14. Mees, 2019: 145
15. Mees, 2019: 147
16. Mees, 2019: 14
17. Mees, 2019: 52
18. Eagles, 2018: 139
19. Bartrum, 1993:122
20. Yorke, 1990: 135
21. Swanton, 2001: 18

Chapter 7: Kings and Kingdoms

1. Bede, book 4.13
2. Hooke, 1985: 17
3. Bede, book 5.23
4. Hooke, 1985: 17

5. Bede, book 4.23
6. Rippon, 2018: 269
7. Rippon, 2018: 284
8. Rippon, 2018: 352
9. Rippon, 2018: 285
10. Rippon, 2018: 103
11. Rippon, 2018: 240
12. Yorke, 2013: 46
13. Bailey in Bassett, 1989: 122
14. Blair in Bassett, 1989: 97
15. Bailey in Bassett, 1989: 111
16. Charles-Edwards, 2014: 444
17. Loveluck and Laing, 2011: 539
18. Yorke, 2013 :74
19. Loveluck and Laing, 2011: 541
20. Dumville in Bassett, 1989: 215
21. Dumville, 1993: III.5
22. Dumville, 1993: III.9
23. Carver, 2019: 639
24. Newton, 1994: 30
25. Dumville in Bassett, 1989: 218
26. Dumville, 1993: III.9
27. Marsden, 1992: 27
28. Dumville, 1993: III.7
29. Carver in Bassett, 1989: 156
30. Oousthuizen, 2019: 96
31. Rippon, 2018: 318
32. Rippon, 2018: 266
33. Rippon, 2018: 284
34. Newton, 1994: 13
35. Newton, 1994: 27 & 29
36. Newton, 1994: 116-117
37. Newton, 1994: 142-144
38. Newton, 1994: 109
39. Manco, 2018: 183
40. Rippon, 2018: 327
41. Dumville in Bassett, 1989: 140
42. Zaluckyj, 2013: 21
43. Bede, book 1.15
44. Hooke, 1985: 17
45. Bede, book 5.23
46. Higham and Ryan, 2015: 142
47. Hirst and Scull, 2019:13
48. Pollington, 2008: 15

Endnotes

49. Pollington, 2008: 53
50. Pollington, 2008: 64
51. Pollington, 2008: 19-21
52. Pollington, 2008: 28–9
53. Pollington, 2008: 87
54. Pollington, 2008: 108
55. Bede, book 1.15
56. Evans, 1952: 101-113
57. Pollington, 2008: 64
58. Pollington, 2008: 243
59. Pollington, 2008: 57–9
60. Pollington, 2008: 31
61. Pollington, 2008: 237
62. Carver, 2017: 38
63. Carver, 2017: 32
64. Carver, 2017: 41
65. Carver, 2017: 121
66. Carver, 2017: 138
67. Hirst and Scull, 2019: 30
68. Hirst and Scull, 2019: 80–1
69. Hirst and Scull, 2019: 93–7
70. Hirst and Scull, 2019: 14
71. Pollington, 2008: 63
72. Bede, book 2.12
73. Bede, book 2.15
74. Bede, book 3.8
75. Bede, book 3.1
76. Bede, book 2.20
77. Bede, book 3.1
78. HB chapter 65
79. White, 2007: 203
80. Keys, 2000
81. Procopius, *Anekdota*, 23.20f
82. Charles-Edwards, 2014: 216